WHERE NORTH MEETS SOUTH

WHERE NORTH MEETS SOUTH

Cities, Space, and Politics
on the U.S.–Mexico Border

Lawrence A. Herzog

CENTER FOR MEXICAN AMERICAN STUDIES
UNIVERSITY OF TEXAS AT AUSTIN • 1990

A CENTER FOR MEXICAN AMERICAN STUDIES BOOK

Editor: Víctor J. Guerra
Editorial Assistants: Martha Vogel, Hope Woodward
Book Design: Víctor J. Guerra, Martha Vogel

Published with the collaboration of the Institute of Latin American Studies, University of Texas at Austin.

Distributed by arrangement with University of Texas Press / Box 7819 / Austin, TX 78713.

Library of Congress Cataloging-in-Publication Data

Herzog, Lawrence A.
   Where North meets South : cities, space, and politics on the U.S.–
Mexico Border / Lawrence A. Herzog
      p. cm.
   Includes bibliographical references.
   ISBN 0–292–79049–X — ISBN 0–292–79053–8 (pbk.)
      1. Mexican-American Border Region—Geography. 2. Cities and towns—Mexican-American Border Region. 3. Urbanization—Mexican-American Border Region. 4. Anthropo-geography—Mexican-American Border Region.   I. Title.
      F787.H47 1990
      917.2'109732—dc20   89–71205

Frontispiece: Aerial photograph, 6 February 1988, of the San Ysidro–Tijuana border crossing, looking southeast over the Tijuana River Zone. *Copyright © Aerial Fotobank, Inc. San Diego, California.*

To my family,
and to the memory of our ancestors
who came from a border town on another continent.

CONTENTS

TABLES

FIGURES

PREFACE

Urbanization of Int'l Boundaries

This book embraces an emerging paradox of human geography: the growth of cities along international boundaries. For many years the world system was ordered in such a way that international boundaries remained essentially free of human settlement. In the last three decades, however, the axioms of traditional geopolitical organization have been shattered; in a number of areas of the world, including the United States–Mexico, United States–Canada, and western European border regions, boundaries have come to house large-scale cities.

The urbanization of international boundary areas presents a bold, new research agenda for social scientists. The implications for theories of urban space, politics, and planning represent one area of inquiry that has gone relatively unexplored. In the U.S.–Mexico case, the growth of border cities has generated more than increased population density at the boundary line; it has spawned a series of economic and functional circulation patterns between "twin" cities that appear to eclipse the traditional screening functions of boundaries. Thus, it might be assumed that the *de jure* functions of the boundary are fading, giving way to new territorial political communities with some degree of autonomy and jurisdiction over their transnational living space. Experiments with the notion of a "frontier planning region" have been debated in the literature on Western European transfrontier cooperation for some time (Quintin, 1973). Yet, as this book points out, despite the overlapping of urban societies around a boundary, national sovereignty is alive and well, and divergent political systems continue to exercise their separate controls over divided territory. On the U.S.–Mexico border, the boundary appears to be intact, a formidable wall dividing North and South.

The urbanization of international boundaries raises new questions for human geographers, planners, and scholars of international relations. First, what is the changing role of international boundaries in territorial planning and international law? This question has been raised in the political geography literature from time to time, but now, more than ever, it needs further discussion. Second, for urban studies and urban geography, the growth of border cities begs explanation within two areas of current debate and discourse: (1) the role of extralocal and global influences on urbanization and urban form, and (2) the ways in which national culture mediates these wider influences to produce what Rapoport (1984) has termed "urban order." In observing both the behavioral and the spatial elements of boundary urbanization, I propose a new urban ecological concept—the "transfrontier metropolis." San Diego–Tijuana, a transborder metropolis of nearly three million inhabitants, offers a microcosm in which the two big questions of urban studies and urban geography can be examined both conceptually and empirically. Several geographers initiated this task more than a decade ago, but without articulating a larger theoretical context for their work (Dillman, 1969; Gildersleeve, 1978). House (1982) produced a most ambitious discussion of the border at the macro level. What remains is to address these questions at the urban scale.

Finally, this book offers discourse for political geographers and scholars of international affairs, especially those concerned with U.S.–Mexico relations. For many years, the international frontier between the United States and Mexico was nothing more than a barren corridor of boundary markers, border gates, and customs houses. That, of course, has dramatically changed in the second half of this century. The transformation of the border zone into a corridor of cities that will collectively house more than ten million inhabitants by the end of the century poses important foreign policy implications for the United States and Mexico. Not only is the border zone inhabited by millions of U.S. and Mexican citizens, it is an important source of revenue for both countries. Management decisions regarding the border environment, criminal justice, drug enforcement and boundary surveillance, trade, and transportation, therefore, must take into account both regional and national interests that, at times, may diverge. More important, most national decisions at the border have transboundary impacts. As a result, the border region itself is becoming a crucial item on the foreign policy agenda. With cities housing the majority of people, investments, and resources vital to the border zone, an understanding of politics, space, and urban development along the border becomes a necessary dimension of this new layer of U.S.–Mexican relations. By examining the comparative urban and political geographies of the region, I hope to shed some light on the contexts within which difficult foreign policy questions will be considered in the approaching decades. Ultimately, this may be one of the few places in the world where urban and environmental planning are elevated to the level of foreign policy.

Change envelops the U.S.–Mexico boundary zone. Border scholars are grappling with the meaning of recent developments on both sides of the border. In Mexico, the financial crisis and collapse of the peso continue unabated while investment in *maquiladora* industrial development grows. Support for the opposition political party (PAN) appears to be on the rise in several northern border states. North of the border, new immigration laws were enacted in the fall of 1986. Narcotics smuggling into the United States continues to draw attention in Congress, raising the question of how far the nation should go in monitoring the boundary. The meaning of these currents of change will be clarified only by the passage of time, and through a better understanding of the border region. In the meantime, it is clear that the border region has become a greater force in the hemisphere. After all, it was no accident that the fourth meeting of the U.S. and Mexican presidents, in 1986, took place in an international border metropolis, Mexicali.

In writing this book, I am indebted to many individuals who generously shared in the various stages of discourse, editing, and rewriting that led up to the final product. Special thanks go to John Agnew, Vivienne Bennett, Hans Briner, Víctor Castillo, Wayne Cornelius, Michael Dear, John Friedmann, Alan Gilbert, Carlos Graizbord, Alejandro Joulia Lagares, David Piñera, Ralph Sanders, and Leslie Sklair. The maps were skillfully drawn by Alejandro Joulia Lagares and Melinda Wedgewood in San Diego and Karen Crowther in Austin. The tables and bibliography were meticulously prepared by Miriam Rico and Lori Sturtz. I am also grateful to my administrative assistant, Mattie McAfee, for her unflagging support on administrative tasks affecting the book. Ricardo Romo and Víctor Guerra, editors at the Center for Mexican American Studies, have been most helpful. For funding assistance, I thank the University of California Consortium on U.S.–Mexico Research (UCMEXUS); and the Academic Senate, Committee on Research, University of California, San Diego.

Portions of some chapters were drawn from material originally published in: *Social Sciences Journal,* Volume 22, Number 3 (July 1985), pages 29–46; *Across Boundaries,* edited by Oscar Martínez, pages 96–116 (El Paso: Texas Western Press, 1986); and *Critica,* Volume 1,

Number 3 (1986), pages 115–134. I am also grateful for permission to use selected materials from the following publications: *Mexican–U.S. Relations: Conflict and Convergence*, edited by Carlos Vásquez and Manuel García y Griego (Los Angeles: UCLA Latin American Center and Chicano Studies Center, 1983), for the use of Table 1, page 328, in Clark Reynolds' essay "Labor Market Projections for the United States and Mexico and Their Relevance to Current Migration Controversies"; *Zonas fronterizas*, by Jesús Tamayo and José Luis Fernández (Mexico, D.F.: CIDE, 1983), for the use of Table A.5.2, page 228; and *Historia de Tijuana*, edited by David Piñera (Tijuana: Instituto de Investigaciones Históricas, UNAM-UABC, 1985), for the use of maps, pages 63 and 65.

1 Introduction

The myth of national sovereignty only persists through ignorance of twentieth century reality.

—J. M. Quintin (1973)

In 1986, two unrelated technological catastrophes in Europe focused world attention on the supranational character of contemporary global geopolitics. At the same time, they hinted at an incipient pattern of human territorial organization—the gradual eclipse of the nation-state as the central unit of decision making and change in the modern world system. When the nuclear reactor exploded at Chernobyl and unleashed a cloud of radiation over western Europe, it quickly became apparent that political boundaries dividing nation-states were meaningless barriers against the movement of deadly radioactive particles. Radiation currents cut a wide swath across national borders, upsetting ecology and endangering life in Poland, West Germany, Yugoslavia, Austria, Italy, and the Scandinavian countries.

Only six months later, a warehouse fire in Basel, Switzerland, caused a thirty-ton toxic chemical spill into the Rhine River, whose watershed blankets three of western Europe's most densely populated nations—France, West Germany, and the Netherlands. The Rhine, one of the most important transport corridors in western Europe and a vital source of water and marine life, was contaminated so severely that its ecosystem may be destroyed for a full decade. A toxic spill from a single factory in one nation may have caused many to suffer.

Both the Chernobyl and Rhine River disasters suggest that it is no longer always possible to confine the by-products of modern technology and production within nation-state boundaries. Ecological systems such as watersheds or air currents have never functioned within the logic of artificial boundaries. In the late twentieth-century world system, where technological achievements in industrial and post-industrial societies often raise the scale of externality effects to a transnational level, it becomes even more difficult to constrain the territorial and ecological dimensions of those effects.

The accidents at Chernobyl and the Rhine River also make it clear that nation-states can no longer expect to seal themselves off from their neighbors by institutionalizing greater defense of their national land boundaries. The world has, indeed, become "smaller." The global geopolitical map is now laced with porous boundaries and "percolated sovereignties" (Duchacek, 1986). We are witnessing, as Gottman (1973) has observed, the decline of the "shelter function" of national borders. Transboundary ecological spillovers are but one manifestation of a deeper transformation in the modern geopolitical system—a transformation highlighted by the evolution of globally interconnected social and economic interests and a corresponding network of transboundary linkages of capital, labor, commodities, information, and ideas.

The changing territorial scale of social and economic phenomena and the subsequent political reorganization of space lead to the underlying purpose for writing this book—to study social, economic, spatial, and political processes operating in an international boundary zone. As world-system relationships alter geopolitical patterns, the role of international borders has changed. So, too, the human geography of border regions is undergoing a transformation. Many international boundaries were negotiated during the formative stages of a system of international law developed in the nineteenth century. Boundaries were geometric lines, etched by transnational treaties, that ran across sparsely populated frontier territory at the edges of nation-states. They were heavily fortified by governments, since they represented, both functionally and symbolically, the outer lining of the sovereign nation-state. During the first half of the twentieth century, two world wars and numerous other global conflicts erupted when the sovereign territorial rights of nation-states were threatened by expansionist regimes with extranational territorial ambitions. In the second half of the twentieth century, however, the traditional functions of boundaries began to unravel. Nuclear rocketry, air power, global communication, and other technologies changed the rules of geopolitics. Cross-national trade, migration, and global transportation have generated a scale of human behavior that transcends the nation-state. In Europe, scholars have been the first to challenge the concept of sovereignty (Anderson, 1982; Gottman, 1973; Quintin, 1973). Following the Rhine River disaster, an official from the United Nations Environmental Program commented that European nations still resist organizing multilateral planning programs for fear of losing national power: "National sovereignty is something states are very reluctant to part with, and monitoring and enforcement provisions are seen as a threat" (*Los Angeles Times,* November 30, 1986).

Of course, international boundaries have never precisely and uncritically divided geographic space at the edge of two nation-states. Throughout this century, neighboring countries have disputed territory along their borders, and many of these conflicts continue (Day, 1982). But where border zones were once functional corridors of defense between nation-states, changes in technology, international politics, and the organization of production have permanently altered their meaning.

In some parts of the world, regions adjacent to boundaries have been dramatically transformed as a result of changes in the function of the border. The border zone between the United States and Mexico is one such place. Here, not only is the boundary increasingly porous, it has become the locus of large permanent urban centers, some of which house more than one million inhabitants. This radical departure from the past opens up fertile ground for research. What are the geographic implications of transborder urbanization? How is city space organized in an international boundary zone that houses various sets of transborder economic and social linkages? What sorts of unique spatial phenomena occur in an urbanized region with a political border running through it? These questions, when placed in the context of the U.S.–Mexico border, become even more intriguing, since it is here where North (industrial, developed society) meets South (Third World, less-developed society).

This book is organized in the following manner: Chapter 2 outlines a general theoretical context for rethinking the meaning of boundaries in human geography. Chapter 3 describes in a rudimentary way dimensions of the macrolevel setting of the U.S.–Mexico border region that are pertinent to the study of urbanization and spatial politics. Chapter 4 provides an entrée into the central portion of the book by theoretically contrasting urban space in two cultures, U.S. and Mexican. Chapters 5, 6, and 7 examine various empirical elements of spatial form and process in the Tijuana–San Diego region.

Cities and the U.S.–Mexico Border

> *And in order to preclude all difficulty in tracing upon the ground the
> limit separating Upper from Lower California, it is agreed that the said
> limit shall consist in a straight line, drawn from the middle of the Rio
> Gila, where it unites the Colorado, to a point on the Coast of the Pacific
> Ocean, distant one marine league due south of the southernmost point
> of the Port of San Diego, according to the plan of said port, made in the
> year 1782, by Don Juan Pantoja, second sailing Master of the Spanish
> fleet.*
>
> —Treaty of Guadalupe Hidalgo

The drawing of the international boundary between the United States
and Mexico, as defined in the Treaty of Guadalupe Hidalgo in 1848
(quoted above; Bevans, 1972), ended a territorial conflict between the
two nations and imposed a two thousand–mile geometric line across
a weakly populated, semibarren region at the edge of two vast
nation-states. Throughout the remainder of the nineteenth century,
and during the first half of the twentieth century, the "borderlands,"
as historian Herbert Bolton (1921) first termed the region, remained a
territory marginal to both U.S. and Mexican society, a traditional
"frontier" between two nations in different stages of development.

In the second half of the twentieth century, a dramatic change
swept across the borderlands. In Mexico, a national economic development program was directed at expanding, economically fortify-
ing, and physically redeveloping cities lying on the northern frontier.
Migrant streams that for five decades had been passing through the
border corridor into labor submarkets located in the U.S. Southwest
began to leave permanent settlers in the towns along the border—
Matamoros, Mexicali, Ciudad Juárez, and Tijuana, among others. On
the U.S. side of the border, a major restructuring of regional economic and political power caused a tilting of capital, resources, and
population toward the previously less-settled zones of the South and
Southwest. In the four decades following World War II, many of the
Sunbelt states (Texas, Arizona, New Mexico, and California) began to
develop nationally competitive economic bases. In both Texas and
California, border cities like El Paso, Laredo, and San Diego experienced considerable growth as part of the larger "rise of the sunbelt"
(Sale, 1975).

By 1980, the borderlands were no longer an arid wasteland, isolated from national life. Economic and social infrastructure abounded. More than seven million inhabitants occupied cities lying directly on the boundary, and over fifteen million people lived within a 120-mile zone of influence around the border. The boundary zone had become a strategic location for specialized economic activities like assembly plants, tourist facilities, services, and commerce. Growth rates of cities and counties along the border exceeded the national averages on both sides.

Yet the urbanization of the border corridor is unique, since it abruptly brings together into a common life space two very different societies, one from the industrial North, the other from the less-developed South. This abrupt confrontation of two disparate cultures leaves its mark on the settlements themselves. Urban space is more than a simple physical container of land uses and people woven together in a functional living environment; it is a repository for social, economic, and political relationships embedded in the larger society. Thus, the nature of urban space at the border reflects more fundamental elements of U.S. and Mexican society and the ways in which those societies utilize urbanized space. The nature of settlement structure at the border also offers clues about U.S.–Mexican interdependence and how it is negotiated in a common environment. This interdependence within a shared geographic space is examined throughout the book.

Transnational Interdependence and Border Urbanization in Global Perspective

What is the meaning of "interdependence" between two countries as interconnected yet different as the United States and Mexico? That is a question that has intrigued scholars of U.S.–Mexico relations for some time. Over the past few decades, writers have struggled to understand such areas of U.S.–Mexico integration as petroleum, foreign investment, trade, in-bond industries, migration, drugs and narcotics, and tourism (Ronfeldt and Sereseres, 1983). Unraveling the meaning of interdependence in U.S.–Mexico relations ultimately requires an understanding of the more general North-South dialogue (Corbridge, 1986) that has been unfolding over the last three decades. This dialogue occurs in a world system that is geopolitically divided between an industrialized, highly developed bloc of nations (North) and a less-developed, semi-industrialized contingent of Third World countries (South). In this book, the border—where North and South meet—is characterized as a setting where the North-South dialogue takes on a distinctly environmental and spatial character, because it is here that the two nations and cultures meet physically and, thus, it is here where the process of interdependence takes on a uniquely geographic form. This form is ultimately negotiated through the political systems of the two countries. Thus, to understand the urban geography of border settlements, one must understand the politics of border space.

The North-South confrontation at the border raises interesting geopolitical questions. For example, how do a Third World and a First World nation negotiate territorial matters at the boundary, when so many social and economic linkages transcend it? What are the politics of space in a border zone? Can territorial planning occur in a region in which the larger inequalities between the two nations come home to roost in the asymmetrical organization of space along the boundary?

These concerns intersect a second dimension of this study: a reinterpretation of the meaning of international political boundaries. These matters are addressed theoretically in Chapter 2, and empirically in later chapters. The North-South connection at the border occurs in the context of a changing world economic and geopolitical configuration. Vast labor, trade, financial, and corporate linkages throughout the world connect people and settlements across international borders with impunity. The scale of world politics has risen far beyond that of the nation-state. This has curious implications for geographic relationships along international boundaries, particularly those where an economy and an urban infrastructure are growing. Chapter 3 examines some of the regional implications of growth along the U.S.–Mexico border.

Culture and Urban Space at the International Border

Regarding cities, there is little question that "culture counts" (Agnew, Mercer, and Sopher, 1984). National cultures impose order on the built environment of cities by shaping them in a manner that embodies the values and beliefs of a society. One finds rather specialized cultural landscapes in traditional Chinese, Mexican, Italian, Muslim, and other cities, as a result of the cumulative effects of indigenous culture being incorporated into the construction of buildings, parks, neighborhoods, and an overall urban structure over time. Defining "culture" as (1) a way of life, (2) a system of cognitive schemata transmitted through symbolic codes, and (3) a set of adaptive strategies for survival within an ecological setting, Rapoport (1984, pp. 50–51) terms the resulting logic of different city structures "urban order."

The importance of the relationship between culture and urban space is magnified on the international boundary between the United States and Mexico. Here, two very different cultures create unique urban spatial configurations. The boundary separates two urban spatial formations that have evolved under different cultural codes and conditions. Yet the physical proximity of these urban formations, as well as the functional, social, and economic ties that connect them, creates an intriguing bicultural urban spatial arrangement. Explanation of the social geography of U.S.–Mexican border cities and of the bicultural elements of the ambience offers a unique addition to the field of urban social ecology. Chapter 4 outlines some theoretical differences between the study of urban space in the United States and in Mexico (Latin America), and Chapter 5 looks at the evolution of spatial form in a case study border urban area, the San Diego–Tijuana region. By sorting out the forces responsible for urban spatial formation on each side of the border, one begins to understand the complexities of the built environment in this bicultural setting.

Politics and Border Urban Space

World-system interdependence, fueled by technological, economic, behavioral, and environmental changes, has a distinct meaning for international borders in the late twentieth century. As one scholar has observed: "Most analysts of contemporary international politics agree that, in general terms, the sovereignty of the nation state erodes through time as it engages in international commerce, finance, investment and communication" (Ojeda, 1983). In some parts of the world, especially western Europe and the U.S.–Mexico border, there are movements to enhance the power of communities around international boundaries, particularly in areas that are growing, or that have something to gain from a stronger cross-border relationship. These movements, often termed "regionalist" (Duchacek, 1986), typically are in conflict with highly centralized, federalist national governments, which tend to be opposed to granting too much autonomy to borderland regions. This has become an ongoing debate in western Europe (Anderson, 1982).

Along the United States–Mexico border, the sanctity of the once-impenetrable political boundary is being eclipsed by a growing system of social and economic transfrontier linkages. These linkages form a transboundary social system (examined in Chapter 6). The social system creates a community of interest around the boundary, and is similar to the regionalist phenomenon in western European boundary areas. It is a system that reaches its zenith in the most densely populated sections along the border. It is anchored by a transnational marketplace, with consumers, capital, and workers creating daily cross-boundary activity systems. These activity patterns are logically defined in space, leaving the impression that functional spatial organization along the border is basically a cross-national phenomenon. Yet this can be misleading; although border urbanization has created sets of linkages that transcend the boundary, the spatial formations are highly sensitive to national culture. More important, one cannot forget that within border urban space is embedded a set of asymmetric relations, from which surplus capital tends to tilt strongly toward the North through a complex economic and financial circuitry. The spatial elements of inequality along the border are everywhere apparent. The volume and content of cross-border flows favor the United States over Mexico. On the U.S. side of the border, it is useful to dissect the urban social fabric in search of clues about the spatial dynamics of Mexican nationals over time. Chapter 6 offers some empirical commentary on the social ecology of Mexican American neighborhoods in one U.S. border city (San Diego).

Urban space in any setting encloses a functional ecosystem— consisting of a physical environment, as well as a social and built environment. On an international border this urban ecosystem becomes more complex, because a political boundary interrupts the ecosystem, imposing an unnatural political organization of space on a natural geographic surface. Although most metropolitan areas display considerable political fragmentation in their spatial organization, the implications for an international boundary have rarely been studied in this context. Chapter 7 addresses the political organization of space in the San Diego–Tijuana region.

The Policy Implications of Border Urbanization

During the decade of the 1980s, the U.S.–Mexico border area has rapidly evolved into one of the most important regions in the Western Hemisphere. The proliferation of historically significant events, including meetings of the presidents of both countries and a growing list of difficult problems in the region, such as drug smuggling, immigration, criminal justice and environmental pollution, have led to a startling increase in media attention to the region.

The data in Table 1 summarize the reporting of border-related issues in major newspapers and magazines in the United States for the period 1980–1986. Using twelve categories for news coverage along the international boundary, one finds that four subjects (not including immigration) dominated reported news in the first six years of this decade: twin plants (*maquiladoras*), environment/pollution, commerce/peso devaluation, and transportation/urban growth. This pattern reflects the basic fact that the U.S.–Mexico border region in the past three decades has been one of the most rapidly urbanizing regions in the world. A growing concentration of people and money

Table 1. U.S.–Mexico Border Issues Reported in Selected Mass Media Publications in the United States, 1980–1986

Issue	Number of Articles
Twin plants/*maquiladoras*	15
Environment/pollution	13
Urban growth/transportation	12
Trade/peso devaluation	10
Drug enforcement/smuggling	8
Business/economic development	7
Energy	5
Poverty/unemployment	4
Technology/computers	3
Tourism	2
Crime/violence	1
Agriculture	1

Source: Dialog Information Services, 1986.

Notes: Immigration excluded as a border issue. Media surveyed include *New York Times, Christian Science Monitor, Wall Street Journal,* and 435 popular magazines covered in *Magazine Index* database.

has led to a restructuring of the borderlands in a way inconsistent with classical views of "frontier regions." The U.S.–Mexico borderlands have evolved into a dynamic region of major metropolitan centers, specialized industry, and large-scale business and economic institutions whose impact resonates far beyond the border zone, permeating and influencing cities, people, and institutions at the national level in both Mexico and the United States. In the United States, therefore, issues such as twin-plant industries, pollution, peso devaluation, and urban growth have received extensive coverage in the national media, because border region issues have been elevated to the level of national concern.

Mexican news coverage of the border region has been equally rigorous, and probably more extensive, although systematic data bases remain unavailable at present. It has long been acknowledged that the border region is one of the key national economic resources in Mexico (Dillman, 1970; Ugalde, 1978). The border region receives considerable attention from Mexico's print media. For example, the nation's leading newspaper, *Excélsior,* has a weekly column called "Frontera Norte" (Northern Frontier). Two other leading national newspapers, *Uno Más Uno* and *La Jornada,* allocate coverage to regions, with the northern border region among those receiving the most attention. So important is Mexico's northern border region that the administration of President Miguel de la Madrid created the Programa Nacional de las Fronteras (National Border Program) within the Ministry of Education. Its function has been to promote media and popular awareness of northern border culture within the nation at large.

If media coverage has signaled the growing significance of the international boundary between the United States and Mexico, no less prolific have been the number of recent scholarly works by social scientists on the subject. Important volumes, such as those by Hansen (1981), House (1982), Jones (1984), Martínez (1986), Nalven (1984), and Ross (1978), have sought to understand this complex bicultural region better. The formation of a national scholarly organization, the Association of Borderland Scholars, of several new journals, and of a number of research centers at campuses in the border regions of both the United States and Mexico is further evidence of a growing attempt to understand this dynamic zone of overlapping cultures.

Such understanding has clearly permeated dialogue between U.S. and Mexican elected officials and the architects of foreign policy in the capitals of the two nations. Policy documents produced by the U.S. Department of State, for example, demonstrate an increase in concern with the role of this region in U.S.–Mexican relations (Storing, 1984). The two nations hold interparliamentary meetings each year. Vital issues affecting U.S.–Mexico relations are discussed by representatives from the U.S. Senate and House of Representatives and from Mexico's Senate and Chamber of Deputies. Recent conferences have demonstrated a greater concern with border-related economic and policy issues, including immigration policy, twin plants, drug trafficking, tourism, border ecology, and pollution (U.S. House of Representatives and Senate, 1983). These topics have begun to occupy a larger share of the agenda in these interparliamentary meetings than they did when the meetings were initiated in the 1960s.

The question of border cities and border urban space will ultimately become a matter of foreign policy for both the United States and Mexico, if it has not already become one. The increasing fragility of the boundary as a barrier to unwanted spillover effects, ranging from polluted air and water to undocumented foreign workers, represents one of the major threads in the fabric of U.S.–Mexico relations. On matters of cross-border sewage spills and air pollution, toxic waste dumping, and water quality management, the United States and Mexico have engaged in numerous bilateral discussions and agreements in the last decade. The more people and economic infrastructure that locate in the region, the more vital will management of the border zone become to the foreign policy agendas of both nations. The immigration issue, of course, has become a crucial area of binational negotiation, as has the narcotics/smuggling matter. Both involve vigilance and maintenance of the border as a protector of national sovereignty. At times, both nations cling to that sovereignty, despite the recognition that social and economic processes transcend the boundary. In the United States, politicians alternately call for bigger and stronger fences or better security from unwanted boundary penetration. One law enforcement leader in San Diego County even went so far as to suggest that the U.S. government consider employing the marines to supplement the understaffed Border Patrol in guarding the boundary (*San Diego Union*, November 30, 1986). In Mexico, the obsession with sovereignty remains strong as well. When the U.S. Drug Enforcement Agency requested in 1986 that Mexico grant its agents permission to cross the border if chasing potential narcotics smugglers, Mexico refused, saying that such a crossing would violate its sovereign rights. Ironically, one hundred years ago, Mexico did allow the U.S. Army the right to chase Indians across the boundary if they were being pursued for having committed some criminal act (Bevans, 1972).

It appears that the border region and its management will very likely become a fixture in the dialogue between the United States and Mexico. One challenge that policymakers will face will be to redefine the meaning of the boundary in light of the world-system relationships that transcend it, and in light of the rapidly changing character of regions around it, especially those that have experienced large-scale urban growth. A better understanding of transboundary urban geography should serve to strengthen the dialogue between officials from both sides of the border who are seeking to relax the tensions surrounding its growth and management.

2 Human Settlements, Space, and International Boundaries in Global Perspective

Territorial borders are quite meaningless for science, and economic interdependence crosses political borders not occasionally, but as a general rule.

—Niklas Luhman (1982)

AT FIRST GLANCE, the study of international political borders seems to encompass a rather parochial body of knowledge. Indeed, until recently, literature on the subject came mainly from classical political geographic studies of boundaries and frontiers. Much of this work, as I review later in this chapter, was done several decades ago. In this chapter I wish to argue that it is no longer sufficient to accept the traditional wisdom about the political geography of boundaries. Border regions should not be analyzed merely as unique regional phenomena. Boundaries are the products of a larger political geographic context. Boundary zones derive their meaning from a role determined by the workings of the world economy. Furthermore, this process has important *territorial* dimensions, which are addressed in this chapter.

Whereas the partitioning of the earth's surface into formal political geographic units (nation-states) has unfolded for several hundred years, in the last few decades social scientists have begun to challenge the notion that the world system is dominated by nation-states. Prominent among these writers is Wallerstein, whose work on the world economy (1974) is built on two important foundations: (1) the call for a more historically based, holistic view of the international political arena; and (2) neo-Marxian critiques of traditional social science explanations of national development (Taylor, 1985). Wallerstein constructs a theoretical edifice around the notion of a single world market fused by capitalist relations of production that have their origins in sixteenth-century Europe. Other writers have posited a global political economy in which the forces of corporate power, aided by technological developments in communications, transport, and industrial production, operate on a worldwide basis that, over time, has altered the traditional meaning of the "nation-state" (Barnet and Muller, 1974; Leontief et al., 1977; Makler, Martinelli, and Smelser, 1982; Strange, 1984). As one study states, with reference to the managers of multinational corporations: "What they are demanding in essence is the right to transcend the nation-state, and in the process, to transform it" (Barnet and Muller, 1974, p. 16).

The territorial implications of global interdependence within the changing world system have received little attention from scholars. Political geography (and geography more generally), with a few noteworthy exceptions, has been slow to respond to the ideas of Wallerstein and other social scientists studying the world system. Gottman (1973) is one of the few important voices in political geography emerging in the last two decades to address the subject of territory and international political economy. He has stated: "New currents in technology, economic demands, and political ideas have injected into the arena disquieting forces that expand accessibility, modify operating structures, and call for the revision of established concepts and principles. The resulting fluidity has turned the present situation into a rather chaotic state of affairs insofar as the meaning of territory and sovereignty is concerned" (Gottman, 1973, p. 154).

Territory, Gottman has argued, now carries with it a "social function" that is derived from a complementarity of interests between the nation-state and the international community. The uses of national territory are tied into an international network of reciprocal relations. Extraterritorial interests, in short, are embedded in national space. The artificial boundaries that once strictly divided national political space no longer have the same impact.

In this book I argue that the emerging complementarity of interests among nation-states has generated new human geographic settlement patterns along international boundaries. This suggests the need for further study of boundaries in the context of the late twentieth-century world political system. Such work is rendered even more compelling by the fact that most political geographic thought about boundaries was developed before World War II, at a time when boundaries were thinly populated corridors of defense separating nation-states. Research and thinking about boundary zones were therefore strongly influenced by political function and demographic character at a moment in time. Boundaries were postulated to generate distorting effects on human behavior, most of which were negative from an economic and policy point of view. For example, they were said to create abnormal market structures for retail trade (Christaller, 1966).

Yet boundaries represent a meeting place of nation-states, and in some areas, the meeting place of the Third and First worlds. As subsequent chapters of this book document, this confrontation has stimulated economic growth and population expansion in some regions. In the most urbanized areas, it has generated unique locational dynamics in space, a specialized social geography, and divergent bicultural morphologies. In the narrative that follows, I wish to begin to unravel the meaning of boundaries in the context of the changing world system.

The Meaning of International Boundaries

Man is forever busy in setting up institutions, systems and machinery to reach his goals and impose order on the environment, and in doing so he must create and control boundaries.

—Raimondo Strassoldo (1982)

Nature abhors fixed boundaries.

—Ellen Semple (1911)

The need to enclose and control territory seems to be one of the fundamental characteristics of sedentary civilizations. Mesopotamian, Roman, and medieval cities were rimmed by walls. Though some cultures rejected the notion of the walled town, most notably the Greeks (Mumford, 1961) and the Incas (Von Hagen, 1957), in general, physical boundaries represent a political act taken to assert control over the environment. In a more complex sense, boundaries represent, in the modern era, a manifestation of nation-state actions to make political power real and explicit by linking it directly to territory (Sack, 1983). Geographer Ellen Semple's observation (quoted above) on the relationship between the drawing of the physical boundary line and the workings of natural ecological processes is one of the ironies of human territorial behavior that continue to haunt the world. The examples of Chernobyl and the Rhine River once again come to mind, as do the acid rain problem on the U.S.–Canada border and toxic waste dumping, sewage spills, and air pollution on the U.S.–Mexico border.

There has been considerable discussion about how one actually defines the physical edge or boundary of a cultural area. Turner's classic study of the American frontier was probably one of the first attempts to construct a sociocultural theory of human territorial behavior on the margins of an expanding nation-state. In describing the expansion of the western United States in the nineteenth century, Turner characterized the expansion zone, or frontier, as the "meeting point between savagery and civilization" (Turner, 1894). He viewed the frontier as a buffer zone, or area of transition, between two cultural heartlands. Following this, scholars began to make a distinction between "frontier," which tended to be equated with a zone or area, and "boundary," which was thought to be a physical line defined by international agreement (Kristoff, 1969; Prescott, 1965). These differences are not merely semantic, they are illustrative of a fundamental feature in the relationship between political boundaries and surrounding territory. The political act of drawing a boundary imposes an artificial line on a landscape whose physical and social geography may overshadow it. Although this dilemma was recognized as early as 1911 by Semple and other geographers, it has become central to the conceptual meaning of boundaries in the post–World War II era.

The concept of a territorial boundary linked to one culture or nation of peoples did not clearly emerge until the modern period of Western history, beginning in the sixteenth century, when the conditions leading to the evolution of nation-states three centuries later were first implanted in western Europe. Most scholars, however, agree that the idea of the territorial frontier can actually be traced back to the Roman Empire (Lapradelle, 1928). During the period of the Roman Empire (first to fifth centuries, A.D.), and during the middle ages, territory was divided up into "kingdoms" or "empires"; the "nation-state," a form of modern political partitioning of space, would not emerge until the nineteenth century.

Although empires or kingdoms were contained within somewhat finite spatial domains, they were not actually bounded by any socially created definition of territorial limits. A clear reference to a form of territorial borders during the Roman Empire has been documented, although there is disagreement among scholars as to the precise meaning of Roman geographic boundaries. Some writers view the Roman walls constructed in Scotland and along the Rhine and Danube rivers as evidence that Roman politicians and bureaucrats were concerned about defining and protecting the limits of the empire (Lapradelle, 1928; Prescott, 1965; Tagil, 1982). Scholars have identified two kinds of territorial lines: *limes imperii*, the fortified or functional boundaries of the empire, and *fines*, the legal borders of the Roman state (Lapradelle, 1928).

It is believed that the *limes* served as floating zones of territorial control, stopping at the confines of barbarian peoples, and physically marking off the limits of Roman territory. They were rarely fixed lines of jurisdiction, since the limits of the Roman state were constantly changing following conquest and war. Tagil (1982) has emphasized the important military function of the Roman walls on the imperial border at the Rhine-Danube river zone, where fortifications served as protection against warlike Germanic tribes to the north. Yet, Murty (1978) believes that although the walls offered material evidence of some kind of empire boundaries, they were often not used for fortification. More important, Murty notes that Rome saw itself as a "universal state." It did not recognize the existence of surrounding states; therefore, in a sense, formal political borders were not necessary (ibid.). The same could be said about many of the Christian empires of the medieval period (Taylor, 1985). Thus, although the Roman Empire may have been the first political culture to introduce the notion of territorial limits, boundaries, rather than serving as formal lines of administrative jurisdiction, appeared to function either as zones of military activity at the edge of conquered regions or as symbolic landscapes defining an approximation of the sphere of influence of the empire. The modern notion of a political border, grounded in international law and respected globally, was still many centuries away.

Nation-States and Sovereignty

It is commonly believed that in western Europe during the period 1600 to 1900, the collective ideas of great writers, philosophers, and statesmen like Locke, Rousseau, Hobbes, and Bodin were an important part of the change that swept Europe into the nineteenth-century era of nationalism and of nation-state consolidation (Merriam, 1972; Rokkan, 1980). By the nineteenth century, as Gottman (1973, p. 53) has noted, territory was regarded not only as crucial to security (shelter), but also as a "receptacle of the economic means of the people." Territory became equated with economic power as a result of a legacy inherited from the earlier feudal period. Before the Renaissance, wealth was generated principally through four means: control of land, control of tolls charged along roads, monopoly of markets, and minting of money (Gottman, 1973). Each of these forms of capital generation was anchored on a geographic basis; that is, to control land, tolls, markets, and currency, it was necessary to control territory. Thus, it is not surprising that as early as the seventeenth century, an interest in rigidly defining and defending the limits of culture areas materialized. Some scholars regard the Peace of Westphalia (1648), which administered the liquidation of the feudal and religious system of the Middle Ages and led to the formulation of many principles of international law, as marking the beginning of the development of the notion of "sovereignty," which would become a key principle underlying the formation of nation-states in the nineteenth century (Gottman, 1973, pp. 44–48; Hinsley, 1966).

Scholars consider the nineteenth century to be the salient time period of nation-state formation, a time when fixed territorial boundaries between nations were physically delimited on the land (Palmer and Colton, 1965). This was also the period in which nationalism flourished, along with the "ideology of nations," described by one scholar as the belief that nations are the only true and natural political units (Tivey, 1981).

The conditions within which nationalism and the formation of nation-states arose have been the subject of considerable scholarly attention (Gottman, 1973; Tilley, 1975; Tivey, 1981). In the seventeenth century, the concept of nation-states was resisted by those interest groups that stood to lose the most from this new form of spatial political organization—the church and the nobility. Some writers, like Hobbes, were pessimistic about the common person's capacity for self-government and therefore argued that sovereign states were needed to prevent complete chaos and self-destruction between competing forces in society (Merriam, 1972). During the eighteenth century, new currents of thought revealed the growing discontent with the divine monarch form of governance, and by the early 1800s, nationalism crystallized among regions dissatisfied with Napoleon's European continentalism (Tagil, 1982). It is thought that the Congress of Vienna, following the defeat of Napoleon, laid the groundwork for the final rejection of monarchic systems of government and their replacement by nation-states.

"Sovereignty," the notion that in any community of people there should be only one source of authority (Navari, 1981), was an important catalyst in the formation of nation-states. Sovereignty actually represents a philosophical concept that can be traced back to Aristotle's work on the need for recognition of a supreme power in the state. It was addressed by many important European scholars over several centuries prior to its heyday in the nineteenth century. It eventually gained popular acceptance as the idea that the state was the ultimate source of authority, law, and legitimate force within its boundaries (Kolinsky, 1981). Kristoff (1969) has argued, in fact, that during the early period of nation-state building, the presence of fixed boundaries represented a sign of maturity and orderliness within a political community, and undefined frontiers were characteristic of less-sophisticated sociopolitical relations, typified by rebelliousness, lawlessness, or the absence of laws. Thus, as the concept of the sovereign state emerged during the nineteenth century, it defined state power on a highly territorial basis. The state retained ultimate jurisdiction over its physical territory. Boundaries became the lines of contention and negotiation within the territorial arena of western Europe, where important changes in the geography of political power would unfold over the next century.

During the late nineteenth century, the formal production of knowledge about boundaries and frontiers began. Friedrich Ratzel (1897), often called the "father of political geography," initiated this body of work with his pioneering book, *Politiche Geographie.* In it he proposed a set of "geographic laws," which explained patterns of world political power on the basis of locational and spatial relationships among nation-states. On the subject of nation-state boundaries, Ratzel offered the analogy of the state as a living organism. The boundary, like the epidermis of animals and plants, was the "skin" of the living state. It served to defend the nation-state against undesirable forces while allowing healthy exchanges, such as commerce and cross-border travel, to occur.

Ratzel's view of the boundary illustrates the dominant thrust of much of the early research about political boundaries. Boundaries were analyzed principally in terms of their role as political and military dividing lines between nation-states. The dominant paradigm of political geography at the beginning of the twentieth century was that territorial political power was negotiated by controlling what some observers have termed the "landpower setting" (Cohen, 1975). Boundaries served to delimit territorial power in a world in which nation-states were the critical unit of negotiation. During the twentieth century, a large body of legal thinking would evolve, placing the concern of land boundaries into the field of international law (Collins, 1970; Gross, 1969). In fact, if one examines the elements of international law, and if one reads through the important cases, it becomes clear that international law essentially consists of a set of global legal principles associated with the governance of space. Some of the most important questions facing international lawyers are *spatial* or territorial ones—the acquisition of land by nation-states, land boundaries, maritime territory, air space, territorial jurisdiction, extradition, and treatment of aliens are all international legal concerns that revolve around territory and jurisdiction over space.

Boundaries and Space in the Twentieth Century

During the twentieth century, the functions of boundaries within the world political system have undergone considerable transformation. National borders have proven to be highly vulnerable to changing social, economic, and political developments within and between nations. The statement "Back of a boundary are not only national interests and ambitions, but a philosophy of international relations" (Boggs, 1940) hints at the context that has defined the meaning of boundaries in this century. Two periods can be identified in characterizing the role of boundaries in the twentieth century: 1900 to 1945, and 1945 to the present.

In the first half of the twentieth century, nation-states negotiated their land-based spheres of influence, often through military confrontation. Two world wars were fought during this period. Border scholars emphasized the defensive, military character of nation-state political boundaries. Spykman (1942), for example, studied the relationship between boundaries and national security. He traced the successive use of earthen walls, brick, masonry, steel plates, and reinforced concrete in the construction of barriers along national borders, especially in western Europe. Equally, Boggs (1940), while giving attention to broader questions about the nature of boundaries across time and space, emphasized the global military and strategic importance of boundaries. By the end of the Second World War, one author who had worked in the U.S. State Department wrote a comprehensive guide for governments and decision makers in the field of boundary making. Interestingly, the book peered into the future by pointing to the need for changes in the concept of national sovereignty and for some kind of supranational control over boundary affairs (Jones, 1945).

Western Europe has been an important arena for the challenging and testing of the relation between boundaries and national defense. Both world wars fought on the European continent reflected instances in which the "shelter function" (Gottman, 1973) of national borders was threatened. Boundaries provided functional lines of defense between countries during a period of territorial expansion and redefinition of the limits of nation-states. An excellent example of the symbolic military importance of borders is the construction of the Maginot line on the French side of the Franco-German border prior to World War II, and the corresponding construction of the Siegfried line on the German side. With both nation-states regarding military invasion as a real threat, what Prescott (1965) has termed the "border landscape" became a zone of military fortification.

Yet, the early part of the twentieth century was not merely an era of territorial expansion. Strassoldo (1982) has noted that boundary making became a hallmark of civilization and progress in the West, with the first half of the present century representing perhaps the most important era in which this national act was exercised. Not surprisingly, much of the scholarly work in this period addressed the problems of boundary changes in a time of expansion and military conflict. Many writers chose a "case study" approach, focusing on disputed boundary zones, boundary changes, boundary delimitation, disputes over natural resources, and the evolution of boundaries (Minghi, 1963).

Since 1950, the functions of international boundaries have continued to evolve in response to changing global economic and political trends. The shelter function of boundaries, so vital to the power struggles that characterized world political geography between the two world wars, has begun to lose sway. Gottman (1973) attributes the "demise of the shelter function" of territorial boundaries to a combination of technological, socioeconomic, and political factors.

Technology has transformed the world political map. New forms of military technology, particularly the development of air power, rocketry, and nuclear power, have changed the rules of territorial competition. Armed confrontation is no longer exclusively land-based. With the advent of nuclear weapons, land-oriented territorial sovereignty has diminished. The possibility of global war and large-scale human loss make boundaries between nation-states far less vital than before. As Gottman states: "The situation of mutual deterrence and the possibility of annihilation of human activity and possibly all life over most of the continents if nuclear war were fully unleashed, obviously calls into question the usefulness of territorial sovereignty in terms of the protection of its inhabitants" (ibid., p. 128).

Other technological shifts have contributed to the decline in the "barrier" functions of boundaries. Satellite communications, radio, and television allow for rapid transfer of information at a scale that easily transcends political borders. Sophisticated forms of transportation and the decrease in the cost of long-distance travel have allowed for frequent and high-volume movements of people and goods across boundaries. Large-scale migrations and the gradual internationalization of trade markets have been important technological innovations in the second half of the twentieth century.

The Globalization of the World Economy

Capitalism as an economic mode is based on the fact that the economic factors operate within an arena larger than that which any political entity can totally control.

—Immanuel M. Wallerstein (1974)

Perhaps the single, critical force most affecting global political geography, and hence the role of international boundaries in the second half of the twentieth century, has been the transformation of the organization of the world economy. Wallerstein (1984) has argued vigorously that this is not a recent phenomenon, but can be traced to the origins of capitalism in western Europe in the sixteenth and seventeenth centuries. Yet, in the late twentieth century, the magnitude of global economic interdependence has reached its zenith. Corporations have increasingly become multinational. Of the one hundred largest economic units in the world, only half were nation-states by 1980 (Makler, Martinelli, and Smelser, 1982, p. 25).

The world economy emerged over a period of several centuries in western Europe; during that period, the nation-state evolved as a legitimate territorial entity. Where nation-states essentially evolved to provide security for regional concentrations of culture groups, the world market formed because national economic interests realized that opportunities for profit existed beyond the confines of their territorial states. The system of mercantilism, for example, was based on the principle that territorial states should claim as much of the world market as possible.

The elements of the world economy today involve a complex web of interrelationships between firms and nation-states. The world market is structured around a global system that brings all national finances under the hegemony of transnational interests. Because nation-states are wedded to an international accounting system and its balance of payments, national finances must deal with global banking and corporate organizations. This has led some observers to claim that nations need a "foreign policy of money," given that "in today's world the management of money, and hence those basic outcomes strongly affected by it, cannot be confined neatly within the territorial limits of individual national political systems" (Calleo and Strange, 1984, p. 91).

One of the reasons why national finances are intimately linked to the world system is that the operating logic of powerful banks and transnational corporations is played out on a global scale (Sampson, 1981; Taylor and Thrift, 1982). This phenomenon has obvious historical roots that can be viewed through the gradual globalization of capitalism. In the early nineteenth century, industrial growth generated new forms of capital concentration and increased commodity exchanges between nation-states. By the late nineteenth century, capital was increasingly concentrated in monopolistic enterprises, and money circulation between nation-states continued to increase. In the twentieth century, the growth of multinational corporations, mainly in the rich northern countries of the world, was accompanied by an increase in the spatial concentration of capital, a steady growth in investments in Third World nations by financial interests based in the industrialized world, and a flow of labor from South (Third World) to North. Overall, the circulation of capital and labor has increasingly become controlled by corporations and financial forces from the industrial heartland of the world (the North).

Capital has now become highly centralized. Of the world's twenty largest transnational industrial corporations in 1980, twelve were based in the United States, three in the Netherlands (two of which

were also based in the United Kingdom), three in the United Kingdom, two in Germany, and two in Italy. The ten largest of these corporations (Exxon, General Motors, Royal Dutch Shell Group, Ford
Motor Co., Mobil, Texaco, British Petroleum, Standard Oil, IBM, and
Gulf Oil) earned over twenty billion dollars in 1978, with net output
averaging around seven billion dollars, or the equivalent of the total
income of some poor nations (Bangladesh, for example) in one year
(Edwards, 1985, p. 197).

In the twentieth century, we also have seen the formation of what
has been termed the "international monetary system" (ibid.). This has
spawned a number of institutions, including the International Monetary Fund (IMF) and the World Bank, that set policies and regulate
the international credit system. One also sees the development of
multistate trade organizations, such as the General Agreement on
Tariffs and Trade (GATT), signed in 1947, the European Economic
Community (EEC), set up in 1959, and the United Nations Conference on Trade and Development (UNCTAD), held in Geneva in 1964,
and dubbed by some as the "trade union of the Third World" (ibid.,
p. 232). Apart from the multistate trade organizations, the introduction of commodity cartels, such as the Organization of Petroleum
Exporting Countries (OPEC) in 1960, reveals how some economic
actors have sought to control the world market for particular
goods, once again generating an extranational logic to the workings
of capital.

Finally, an even more profound understanding of the global nature of the world economy emerges when one looks at the international credit system operating after World War II. When organizations such as the World Bank and IMF were created, they had specific
purposes. The World Bank was to provide multilateral aid for development; the IMF was to act as a "central" bank, regulating exchange
rates and supervising the expansion of international money (ibid.).
When these agencies were created in 1944, their architects did not en-
vision the escalation in the total control over the world economy that
these and other centralized agencies would have. It was not foreseen
that the U.S. dollar would become the international currency and
medium of exchange. In line with the growing integration of the
world economic system, a second important international currency
emerged in the 1970s: "Eurocurrency," an "offshore" or overseas
banking conglomerate that became a competitor to U.S. financial
capital. Over time, the world banking system became more dis-

persed—it was not controlled by one nation or by any one central bank. Even the IMF only controls about 10 percent of world reserves (ibid., p. 182); the remainder of international credit is retained by private banks and financial groups.

The gradual, post–World War II internationalization of finances and economic growth has specific territorial and spatial implications. As the world became more integrated economically, it also became so geographically. Technology allowed a partial conquest of geographic space; thus technological developments such as air freight, telex, and computers began to diminish the impact of distance (transport costs) as a factor of production (Harris, 1983). The elimination of distance/transport costs as a factor of production is a key reason for the changing industrial location patterns that have taken hold globally in the last few decades. Where transport costs and other nonlabor factors once dominated the locational decision process of industrial entrepreneurs, today the cost of labor has become the primary consideration of factory location (Storper and Walker, 1984).

Another factor that must be considered as a territorial outcome of world interdependence is the ecological impact of production. There is little question that, as the scale of production, technology, and international interaction has grown, the outputs of production have become part of a "global ecosystem." The destruction of finite resources within that ecosystem, such as fossil fuels (petroleum), and the destruction of the environment through pollution have generated serious costs for the international economy (Pirages, 1984). One attempt to model the global economy emphasized the importance of pollution, food, and natural resources in input-output relationships between regions across the globe (Leontief et al., 1977).

Global financial interdependence can also lead to global dependence, thus one of the by-products of an international economy has been regional inequality between the Third and First worlds. This inequality has been analyzed in great detail by the "dependency theorists," who believe that the problems of the Third World are derived largely from the development of world capitalism (Wallerstein, 1974). According to dependency theory, capitalism thrived by implanting an economically exploitative system in newly colonized regions, initiating a century of dependent relations leading to underdevelopment (Amin, 1974; Frank, 1978). The economic and territorial ambition of capitalist nations led to a period of imperialism (Smith, 1981) during which the Third World—First World relationship was established to the disadvantage of the former. Despite the resounding cynicism of this school of thought, pragmatic concerns emerge; for example, given the interdependence of the world economy, questions about the economic development of Third World nations cannot be divorced from the world economic system (Brookfield, 1975). Development in the Third World is not simply a matter of following the models established by the Western nations a century earlier; it must be conceived in the context of a politically and economically integrated world system.

One of the linkage forms that generates a great deal of interdependence between the First and Third worlds is labor migration. The flow of labor from poor countries to rich ones occurs because there is a systematic relationship between the supply and demand for labor. The relationship transcends the international political boundary, whether or not nation-states wish to impede it. In many instances, national governments support the migration of labor across their borders, since it serves the needs of national economic interests. This is obviously the case in many First World nations that receive large numbers of Third World migrants—the United States, Canada, Switzerland, Germany, and so on.

It is not surprising, from either a First or Third World perspective, that cross-national labor markets exist. From the point of view of Third World workers, "there is a natural tendency for labour to seek out for itself that location where its labour power can be exchanged for the most desirable wages and living conditions. . . . Within an international capitalist economy, the drive towards equalization of the wage scale occurs through immigration among nations" (Petras, 1980). Thus, just as capital circulates freely among nation-states in search of optimal returns, in an interdependent world so too does labor circulate among different territories in search of a maximum return. The phrase "international division of labor" has been used to describe this south-north flow (Nash, 1983; Sassen-Koob, 1983).

Despite the inequalities engendered in First World–Third World relations, one cannot ignore the far-reaching implications of the global economy: the liberalization of trade and travel, large-scale labor migration, and innovations in high technology that enhance global interaction. Relative prosperity in the Western world during the years 1950–1970 allowed the luxury of spending billions of dollars on research and development, producing many of the technological innovations that contribute to the spatial and economic reorganization of the globe. One by-product of this spatial reorientation has been a change in national policy toward the growth of border zones, allowing for the development of settlements along international boundaries.

Human Settlements, Space, and International Boundaries in the Late Twentieth Century

All state borders are social creations . . . boundaries are essentially "paper walls" created by the contractual relations among states.
—Elizabeth M. Petras (1980)

Given the changes wrought by the steady internationalization of world finances and other integrating forces such as large-scale labor migration, one has to ask the question: What is the role of the international political boundary in the late twentieth century interdependent world system? Transnational economic relationships have altered the scale and nature of global political geography. Nation-states have sought to create organizations and policies to respond to these changes. International agreements on migration, trade, travel, and information exchange are one example. International organizations like the United Nations, World Bank, and International Monetary Fund have produced institutional responses to these changing conditions. Some scholars have observed the effects of interdependence on border regions and the policy options open to nation-states affected by these processes (Anderson, 1982). Others speak of "trans-border regimes" and other innovative forms of governance around boundaries under conditions of complex interdependent association (Duchacek, 1986; Martínez, 1986). Western Europe is at the leading edge of discoveries and experiments, particularly within the European Economic Community and the Council of Europe, organizations whose existence is based on the recognition that cross-border interdependence requires a relaxation of national sovereignty in favor of regional cooperation.

Yet, despite the global industrialist motto "Down with Borders" (Barnet and Muller, 1974), the world system remains compartmentalized into sovereign nation-states. These national units still play a fairly decisive role in the world economy—they exert some control over interest rates, money supply, foreign trade, quotas, and tariffs.

Although new production technologies, finance capital systems, and marketing strategies operate on a worldwide basis, nation-states remain a vital element of the world economy. Politically, of course, they continue to be seen as the only viable form for maintaining world order. In this light, boundaries become essential to the maintenance of territorial integrity and the political organization of a world system that recognizes the sovereign rights of nations. As Taylor (1985, p. 105) states, "A world of sovereign states is a world divided by boundaries."

Changing global conditions suggest the need for continued rethinking of the human geographic relationships generated around international political boundaries. Both the western European and U.S.–Mexico boundaries have been severely affected by changes in technology, economics, and power relations. Cross-border movements of labor, commodities, and capital continue to grow. Ten years ago, scholars documented the number of transborder commuter workers in western Europe to be about one-quarter million (Ricq, 1982). A similar number may engage in this activity along the U.S.–Mexico border, although precise data are difficult to obtain. The late twentieth-century world arena has become a place of porous boundaries. Trade, migration, communications, technology, and culture link nation-states together, often in a way that offsets the traditional role of the political border. Furthermore, modern military technology has modified the importance of land boundaries.

The boundaries of western Europe and the U.S.–Mexico borderlands have been transformed from isolated buffer zones into highly urbanized regions with formidable concentrations of resources, capital, economic activities, and institutional mechanisms for further growth. As we shall see in the next chapter, the U.S.–Mexico border region, in particular, has become one of the most important economic regions in the Western Hemisphere, as well as a source of political controversy for the two nations.

The meaning of the international boundary itself as a spatial setting is a subject that few have considered. Yet the transformation of many border zones from sparsely settled frontiers to urbanized spheres of economic growth suggests a need for a better understanding of the urbanization process along the international boundary.

It is useful to recall the limitations of the theoretical body of knowledge on international boundaries inherited from a generation of political geographers. As mentioned earlier, prior to World War II, political geographers typically studied the military or strategic significance of boundaries in the larger analysis of power relations between nation-states (Minghi, 1963; Prescott, 1965; Spykman, 1942). Boundaries were viewed as essentially unstable. With the nation-state serving as the principal unit of analysis in political geography (Johnston, 1982), empirical research was of a general nature. Only case studies of the redrawing of boundaries occasionally surfaced.

Many early researchers emphasized the restrictive nature of borders, viewing them as obstructions to "normal" patterns of economic activity. Christaller argued that international boundaries imposed a set of uncertainties on the organization of economic space. Boundaries tended to distort the size and spacing of trade areas, thus causing locational problems for consumers and retailers (Christaller, 1966, p. 96). Losch (1954, p. 199) addressed borders in a discussion titled "Economic Regions under Difficult Conditions" and essentially compared political boundaries to the edges of market areas, noting that "both break up the regular meshes, which are then replaced by relatively uneconomic areas." Hoover (1948) believed that borders impeded both the migration of factors of production (labor, capital, and enterprise) and the exchange of commodities. He outlined a variety of ways that boundaries obstruct trade, including tariffs, the expense and time required to administer boundary regulations, and differences in tastes, customs, and language. He noted that "trade across boundaries is ordinarily slower, more complicated, more roundabout, and therefore more costly" (ibid., p. 225).

It was only after World War II, as I noted earlier, that scholars began to view boundaries more simply as forces of interruption or conflict. For a time, questions about the political-military significance of boundaries were replaced by those involving what House (1968, p. 331) has termed "normal boundary contact between states." The literature became inundated with case studies of boundary zones over the next two decades.

One salient group of border researchers emerged in Europe in the post–World War II period. The work by these scholars reflected, in part, a response to the political geography of border regions in western Europe. Most of this century in western Europe has seen a gradual shift away from absolute national sovereignty toward recognition of an integrated European system. This became the central theme in the European literature on borders (Anderson, 1982; House, 1968;

Quintin, 1973; Strassoldo and Delli Zotti, 1982). Changing technologies and economic relationships caused researchers to focus their attention on the increasing permeability of political borders and the resulting growth in the magnitude of exchanges of workers, consumers, products, and capital (Anderson, 1982). They also realized that the compact political geography of western Europe and the historic juxtaposition of ethnic systems, culture, language, and religion all contributed to the pattern of societal integration across political borders (House, 1968, pp. 334–344; Tagil, 1982).

As is the case along the U.S.–Mexico border, western European boundary zones have become more urbanized in the post–World War II era. Cities that have grown along European boundaries include Lille, Trieste, Basel, Geneva, Strasbourg, and Liège-Maastrict-Aachen. This proliferation of urban settlement clusters has typically been accompanied by an increase in sets of transboundary spatial and economic linkages, including commuter worker flows, trade, and exchange of capital and technology.

The increase in the degree of functional interdependence has been addressed by European scholars in a variety of ways. Some have focused on the cross-border economic impacts of activities on either side of the boundary (House, 1968; Sayer, 1982). Others have been preoccupied with the legal and political aspects of transfrontier cooperation (Anderson, 1982; Dupuy, 1982; Hansen, 1983; Strassoldo, 1982). Still others have examined border zones as functional planning regions whose importance overshadows the political line itself (Quintin, 1973; Strassoldo, 1982). In the Council of Europe, a parliamentary organization connected to the EEC, European nations, beginning in the early 1970s, sought to establish an applied research agenda on the nature of border region problems, as well as experimental solutions to these problems through multilateral transfrontier cooperation agreements. Among those agreements are transnational commissions set up to deal with pollution on the Rhine River, Lake Geneva, and other areas (Council of Europe, 1977, 1979, 1982).

Whereas western European borders have provided one important example of the evolution of urban space around international borders, the U.S.–Mexico border region offers an even more striking example. During the period 1950–1980, this was one of the fastest-growing regions in the world. The implications of border urbanization are clearly distinct from those in western Europe. Substantial differences in culture and levels of economic development, as well as a history of borderlands conflict, mark the region (Friedmann and Morales, 1984). The philosophy of European integration that led to the formation of the European Economic Community does not have a counterpart in North America. Although urbanization has occurred on either side of the boundary, and interaction flourishes, the meaning this has in terms of the organization of space still remains to be understood. On a regional scale, Hansen (1981, pp. 22–30), in reviewing growth pole literature and location theory as they apply to border regions, found these bodies of knowledge to be inadequate for understanding the economy of border regions. Still less conceptual or theoretical guidance exists for understanding the organization of urban space along borders.

What is needed is a spatial approach to the study of international boundaries. Such an approach would analyze both the impact of the boundary on the settlement space around the political border and the complex social and economic formations that become embedded in settlement space because of unique locational, political, and other attributes of the border zone. This would build on Prescott's (1965, pp. 90–108) classical concern with "border landscapes" and Lapradelle's (1928) emphasis on "*le voisinage,*" or the border zone. The idea would be to go beyond landscape studies to probe the political and institutional processes that shape human geographic forms along the boundary, as well as the forces that cause those processes to overlap across the border. One might hypothesize that international boundaries impose some measurable impact on settlements within a given area of influence. These impacts may include land-use structure, the location of economic activities, transport networks, population distribution, and retail service locations. Minghi (1963, p. 428) regarded research of this nature as important and, in his review of literature on border studies in the 1960s, observed that an important direction of future research should be to consider the role of boundaries "in determining spatial patterns of selected behavioral activity."

In sum, political geography has generated an important bank of historical information about borders, yet in the two decades since Prescott and Minghi called for more work on border land-use patterns and landscape analysis, little new research has appeared. One reason for this lack is that modes of thinking from the past (for example, a preoccupation with the destabilizing effects of boundaries) may have carried over into the conceptual approaches taken by scholars interested in border regions. As subsequent chapters in this book seek to make clear, analysis of border space (border cities) within the context of the global economic system must transcend the narrow perspective of "boundary studies" traditionally employed by political geographers and others. The study of border space requires an analysis of extralocal forces and a sensitivity toward the cross-cultural dimensions of border regions.

3 The Formation of an Urban System along the U.S.–Mexico Boundary

In the spirit of a new people that is conscious not only of its proud heritage, but also of the brutal "gringo" invasion of our territories, we, the Chicano inhabitants and civilizers of the northern land of Aztlán, from whence came our forefathers, reclaiming the land of their birth and consecrating the determination of our people of the sun, declare that the call of our blood is our power, our responsibility, and our inevitable destiny. . . . Aztlán belongs to those that plant the seeds, water the fields, and gather the crops, and not to the foreign Europeans. We do not recognize capricious frontiers on the bronze continent. . . . Before the world, before all of North America, before all our brothers in the bronze continent, we are a nation, we are a union of free pueblos, we are AZTLAN.

—El Plan de Aztlán

CHICANO WRITERS AND HISTORIANS have said that the U.S.–Mexico borderlands are a place of singular cultural origins. Before the U.S.–Mexican War of 1846, all of the southwestern territory—including the present-day states of California, New Mexico, Arizona, Texas, and Colorado—was part of Mexico. Some scholars believe that the borderlands region was inhabited by the (pre-Aztec) predecessors of the Nahuatl culture, who migrated into the Valley of Mexico in the thirteenth century. They claim that records left behind speak of a place between two rivers, which may have been the Gila River in Arizona and the Rio Grande in Texas (Valdez and Steiner, 1972). Although this notion is disputed by other scholars and archaeologists, it remains possible that Aztlán, the mythical land of Aztec ancestors, may actually have been the region that is now the Southwestern United States. This injects an element of ethnic loyalty into the cultural mosaic one finds in the borderlands today, typified in El Plan de Aztlán, written by Chicano activists in 1969, and quoted above (ibid.).

Figure 1. The U.S.–Mexico Border Region

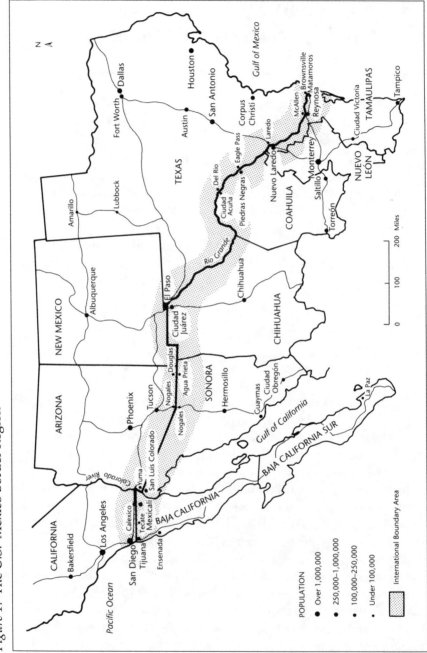

The modern boundary that separates the two nations is hardly a logical one in terms of ecology, culture, and history. Today, the area commonly labeled the U.S.–Mexico border region (Figure 1) encompasses (to the north) the states of Texas, New Mexico, and Arizona, as well as southern California. In Mexico, it includes the states of Tamaulipas, Nuevo León, Coahuila, Chihuahua, Sonora, and Baja California. The international boundary is a jurisdictional line nearly two thousand miles long that runs roughly through the middle of this region, from the Gulf of Mexico to the Pacific Ocean. For nearly one-half the distance the boundary is physiographic, following the natural contour of the Rio Grande. At El Paso, it becomes a geometric line, cutting across the Sonoran and Mojave desert regions and over the coastal sierra until it reaches its westernmost terminus at San Diego–Tijuana.

U.S. economic interest in the borderlands region led to Anglo immigration and settlement of the area in the early 1800s. When the United States sought to annex Texas in the 1840s, armed conflict broke out between Mexico and its northern neighbor. Mexico's defeat led to the signing of the Treaty of Guadalupe Hidalgo in 1848, in which the present states of California, Arizona, New Mexico, Texas, Nevada, Utah, and parts of Colorado, Kansas, Oklahoma, and Wyoming were ceded to the United States in exchange for a cessation of hostilities, the withdrawal of U.S. troops from Mexico, and a payment of fifteen million dollars (Bevans, 1972).

The signing of the Treaty of Guadalupe Hidalgo and the subsequent drawing of the international boundary begin the history of the bicultural border zone as we know it today. At its inception, the line cut across uninhabited terrain—deserts, river valleys, mesas, canyons, and mountain chains. In the middle of the nineteenth century, the core populations of the United States and Mexico resided in their northeast and central plateau regions, respectively. The boundary was simply an artificial line cutting through an ecological region, divided politically for the first time at mid-century. In the beginning, the border zone was not meant to house large cities. It was a territory that mirrored Turner's (1969) conception of the frontier, a region on the edge of civilization, or what House has described as a place of "scarce natural resources in a forbidding environment" (House, 1982, p. 56).

As Table 2 shows, the principal treaties addressing the border region in the nineteenth century and in the first half of the twentieth,

Table 2. Principal Treaties and Other Bilateral Agreements,
U.S.–Mexico Border Region

Year Signed	Treaty/Agreement	Description
1828	U.S.–Mexico Boundary Line	Defined boundary at Arkansas and Red rivers
1831	Amity, Commerce and Navigation	Opened ports to citizens of both nations; gave security and equal rights to citizens residing in either nation; allowed for ease of passage by citizens of both nations
1848	Guadalupe Hidalgo	Ended U.S.–Mexico War; established new international boundaries at Rio Grande, Gila River, and port of San Diego
1853	Gadsden Treaty	Revised fifth article of Guadalupe Hidalgo treaty to include additional lands south of Gila River within U.S. jurisdiction
1884	Boundary Waters: Rio Grande and Rio Colorado	Defined political border along Rio Grande and Rio Colorado
1889	Boundary Waters: Rio Grande and Rio Colorado	Formation of International Boundary Commission (IBC) to address boundary disputes and problems along two rivers
1906	Distribution of Waters of Rio Grande	Agreed on equitable distribution of Rio Grande water for irrigation purposes
1910	Chamizal Arbitration	Resolved land jurisdiction problem for Rio Grande in the Ciudad Juárez–El Paso region
1925	Prevention of Smuggling	Agreement to exchange information to prevent smuggling
1944	Utilization of Waters of Colorado, Rio Grande and Tijuana Rivers	Outlined agreements on water management along three major boundary rivers; reorganized IBC to become International Boundary and Water Commission (IBWC)

Continued on facing page

Table 2 (continued).

Year Signed	Treaty/Agreement	Description
1952	Aviation	Agreed to facilitate flight notifications on nonscheduled private, commercial, or industrial flights across U.S.–Mexico border
1960	Construction of Amistad Dam	Agreement to build Amistad Dam on Rio Grande to form part of system of international storage dams
1970	Economic and Technical Cooperation	Agreed to designate officials and maintain contact on matters of economic and social development of border area
1972	Emergency Delivery of Colorado River Water to Tijuana	Agreement by IBWC facilitating transport of Colorado River water to Tijuana on an emergency basis
1973	Colorado River Salinity Problem	Identified solution to border problem of salinity of the Colorado River
1978	Environmental Cooperation	Agreed to cooperate on environmental and transboundary problems
1979	Housing and Urban Development	Agreed to cooperate and seek technical exchanges in housing/urban development, especially in urban areas along international border
1980	New River Sanitation Problem	Recommendations for resolution of New River border sanitation problem at Calexico, California

Sources: Bevans, 1972; U.S. Department of State, 1987.

were concerned with boundary definition and maintenance in an area devoid of population. During the second half of the twentieth century, however, treaties and negotiations over the boundary took on a different character—they began to reflect dramatic changes unfolding along the border and in the larger region. The transformation process involved the gradual formation of urban settlements in and around the boundary. From 1950 to 1980, border cities were among the fastest-growing urban areas on the continent. As thousands of inhabitants began to occupy the region, the United States and Mexico for the first time were faced not only with simple boundary maintenance questions, but with management problems for a border region populated by larger and larger numbers of U.S. and Mexican citizens. Thus treaties emerged dealing with economic and cultural exchange along the border (1970), environmental cooperation (1978), housing and urban development (1979), and the New River sanitation problem (1980).

The gradual settlement of the border area after 1848, leading up to large-scale urbanization in the second half of the twentieth century, is part of the changing regional dynamics of North America. The dramatic economic transformation of this zone in the twentieth century contrasts rather starkly with historian Charles Lummis' (1925) description of the nineteenth-century border zone as the "land of sunshine, adobe, and silence." In the twentieth century, the borderlands attracted industry for the first time (Dillman, 1983); tourism and trade also proved to be vital sources of wealth (James, 1983; West and James, 1983). These new activities, in turn, generated multiplier effects by attracting other new forms of economic activity to the area. The border region became economically viable as government, private investors, and other agents of economic growth discovered its value-enhancing locational advantages. The locational attributes of the border enhanced the demographic restructuring in the region, most notably at the borderline itself. Migration from the interior of Mexico to the border and subsequently into the U.S. Southwest became the anchor for population change in the region. Along the boundary, beginning after World War II, a process of migrant passage and return to and from the Mexican border towns took its toll on the Mexican border cities. By 1980, there were three Mexican border cities with over one million inhabitants.

This growth partly contradicts the classical ideas about border regions discussed in Chapter 2. The process of demographic transformation from rural to urban settlement along the two thousand–mile boundary represents a precedent-setting form of regional change for political boundaries. Although many scholars have treated the growth of the region in a macro sense (Hansen, 1981; House, 1982; Sale, 1975; Urquidi and Méndez Villareal, 1978), only a handful (Dillman, 1970; Hiernaux, 1986; Martínez, 1978) have looked specifically at the urbanization process. What remains to be understood is the human geographic implications of the boundary urbanization process. This chapter looks at the regional dimensions of borderland urban growth.

The growth of frontier cities has been largely determined by developments confined within the national borders of the United States and Mexico. Despite the transborder historical and cultural ties of the region, the growth of cities on each side of the boundary mainly occurred as a result of social, economic, and political forces native to each sovereign nation. The boundary line drawn in 1848 divided the destinies of territory on either side of it: Mexican cities grew as a result of processes operating in Mexico, and U.S. cities reacted to forces within the United States. Over time, regional development became infused with meaning in two very different contexts, north and south of the boundary line. Two vastly different public and private decision-making systems exercised authority over the use of space along the border. By the end of the century, these separate political authorities would clash over the management of common terrain.

National Contrasts: Northern Mexico and the U.S. Southwest

Northern Mexico

Northern Mexico's rapid demographic and economic growth in the twentieth century stands in stark contrast to its importance to the nation in the four previous centuries. During the period of Spanish colonization, from the sixteenth to the nineteenth centuries, Mexico's central plateau region dominated the territorial priorities of the Spanish government. From 1521 to 1810, Spain imposed a rigid administrative system on the Mexican provinces. Regions that offered a high potential for profit, such as the food-producing basins around Mexico City, Puebla, and Guadalajara, or the silver-mining regions in the Bajío and Sierra Madre Occidental, were provided with labor and resources for growth. Within this territorial planning system, the urban hierarchy of colonial Mexico was segmented into three functional city prototypes (Unikel, 1978): (1) administrative cities in the central plateau (Mexico City, Puebla, Guadalajara), (2) port cities for exporting resources to Spain (Veracruz, Acapulco), and (3) mining cities (Guanajuato, San Luis Potosí, Pachuca, Zacatecas). Given the spatial constraints of limited land transport, the territorial limits of Mexican growth during the colonial era were confined to the hinterlands of this system of cities, all of which remained within the core area of central Mexico. From the view of the national political organization of space, this meant that northern Mexico occupied a position of very low status, which was clearly not enhanced by the ecological inhospitality of the arid border zone. One can argue that this historical pattern of regional growth established a precedent of political and economic primacy in the central plateau region, a pattern that continues to structure the territorial priorities of the Mexican government today, despite dramatic shifts in the locational decisions of individuals, firms, and planners, and, indeed, in national demographic structure. Central Mexico remains the core of the nation politically, economically, and culturally.

Northern Mexico did not really begin to emerge from its marginal past until the late nineteenth century, when the construction of the national railroad system during the Porfirio Díaz administration allowed greater communication between northern and central Mexico (Appendini and Murayama, 1972). Although the rail system essentially fortified Mexico City's stronghold over the national economy, it did allow northern Mexico to develop an autonomous economic base for the first time in its history. One important component of that economic base was the development of commercial ties with the United States. Other important economic gains were made through the establishment of centers of cotton production in Matamoros, oil in Tampico, and steel in Monterrey.

Monterrey offers one barometer of the changes affecting northern Mexico in the late nineteenth century. Its population shifted dramatically between 1880, when it was a small city of about sixteen thousand inhabitants, nineteenth-largest in Mexico, to 1960, when it ranked as the third-largest settlement in Mexico, with over one-half million residents. The city possessed some site advantages that would have allowed moderate expansion, for example, accessibility to major Mexican ports on the Gulf of Mexico and to the U.S.–Mexico border, and proximity to natural resources such as iron ore, coal, and natural gas, as well as good supplies of fresh water (Herzog, 1978).

Yet these factors alone could not have caused the city to grow into the second major industrial center of Mexico, and one of the nation's three most important cities. Monterrey's ascendance can be attributed to changes in the late nineteenth century that allowed northern Mexico to exploit some of its advantages over central Mexico; proximity to the United States was perhaps the most important of these advantages. Under the Porfirio Díaz administration, Monterrey cultivated a growing class of industrial entrepreneurs and investors, who developed some autonomy from Mexico City's elite financial class. Over time, the Monterrey bourgeoisie developed financial ties with U.S. elites and received tax breaks, low-interest loans, and other financial incentives from the Mexican government. Gradually, small, successful industrial enterprises grew into large ones as Monterrey's elite was able to gain access to national interests. During the late nineteenth and early twentieth centuries, Monterrey's development was controlled by powerful families, some of them foreign-born (including U.S.). These families developed large-scale industrial enterprises in the steel, beer, glass, textile, and construction industries. By 1960 Monterrey had become the third-largest city in Mexico, the most powerful city in the North, and an important force in the changing regional dynamics of the nation, changes that saw the emergence of northern Mexico as a rival to central Mexico in terms of investment and regional growth.

If one looks at the distribution of Mexico's population from the late nineteenth century to the post–World War II era, the importance of regional shifts from central Mexico to northern Mexico are highlighted. In 1880, only three cities in northern Mexico were among the largest twenty-five cities in the nation—Saltillo, Monterrey, and Hermosillo. During that period, the nation's population, resources, and priorities were clustered in central Mexico—the largest cities being Mexico City, León, Puebla, and Guadalajara. This rank-size distribution reflects the legacy of the Spanish colonial urban system. By 1920, the skewing of people and resources toward the central plateau and southern Mexico had not changed dramatically. With the exception of Monterrey, the largest cities were still in the traditional core—Mexico City, Guadalajara, Puebla, and San Luis Potosí.

It was not really until the post–World War II era that changes in technology and the growth of new local and national markets for Mexico's products allowed the northern Mexico region to emerge as a zone of production and settlement rivaling the central plateau. During the postwar era, commercial agriculture in northern Mexico began a period of dramatic growth, especially in the states of Sonora, Sinaloa, and Baja California. One contributing factor in this rural development shift was that the social revolution of 1910 encouraged agricultural development away from the traditional core area of central Mexico. Agrarian reform programs specifically sought to redistribute lands in states outside the nation's urbanized nucleus—this, in part, in order to enhance colonization efforts in these areas (Barkin, 1970).

A second important economic activity that contributed to the growth of northern Mexico was the expanding transborder trade linkages that evolved in the post–World War II era. (These are discussed in more detail later in this chapter.) So important did these linkages become that, by the 1960s, the Mexican government created a national border development program, PRONAF (Programa Nacional Fronterizo), whose purpose was to enhance the productivity of the region by improving its infrastructure (Dillman, 1970). By 1960, ten of Mexico's twenty-five largest cities were located in northern Mexico, and of these, four (Ciudad Júarez, Mexicali, Tijuana, and Nuevo Laredo) were cities lying directly on the boundary. By the 1970s, per capita incomes in many of northern Mexico's municipalities began to exceed averages in other parts of the country, demonstrating the region's continued growth in importance (Urquidi and Méndez Villareal, 1978).

The U.S. Southwest

The growth of the U.S. Southwest, principally the states of California, Arizona, New Mexico, and Texas (Figure 1), can be viewed within the perspective of long-term evolutionary shifts in the regional structure of the United States. These shifts were tied to the changing relationship between technology, especially in the area of transportation, and the regional spread of population (Borchert, 1967). As the nation evolved from one with an urban system concentrated along the Atlantic coast (pre-1790) to one with river transportation (1830), new settlements emerged in the interior along the Mississippi, Ohio, and Missouri rivers. During the "iron rail" period, cities in the Midwest (Chicago, Detroit, Milwaukee, and Cleveland) were added to the nation's urban system. In general, the nineteenth century was a time in which the northeastern region of the United States dominated the spatial orientation of the nation, with leading cities at the turn of the century being New York, Philadelphia, Pittsburgh, Detroit, and Boston. The Northeast controlled decisions about investment and government infrastructure and thus dictated the tempo of labor, capital, and resource mobility.

However, it is also clear that westward migration and expansion into the southern and western regions were important elements of nineteenth-century regional dynamics. The standardization of rail gauges in the 1870s allowed for the construction of transcontinental rail systems that linked regions for the first time, subsequently opening up investment and development in areas of untapped natural resources, especially in the West and Southwest. Thus, the period 1870–1920 was a time when the infrastructure for regional change was put in place, and several western and southern cities, such as San Francisco, Los Angeles, Atlanta, and Denver, began to establish their importance as regional growth centers.

It was in the period 1920–1960 and beyond, however, when the most dramatic shifts in the spatial organization of the U.S. economy and urban system occurred. During this period the construction of a federal highway system, the emergence of trucking, and the development of a national air transport network allowed extensive spatial deconcentration of the U.S. population, away from the densely urbanized Northeast-Midwest to the South, West, and Southwest. The most notable shifts were marked by the development of new centers of production, resources, and population, such as the financial and business center in Atlanta; the Gulf Coast–Texas–Oklahoma petrochemical industrial area (Dallas, Houston, New Orleans); the Los Angeles–Long Beach–San Diego conurbation; the development of the San Francisco–Bay Area metropolitan region; and the emergence of new Sunbelt cities (Phoenix, Miami–Ft. Lauderdale, San Antonio, Jacksonville, Tampa–St. Petersburg).

Severely altered population distribution patterns underscore the nature of these regional shifts since the Second World War. From 1950 to 1980, population growth in the South surpassed the national mean, and expansion in the West occurred at more than twice the national average. At the same time, both the Northeast and North Central regions experienced rates of population change below the national average.

These trends confirm the now-popular assertion of a new regional transformation in the United States, with the "rise of the southern rim" (Sale, 1975), and the growth of the U.S. Sunbelt (Sawers and Tabb, 1984). The population redistribution from the traditional "frostbelt," or northeastern manufacturing belt, to the South and West did not occur as a result of any single factor (such as transport technology, although this certainly dictated the rhythm of changes in the urban system during the nineteenth century), but, rather, through a complex series of interrelated factors: the migration of various population interest groups (armed forces, elderly, amenity-seeking residents); federal government policies; lower land, energy, and living costs; the growth of new markets and an expansion in the regional industrial base (Weinstein, Gross, and Rees, 1985).

The expansion of the economic base of the South and West probably created much of the impetus for the dramatic shifts in the flow of people, resources, and capital to this region during the last five decades. The development of the main economic activities of the region, principally agriculture, defense, technology, petroleum, real estate, and the "leisure industry" (tourism and recreation) benefited, in part, because demand for the consumption of goods and services shifted away from traditional manufacturing activities toward the tertiary and quaternary sectors in the middle part of this century. As a result of an increase in "post-industrial" (Bell, 1976) economies, such activities could be produced at an advantage in the South and West, thus displacing some of the regional power that the Northeast had held earlier in U.S. history.

The emergence of the Sunbelt illustrates how the market can have a larger influence on regional economic and demographic restructuring than any other force. Public policy, for example, did little to stimulate the growth of the Southwest—this region has never been a particularly high priority area for investment decisions made in Washington, D.C. The Sunbelt rose, not so much because of a conscious shift in public policy, but because a set of economic activities found locational and other advantages there. In short, the Southwest shed its frontier past and became competitive with other productive regions of the United States.

Economic Base of the Borderlands Region

The evolution of an urban system in the borderlands region hints at a more fundamental transformation of the regional economy. Most scholars acknowledge a direct relationship between regional economic development and urban growth (Friedmann, 1972). Cities are typically the driving force in the transformation of a region's economy. They provide a central place for the concentration of resources, technology, infrastructure, and capital utilized in the maximization of a region's production potential. They are frequently the nucleus of technological and other innovations, which may then spread across regions.

Table 3 offers an overview of the economies of borderland states in the United States and Mexico. In the Mexican states, one sees that the manufacturing, commerce, and service sectors employ more workers than the national averages, a reflection of the propensity in border states for economic activity in *urban* areas. Nearly all of the manufacturing activities in the Mexican border states are derived from the assembly-plant program, which allows foreign corporations to utilize Mexican labor to assemble products that are then shipped to their final market destinations outside of Mexico.

On the U.S. side of the boundary, manufacturing represents a lower percentage of employment in border states (16.9) than in the remainder of the United States (22.1). Yet the construction, trade, and

Table 3. Employment by Sector, Border States (%)

Sector	Employment in Border States	National Total
Mexico (1975)		
Agriculture	47.7	64.3
Mining	1.8	.4
Manufacturing	23.9	16.3
Commerce	15.6	11.7
Services	11.0	7.3
Total	100.0	100.0
United States (1978)		
Agriculture	1.2	.7
Mining	1.5	.8
Manufacturing	16.9	22.1
Construction	6.0	5.4
Trade	22.6	21.5
Services	21.6	20.8
Other (incl. gov.)	30.2	28.7
Total	100.0	100.0

Source: Anderson, Clement, and Shellhammer, 1980.

service sectors all employ higher than the national averages. One must also acknowledge the lower proportion of agricultural workers in the U.S. border states (1.2 percent) as compared to Mexico (47.7 percent). Yet, even the Mexican proportion will continue to decrease as more people leave the rural towns for jobs in industry and services in the cities.

The economic base of U.S.–Mexico border cities is as complex as the various subregions that divide the two thousand–mile border region. On the Mexican side of the border, a number of cities display growing manufacturing sectors, most notably Tijuana, Piedras Negras, and Nuevo Laredo. Agriculture continues to be an important source of employment on the Mexican side of the border, especially in Mexicali, Ensenada, and the Lower Rio Grande Valley cities of Reynosa and Matamoros. In these cities, agriculture continues to account for more employment than industry, contradicting prevailing theories of urban growth, which typically assume that industry replaces agriculture as the driving force of the settlement economy.

Another important characteristic of the economic base of border cities is the dominant role of the tertiary sector. It is now clear that retail/wholesale trade, government, education, and services are becoming the dominant economic activities of the border cities. Neither industry nor agriculture alone has established locational attractiveness for capital and labor migration to the border cities. Rather, it is the strategic importance of activities such as tourism, retail trade, construction, and specialized services that have increasingly fueled these urban economies. On the Mexican side of the border, the sum of tertiary activities for most border settlements (construction + retail/wholesale trade + services + government) far surpasses the national figure of 31.3 percent (Secretaría de Industria y Comercio, 1976). In most cases, these activities, taken together, represent more than half of the total employment in these cities. Some, such as construction and personal services, are simply concomitants of urban growth, yet others reflect the penetration of U.S. markets by Mexican border cities. In addition, there exists a large category of service and commercial employment that goes unrecorded—the informal or street economic activities, typified by vendors of goods and services who work periodically at different locations.

On the U.S. side, the tertiary economy has become equally important, although for different reasons. The retail trade sector has grown, with some linkages to Mexican markets. Services such as real estate, finance, and insurance represent a large proportion of the tertiary growth in border settlements, as does tourism, which attracts both a regional and a national market because of the climate, physical amenities of the Sunbelt, and the proximity of Mexico. Construction activities, education, and real estate are concomitants of high urban growth rates. In many cases, employment in government far outdistances national urban figures, due to the location of large military bases and operations along the border near cities like Las Cruces, El Paso, Yuma, and San Diego. Some of these cities also employ large numbers of civilians in activities that support military base operations (ship repair, construction and manufacturing contracts, food and other services).

Perhaps the most striking characteristic of the border cities is the economic asymmetry at the boundary. In Mexico in 1960, for example, border municipalities averaged about $640 (U.S.) in per capita income per year, approximately one-fifth the average income in the United States for the same year. Still, the Mexican figure represented more than twice the average per capita income of other cities in Mexico, suggesting that Mexican border cities are prosperous relative to the rest of the nation. Proximity to Mexico, however, appears to bring down the per capita income levels in many U.S. border cities. Wage levels in 1977 for border towns such as Calexico, Eagle Pass, Laredo, and Brownsville tended to represent only one-half the average wage levels for the respective states. As one moves away from the border (El Centro, Yuma, or Tucson), or in cities that have a more diversified economy (San Diego), per capita incomes rise substantially.

The spatial distribution of urban per capita incomes presents an interesting set of patterns. In Mexico, per capita income is relatively homogeneous across the boundary region, with the exception of Tijuana (where it is higher). Mexican spatial variation has a north-south orientation, rather than an east-west one. As one moves into the interior, per capita incomes decrease. In the United States, the opposite is true. As one moves away from the border, incomes tend to rise, except in cities where a higher proportion of Mexican American workers live (San Antonio, for example). In addition, per capita incomes rise as one moves from east (Texas) to west (California). Hansen (1981, p. 75) has noted that much of this urban income pattern is correlated with ethnicity. A strong negative correlation between income levels and Hispanic settlement can be documented in U.S. towns and cities across the two thousand–mile border.

The economic asymmetry between the two nations does not end at the boundary—it spills over into the United States and, with a few exceptions, leaves a belt of socioeconomically depressed areas (relative to the rest of the United States) along the immediate border on the U.S. side. Ironically, on the Mexican side, the ability to earn U.S. dollars in service activities such as tourism, auto repair, or entertainment has created a belt of prosperous border towns just south of the boundary. The coexistence of these two sets of settlements with contrasting characteristics reflects one of the important peculiarities of borderlands settlement space at the international political line.

The evolution of the borderlands economy flies in the face of traditional theories about the economies of border zones. In the work of such theorists as Christaller and Losch, and others, the boundary line was seen as being a disruptive force—cutting off the city-hinterland market relationship, interrupting supply networks, distorting trade relations, and debilitating the effects of a growth pole (Hansen, 1981). The international political boundary zone was viewed as a fragile and politically sensitive region that would present a set of continual political and institutional barriers to private investment and economic growth. Yet, by the late twentieth century, the development of the U.S.–Mexico borderlands economy suggests that the opposite can occur. In what was once an arid, resource-poor frontier at the edge of two nation-states, a vital, dynamic economic base has emerged around the development of a regional system of cities, within which a subsystem of border cities has gained increasing importance.

The Borderlands Urban System

The emergence of a system of cities in the borderlands region illustrates how this region has moved from a nineteenth-century frontier zone at the margin of national territory to a twentieth-century area of economic dynamism. The appearance of cities on the landscape of the border region is a barometer of the transformation of the region's economy. The borderlands urban system, as it grew and spread over the territory of the U.S. Southwest and Northern Mexico, has displayed increasing integration, both within the United States and Mexico, and across the international boundary. The strengthening of intraregional ties can be correlated with the gradual improvement and diversification of the regional economy and the region's expanding importance to the hemisphere.

Cities ultimately represent an essential propulsive force in extending economic influence over a region. They become the loci of production, consumption, power, innovation, technology, and knowledge. Much of the earliest work on city systems sought to discover correlations between mathematical city-size distributions and levels of economic development (Berry, 1961), or relationships between urban size and efficiency (Alonso, 1971). Yet, much of this kind of research has proven to be inconclusive. Others have recognized the importance of territorial politics and power in dictating the growth of city systems (Friedmann, 1972), while it is generally acknowledged that public sector decisions, especially those made at the state and federal levels, extend considerable influence over the growth of an urban system.

The unusually high growth rate of the border urban system is highlighted in Table 4. On both sides of the political boundary, mean annual growth rates have far surpassed the national averages. In the United States, during the decade of the 1970s, growth rates for the largest U.S. border cities were three to four times greater than the national average. Obviously, this growth figure did not entirely result from proximity to the border, particularly in the cases of San Diego and Tucson, cities with diversified economic bases. Still, it remains significant that growth rates were abnormally high on the U.S. side. Along the northern Mexican border, growth rates in the decade 1960–1970 were one-and-a-half to two times as large as the national average in most of the region's principal border cities. Between 1970 and 1983, this growth continued.

Overall, the Mexican cities along the border grew at faster rates than their U.S. counterparts. Also, it is quite likely that the Mexican population estimates may be undercounted for two reasons: first, many new immigrants to Mexican border cities live on property that is not registered by the government and thus may be excluded in census population counts; second, there is a substantial population of border residents that migrates seasonally to employment opportunities north of the border, and therefore may be missed by census takers. In any case, it seems clear that border cities have become an important part of Mexico's national population picture. Of the fifteen largest cities in Mexico, eight are cities located in border states; of

Table 4. Population Growth of Principal U.S. and Mexican Border Cities

	Average Annual Growth Rate	
	1960–70	1970–80
U.S. Cities		
San Diego	3.1	3.7
Tucson	3.2	5.1
Las Cruces	1.6	3.8
El Paso	1.4	3.4
Laredo	1.2	3.6
McAllen	.03	5.6
Brownsville	−.07	4.9
United States	1.7	1.0
Mexican Cities		
Tijuana	6.2	6.6
Mexicali	4.2	4.1
San Luis Colorado	5.8	6.2
Nogales	3.3	3.6
Ciudad Juárez	4.5	4.8
Nuevo Laredo	4.9	5.2
Reynosa	6.4	6.8
Río Bravo	8.3	8.9
Matamoros	4.1	4.4
Mexico	3.3	3.2

Sources: U.S.: U.S. Bureau of the Census, 1986; Mexico: Banamex, 1983, pp. 48–49.

these, three are cities lying directly along the border. By comparison, the importance of border region cities in the United States to the larger national urban system is far weaker than in Mexico. Only three U.S. cities out of the top fifteen lie in border states, and of these, none is a border city.

Table 5 offers population figures for the border region urban system including the subset of immediate border cities within that larger regional system. Several patterns emerge from Table 5. For cities lying on the boundary, population is greater in cities on the Mexican side, with the exception of San Diego, a city with a diverse economy tied to its naval base, physical amenities, and proximity to markets in

Table 5. Rank-Size Urban System, U.S.–Mexico Border Region

United States		Mexico	
City[a]	1980 Pop.	City	1983 Pop.
Los Angeles/Long Beach	11,497,568	Monterrey	2,651,000
Dallas/Ft. Worth	2,930,516	• Ciudad Juárez	750,600
Houston	2,735,766	• Tijuana	636,900
• San Diego	1,861,846	Torreón	603,300
Phoenix	1,509,052	Tampico	546,000
San Antonio	1,071,954	Chihuahua	478,400
Austin	536,688	• Mexicali	446,900
Tucson	531,443	Hermosillo	410,700
• El Paso	479,899	• Reynosa	321,900
Albuquerque	419,700	Saltillo	318,500
Bakersfield	403,089	• Nuevo Laredo	287,000
Corpus Christi	326,228	• Matamoros	240,100
• McAllen/Edinburg/		Obregón	236,400
Mission	283,229	Monclova	180,100
Lubbock	211,651	Ensenada	179,900
• Brownsville/Harlingen	209,727	Ciudad Victoria	167,800
Amarillo	173,699	• Río Bravo	118,900
• Laredo	99,258	Guaymas	114,600
• Las Cruces	96,340	Piedras Negras	113,700
Santa Fe	93,118	• San Luis Colorado	109,800
• Del Rio	30,000	• Nogales	82,200
• Eagle Pass	20,000	• Ciudad Acuña	41,900
• Nogales	16,000	• Agua Prieta	34,400
• Calexico	14,000	• Tecate	30,500
• Douglas	13,000		

Sources: U.S.: U.S. Bureau of the Census, 1984; Mexico: Banamex, 1983.

• = city on international boundary.

a. Standard Metropolitan Statistical Area (SMSA).

southern California. Otherwise, the immediate Mexican border cities outdistance their U.S. counterparts substantially. This reflects, more than anything else, Mexico's greater dependence on the United States. This dependence has transformed the border cities into reception areas for Mexicans seeking employment in the United States. Over time, many in-migrants have stayed in the border cities and found employment there as the economies expanded and diversified. In the United States, after San Diego, El Paso, McAllen, and

Brownsville, populations fall off below 100,000. Yet in Mexico, nine border cities have over 100,000 inhabitants.

One also sees similar patterns at the regional level. Again, many of the U.S. border cities fall at the bottom of the regional rank-size hierarchy, whereas Mexican boundary cities are skewed more toward the middle and top. Several important patterns of population distribution can be identified (see also Figure 1). Population tends to be concentrated in two major subregions: the California–Baja California border zone, and the northern Mexico/Monterrey–Lower Rio Grande area. In the California–Baja California area, one finds several high-order metropolitan centers, including Los Angeles, San Diego, Tijuana, and Mexicali; in the Lower Rio Grande (Texas) and northern Mexico region, one finds Monterrey to the southwest, and a number of growing border cities like Brownsville–Matamoros, McAllen–Reynosa–Río Bravo, and Laredo–Nuevo Laredo. A large number of high-order cities are nearby (San Antonio, Corpus Christi, Tampico, and Torreón).

Much of the borderlands between the two urbanized subregions of California–Baja California and northeast Mexico–South Texas is sparsely populated, with the exception of corridors of linked cities in Arizona and Sonora (Phoenix–Tucson–Nogales–Hermosillo–Guaymas) and New Mexico and Chihuahua (Albuquerque–El Paso–Ciudad Juárez–Chihuahua). The fact that the border region is divided into essentially four subregions, each with its own subsystem of cities, illustrates how the borderlands have evolved into a region that is in significant ways spatially integrated in a north-south manner (transboundary/transnational) rather than in a west-east manner (national). Yet at the same time, the distributional patterns emphasize the degree to which Mexico has more at stake in these emerging transboundary linkages and thus has developed a system of immediate border cities with larger populations than the U.S. "sister" cities just across the border.

Industrial Location

Industrial location has become an important determinant of the growth of the urban system along the border. Although classical industrial location theory suggests that international borders will be highly unattractive to a firm's locational priorities, since the border would cut off the market and create additional institutional costs (and risks) for the transport of goods (Christaller, 1966; Losch, 1954), the modern U.S.–Mexico border region has seen the evolution of conditions that classical location theorists could not have foreseen. Mainly, the boundary region has evolved as an area in which labor is both cheap and highly mobile. This has been the principal incentive for the development of the assembly-plant industrial development program on the Mexican side of the boundary.

The Border Industrial Program (BIP) was created in Mexico in the mid-1960s to help relieve unemployment in border cities. It was part of a national strategy to strengthen the border region economy through PRONAF, or the National Border Program. The aim was to create institutional conditions to foster industrial development along the border. Although Mexico realized that the border region could not fully draw industrial capital away from the heartlands of industrial development in the hemisphere, it saw the potential to attract capital for assembly plants, or *maquiladoras,* which would assemble industrial goods, principally for multinational corporations (Fernández Kelly, 1983; House, 1982).

By the late 1980s, assembly plants had become the cornerstone of the manufacturing sector along the northern Mexican border. In 1987, these plants employed about one-quarter million Mexican workers, clearly the fastest-growing sector in the entire region (Banco de México, 1987). Cities like Nogales, Matamoros, and Nuevo Laredo, which were not economically dynamic otherwise, owed their growth in large part to the development of this specialized, labor-intensive economic sector.

The long-term viability of the assembly-plant program has been severely questioned, however. The *maquiladora* process represents only the final stages of industrial production and does not allow northern Mexico to enjoy the backward and forward linkages that normal industrial development generates (Fernández, 1977). For example, all of the inputs to the assembly of electronic goods (glass tubes, circuit boards, and so on) are produced in the United States, and all of the technological outputs (research and development) associated with the electronics industry are also generated on the U.S. side of the border. Finally, the principal markets for the finished goods are located north of the border. Thus, northern Mexico gets only the employment generation of the *maquiladora,* and little more (Tamayo and Fernández, 1983). Although much discussion of the spread effects of assembly plants in the form of development of technical skills, managerial talent, and pilot manufacturing outlets took place early on, hardly any of these kinds of benefits have trickled down from the *maquiladora* program.

More important, the program is controlled by foreign capital, and its main locational incentive is cheap labor, making this sector "footloose." In 1975, for example, Mexico remained a leader in the electronics sector, but was already facing stiff competition from less-developed nations in other sectors, such as textiles and clothing. The number of nations involved in the foreign assembly process is increasing dramatically (Table 6). Whereas in 1972, only Mexico, Taiwan, Singapore, Hong Kong, and South Korea were substantially involved, by 1978, at least eleven nations, including Brazil, El Salvador, and the Philippines, earned more than twenty million dollars in export value from these activities. Although Mexico held its own in terms of the percentage of total imports by the United States, the extension of these "export enclaves" into new cheap labor zones illustrates both the high mobility of such operations and the vulnerability of the northern Mexican border region to losing its hold on this im-

Table 6. Value of U.S. Imports from Selected Less-Developed Nations (millions of dollars)

Country	1972 Import Value	%	1978 Import Value	%
Mexico	170.3	32.6	715.3	32.9
Taiwan	162.1	31.0	392.6	18.0
Singapore	66.6	12.7	193.3	8.9
Malaysia	0.2	—	188.1	8.6
Hong Kong	73.1	14.0	182.4	8.4
Brazil	3.5	—	123.3	5.7
South Korea	21.6	4.1	117.8	5.4
Other	13.5	2.6	97.1	4.5
Philippines	6.3	1.2	72.5	3.3
El Salvador	0.3	—	44.3	2.0
Haiti	5.1	1.0	28.7	1.3
Dominican Rep.	0.3	—	20.1	0.9
Total	522.9	100.0	2,175.5	100.0

Source: Tamayo and Fernández, 1983, p. 228.

Notes: Assembly of machinery, electrical equipment, and textiles occupies about three-fourths of total value of imports. Percentages are rounded unless otherwise noted.

portant sector. As a result, Mexico extended the geographic area of eligibility for the assembly plant program from the original zone of 12.5 miles from the boundary to the entire nation. Recent data suggest that some *maquiladoras* are beginning to locate in the nation's interior (about 17 percent of all *maquiladoras* in 1987; see Sinkin and Marks, 1988). If this trend continues, it could eventually neutralize the geographic dominance of the northern border in this economic sector (Grunwald and Flamm, 1985).

Furthermore, a number of writers have commented on the limitations of the assembly-plant program as a source of long-term employment stability along the border. It has been shown that between 65 and 90 percent of all employees in border city assembly plants are women between the ages of sixteen and twenty-four (Fernández Kelly, 1983; Tamayo and Fernández, 1983). Women supposedly have the skills needed for assembly work, but others speculate that they are hired because they are easier to train, partly as a result of their lack of knowledge of labor laws and union organization. By hiring women, however, the *maquiladora* programs have not resolved the unemployment problem along the border; they have simply created a new "artificial" labor force. Yet there can be no question that, despite these limitations, the border industrialization program has injected jobs and income into the border region, thus contributing to the growth of the urban system on the Mexican side of the boundary.

On the U.S. side, changes in the nature of industry created locational advantages in the Southwest that contributed to the growth of cities. Although, in the past, transport of traditional industrial goods (heavy durables) to the northeastern markets would have eliminated the Southwest from consideration in location decisions, the development of new economic sectors in manufacturing—principally high-technology industries like computer goods and electronics—has changed the locational formulas of U.S. firms. Even corporate headquarters have shifted their locational priorities toward the Sunbelt (Suárez Villa, 1984). Furthermore, the availability of (often illegal) Mexican labor on the U.S. side of the border in such industries as garment production cannot be discounted as a locational factor in the siting of new industries in the Southwest, even though this might not be stated officially. Taken together, these factors must be recognized as part of the momentum in the shift of population and resources toward the Southwest.

Spatial Interaction and Transboundary Economic Space

Discussion in this chapter has characterized the borderlands urban system as a set of points (urban centers) in regional space with an identifiable economic structure. It has been suggested that two distinct urban systems formed on either side of the border, each with economic properties derived within a separate national context. Although some similarities can be accounted for by the sharing of the boundary and common geographic resources, for the most part, northern Mexico is a substantially different region than the U.S. Southwest; each has different economic priorities, and each has evolved at a level compatible with its national setting.

What has not yet been addressed here is the gradual evolution of linkages between the national subsystems of cities north and south of the border. These linkages are part of a transboundary economic system that involves growing volumes of intercity exchanges of goods, services, people, workers, technology, and capital across the U.S.–Mexico border. Such linkages occur at the regional scale, that is, between northern Mexican cities and southwestern U.S. cities, as well as at the local or immediate level, that is, between paired U.S. and Mexican cities lying directly along the border. (The latter is discussed in Chapter 6.)

Transboundary economic space in the U.S.–Mexico borderlands can be viewed as an overlapping of product, service, and labor markets across the international political line. As the boundary region on either side has become more populated, and as its economy has diversified, these transborder economic linkages have become both larger and more complex. Growing transborder economic interaction reflects the fact that the United States and Mexico have become important trading partners. Mexico exports about 65 percent of all its merchandise to the United States, while 60 percent of all its imports come from there. After Canada, Japan, Germany, and England, Mexico is the fifth-largest export market for U.S. merchandise (James, 1983, p. 154). More important, most import and export occurs in the borderlands region. Table 7 shows that in 1980, 86 percent of all U.S. exports to Mexico originated in the border states, and 69 percent of all goods imported went to destinations in the U.S. border states. Thus when we speak of U.S.–Mexico economic relations, a significant portion of these exchanges occur through geographically determined

Table 7. U.S. Trade with Mexico, 1980 (millions of dollars)

	U.S. Exports to Mexico			U.S. Imports from Mexico		
Product	From Border States	Total	% from Border States	To Border States	Total	% to Border States
Animal & plant	1,855.9	2,533.3	73.0	1,360.8	1,469.5	93.0
Wood & paper	563.6	575.6	98.0	159.6	161.5	99.0
Textiles	325.9	332.8	98.0	248.3	267.8	93.0
Chemicals (petroleum, gas, etc.)	1,507.7	1,747.2	86.0	3,694.6	6,886.6	54.0
Nonmetallic minerals	216.8	258.5	84.0	161.0	177.3	91.0
Machinery & transport equipment	7,857.8	8,538.7	92.0	2,336.6	2,804.1	83.0
Other	834.6	1,154.9	72.0	673.7	725.7	93.0
Total	13,162.3	15,141.0	86.0	8,634.6	12,492.5	69.0

Source: Security Pacific National Bank, 1981, p. 10. Reprinted in J. Ramírez A. and V. Castillo R., 1985.

supply-and-demand relationships native to urban centers in the borderlands region.

Exchanges of factors of production (labor, capital, raw materials, managerial skills), finished products, and services determine the nature of transboundary economic space. Because transboundary input-output data are difficult to collect, we can piece together only some elements of the transboundary economic system using other crude measures.

In general, the cross-border exchanges penetrate virtually all sectors of the borderlands economy. More than half of Mexico's exports to the United States in 1980 were in the primary sector merchandise category (agriculture, 9.3 percent; minerals and metals, 5.9 percent; petroleum, 42 percent). Although petroleum does not come from northern Mexico, about half of all the imported petroleum goes to U.S. border states. Agriculture displays even stronger linkages, with much of the exchange of Mexican farm products coming from the border states of Sonora, Baja California (fruits, vegetables, cotton) and the Lower Rio Grande Valley in Tamaulipas (Schramm, 1984). Of all merchandise exported by Mexico (and two-thirds of this goes to the United States), primary products dominate; only 7.8 percent of Mexico's total exports in 1980 were in manufactured products.

The tertiary sector is growing rapidly in Mexico and the border region. The growth of Mexico's border cities and the expansion of their economies have been fueled by the development of strategies to capture the U.S. markets in the areas of retail trade, tourism, assembly of manufactured parts (electronics, clothing), and other services. In 1980, slightly more than one-third of all Mexican export income was derived from these activities, and much of this is income captured along the international border. Thus, for example, one finds that between 1960 and 1982, Mexican border cities experienced overall favorable trade balances, although the "retention coefficients," the ability to retain trade-related income on the Mexican side of the border, fell off considerably in the 1980s (Table 8). By 1980, for every dollar earned on the Mexican side of the border, about eighty-four cents was respent in the United States. In 1982, it was estimated that more than ninety-one cents on every dollar earned in Mexican border cities went back into the United States. Mexican border cities have generally prospered through decades of commercial integration into the U.S. economy. This integration produced largely positive trade balances, although some trade deficits have occurred.

Despite these overall healthy transactions, Mexican border cities generally suffer because of an abundant drainage of capital back into

Table 8. Border Transactions, Mexico, 1960–1982 (millions of dollars)

	Income	Expenditures	Balance	Retention Coefficient (%) [Balance ÷ Income]
1960	366.0	221.0	145.0	39.6
1965	449.5	295.2	154.3	40.9
1970	878.9	585.0	293.9	33.4
1975	1,541.6	957.7	583.9	37.9
1980	3,722.1	3,129.6	592.5	15.9
1982	4,149.2	3,756.6	392.6	9.4

Source: Banco de México, 1982.

the United States (as shown by the low retention coefficients in the 1980s). Some researchers claim that this is the result of becoming too dependent on the United States commercially and of an absence of government policy in Mexico for controlling border trade (Tamayo and Fernández, 1983). In 1972, between $600 million and $740 million was spent by Mexican consumers in towns on the U.S. side of the border (ibid., p. 107). This virtually neutralizes any overall gains made through commercial transactions with the United States.

Thus, although a transnational economy operates over the U.S.–Mexico border, it is an economy that is highly unequal from south to north. True, Mexican border cities have average income levels that exceed the rest of the nation, but dependency on the United States combined with a lack of alternative wealth-creating activities leaves the Mexican border highly vulnerable to U.S. economic fluctuations, as well as to pressures from the larger national economy. National economic policies, such as peso devaluation, have their greatest impact along the border (Mungaray and Moctezuma, 1984). Other policies such as free trade zones offer the possibility of improving the area's economic vitality, but have not been implemented with sufficient force (Tamayo and Fernández, 1983).

Finally, one of the truly integrating forces that tie together northern Mexico and the U.S. Southwest is labor. Migration streams from Mexico into the Southwest have long been recognized as being vital to the U.S. border economy (Bustamante, 1978; Hansen, 1981). Mexican workers built the infrastructure of the Southwest, including railroads, irrigation systems, factories, highways, and buildings. The migration of undocumented Mexican workers into the United States has become so extensive that a contingent of social scientists has emerged to research the long-term implications of immigration for social, economic, and regional life in U.S. receiving communities and in Mexico's sending areas. In 1984, one group of these scholars took on the task of explaining the spatial logic of cross-border undocumented Mexican migration to the United States at both the macro and micro levels (Jones, 1984).

Today, the border region continues to reflect a logical relationship between cheap Mexican labor and increased economic efficiency in production on the U.S. side of the border (Reynolds, 1983, 1984). Despite all the U.S. rhetoric about immigration control and national sovereignty, U.S. capital benefits from cheap (illegal) Mexican labor. These benefits have accrued over time. As Table 9 estimates, by 1975

Table 9. Mexican Contributions to the U.S. Labor Pool (thousands)

	1940	1950	1960	1970	1975
Mexican labor force	5,858	8,345	10,213	12,955	15,400
Legal and undocumented temporary migrant workers (per year)	300	500	500	600	900
Cumulative stock of permanent undocumented workers	—	500	1,000	1,550	1,925
Cumulative stock of legal immigrant workers	—	30	210	470	650
Total Mexican workers in U.S. labor pool	300	1,030	1,710	2,620	3,475
Mexicans working in U.S., as share of Mexican work force	5.1%	12.3%	16.7%	20.2%	22.6%

Source: Reynolds, 1983, p. 328.

Note: "Mexicans in the U.S." refers to all legal and illegal immigrants who entered the U.S. between 1940 and 1975 and their offspring, regardless of place of birth.

as much as one-fifth of the entire Mexican labor force may have been working at one time or another in the United States. A figure of nearly 3.5 million Mexican workers (legal and undocumented) in the U.S. work force is rather startling. These workers are drawn to distinct labor markets, principally in the Southwest, including corporate farming operations and a variety of urban semiskilled and unskilled work.

Summary: Boundary Cities and Transborder Urban Space

The borderlands region has been dramatically transformed in the late twentieth century. Shifts in the distribution of population, resources, capital, and political power have permanently altered the demographic and economic structure of the border region. The growth of important urban centers in the border states of both nations is one element of the changing geography of the border region. The evolution of transboundary economic linkages is a second.

One interesting geographic development has been the growth of a corridor of densely populated cities and towns along the international frontier. In this corridor, the emerging U.S.–Mexican economic and social relationships that have evolved in the larger border region are brought into sharper focus. Along the border these relationships are intensified and directly affect the economic well-being of the settlements and the ability of local, regional, and national governments to construct physical, social, and economic planning policies in the interests of local inhabitants. In short, boundary cities illustrate the problems and opportunities of U.S.–Mexican relations in the borderlands (House, 1982). Boundary cities have become so functionally intertwined that their futures are inextricably bound, whether or not the two national governments are able to devise formal procedures for addressing border-related problems.

The boundary has evolved into a unique linear zone of high-density urban formation. This formation is typically bicultural; that is, urban growth has occurred on both sides of the boundary, reflecting the degree to which economic interests overlap the artificial political boundary, although with the exception of San Diego, considerably more population lies on the Mexican side.

Martínez has shown that the skewing of population toward the Mexican side of the border is explained by the dual role those cities play in the migration process: they are both "springboards" into the United States, and "receptacles" for workers returning voluntarily or through deportation (Martínez, 1977). Equally compelling as an explanation are arguments about the growing sophistication and diversification of the border economy and the opportunities, albeit unequal, for capital formation on both sides of the border.

The transboundary economic space is perhaps most vibrant at the border itself. Here, a number of sectors display tremendous dynamism: trade, tourism, and assembly plants, for example. In the area of tourism, Mexico earned over one billion dollars in 1980; two-thirds of these transactions occurred along the border (Dillman, 1983, p. 241). Although "symbiotic" has been used to describe the common cross-border economic interests of U.S. and Mexican paired settlements (Dillman, 1969), clearly there are enormous imbalances in wealth earned at the boundary, with Mexico being the unequal partner (Hiernaux, 1986; Tamayo and Fernández, 1983).

Nevertheless, an important quality of boundary urban spatial formation is a kind of functional integration that is generated through an economic system operating over a transnational spatial surface. The recognition of a unique type of functional interdependence is established through the use of the term "twin city," which implies that the settlements formed as a result of the same origins. This has indeed often been the case, as historians have shown (McWilliams, 1968; Martínez, 1978). McWilliams (1968) was one of the first scholars to recognize the transborder nature of settlement formation by stating: "From El Paso to Brownsville, the Rio Grande does not separate people, it draws them together. Along the river, as along the entire border, the towns are twins, and Siamese twins, in some cases, for many have interconnecting communications. . . . throughout south Texas, back from the border, most of the towns are twins: an American town and Mexican town being joined together" (p. 61).

The existence of an international boundary no longer serves to hinder growth; quite the contrary. The border as a region has seen enormous changes in its economic base and its overall contribution to the national economies of both the United States and Mexico. As a geometrical line, it has ceased to be merely a jurisdictional indicator. Instead, changing regional forces have allowed businesses on both sides of the border to prosper. An important outcome has been the development of transboundary economic space and, within this, a system of paired cities hugging the international political boundary line. High-density formation, economic interdependency, and location within separate national jurisdictions create a rather complicated spatial organization, one that has been characterized by one scholar as "peculiar" (Hiernaux, 1986, p. 35). It is this spatial organization and its political-geographic and policy implications that are central to the next chapters of this book.

4 Urban Space in Cross-cultural Perspective

All different urban orders are related to, and are a function of, culture.
—Amos Rapoport (1984)

CHAPTER 3 SUGGESTED THAT, despite well-documented evidence of increasingly stronger transboundary economic linkages in recent decades, the evolution of the U.S.–Mexico border region was mainly determined by forces indigenous to the two national cultures that had jurisdiction over the areas divided by the political boundary. The same can be said for the urbanized zone located on the border. If one is to study the structure of settlements at the boundary, one must assume that these structures were formed through decades of cultural, economic, social, and political input from forces native to each culture. Thus, to fully understand the nature of urban space on the U.S.–Mexico border, it is necessary to explain more generically how two cultures, one from the developed, affluent, technologically advanced North, and the other from the less-developed, industrializing South, shape city structure on either side of the boundary. This chapter examines some of the cross-cultural contrasts between theories of urban space in the United States and those in Mexico.

The North American Theoretical Context

Most theoretical discourse about urban spatial structure has been generated in the context of the North American (Anglo-American) cultural setting. One finds, for example, that many standard urban geography textbooks offer theories and concepts mainly associated with the North American region (Hartshorne, 1980; Palm, 1981; Yeates and Garner, 1980). Any framework for analyzing urban spatial structure, therefore, must acknowledge the critical role of North

American urban theory. It should be noted, however, that some authors have recently argued that the term "North American city" is misleading, since there are actually important differences between U.S. and Canadian cities (Goldberg and Mercer, 1986).

Bourne (1982) provides a useful generic discussion of urban spatial structure in which he offers a three-tier definition of space: (1) urban form (spatial patterns of elements such as land use or buildings); (2) urban interaction (linkages or interrelationships that integrate pattern and behavior of individuals, land uses, and so on); and (3) "organizing mechanisms," or rules that link subsystems of interaction and formal pattern together.

Urban form and interaction vary significantly across culture; therefore, it would appear, one ought to find a variety of culturally based theoretical formulations on the "organizing mechanisms" that explain form and behavior. Yet such is not the case. The fact is that the bulk of urban theory from which economic, spatial, and other rules have been derived to explain form and function is rooted in the empirical analysis of U.S. cities. Korcelli (1982), for example, laments the fact that both social area models and theories of urban land rent have tended to explain cities in Western market societies, whereas socialist cities, among others, have not been adequately studied. Agnew (1978) has shown that the concept of homeownership, and thus the behavior of housing markets, varies considerably when one compares cities in Great Britain and the United States. Still other scholars have sought to identify unique cultural factors determining urban structure in such diverse areas of the world as China (Murphey, 1984), the Middle East (Abu Lughod, 1984), Japan (Allinson, 1984), western Europe (Claval, 1984), and other world regions (Agnew, Mercer, and Sopher, 1984).

There is no question that urban spatial theory has been virtually overrun by writers formulating paradigms in the context of North American cities. One can point to a number of "organizational rules" that have emerged from urban spatial theory in which the U.S. city was utilized as a basis for generalizing about the internal structure of the city.

Transport Technology and Spatial Structure

A dominant theme in research on urban spatial structure has been the relationship between transport technology and land use. For the U.S.

city, Borchert (1967) and Warner (1962) have argued that as technology evolved from travel by horse and foot to electric streetcars and rail to elite automobiles and, finally, to ubiquitously consumed automobiles, so too did the use of land change. Each technological shift in the capacity to travel within urban areas caused a shift in the decisions regarding the location and density of land uses. Over longer periods of time, measurable shifts occurred in housing-market dynamics, location of commercial and industrial uses, and overall spatial orientation of the city. Discrete periods of intraurban transport modes, and corresponding morphological prototypes have been identified in this literature (Adams, 1970).

Generally speaking, scholars recognize that the development of automobile technology and relatively low-cost fuel for mass consumption has contributed to the evolution of a dispersed, freeway-oriented urban spatial fabric in contemporary U.S. cities. Suburban rings surrounding old inner-city cores have become dynamic locations not only for residences, but for industry, retail activity, cultural facilities, offices, and other important urban activities. The suburban regions of North American metropolitan areas have become as complex and vital to city life as inner-city business districts were at the turn of the century. Suburban space has generated new conceptual questions for North American urban theory, as the social, economic, political, and spatial impacts of suburban areas on the city have grown (Muller, 1981). Suburban places reflect U.S. cultural values about private property, as well as more general philosophies regarding privatism (Warner, 1972). Equally, they tend to reflect U.S. aesthetic preference for rural landscapes, which may be traced to the image of the English country landscape (Duncan and Duncan, 1984).

The Role of the Central Business District

A second important element in the development of urban spatial theory has been the role of the central business district. Most scholars recognize that the traditional nucleus of the city was once the fulcrum of urban spatial organization (Sjoberg, 1960) and, therefore, must be understood in any legitimate theory of urban space. The earliest research on this subject came from urban land economists. Beginning with the work of Von Thunen (Hall, 1966) on the relationship between rural land uses and the central market, economists like Alonso (1965) constructed an edifice of theory regarding land-rent patterns around the central business district (CBD). Alonso proposed that land users of different categories and social classes would trade off their utility needs (size of property) with proximity to the CBD. In this way, land-rent gradients around the dominant center could be identified.

A second major thrust in the study of North American CBD's sought to understand their changing functional role within the larger ecological structure of evolving metropolitan areas (Bowden, 1971; Murphy and Vance, 1954). During the 1950s and 1960s, federal intervention in the redevelopment of the inner city unleashed a large literature on the failures of "urban renewal" (Gans, 1962; Hartman, 1974). Subsequently, there has been considerable debate over the spatial decentralization of U.S. urban areas and the future of the downtown in light of emerging suburban activity centers. Hall (1984) has argued that the pattern of automobile-dependent, suburban cities will continue and that the role of the CBD in the United States will continue to weaken as energy availability, compact vehicles, and computer technology further render the downtown location less strategic within the overall structure of North American metropolitan areas.

The Economic Structuring of Space

Following the work of land economists, other scholars—including urban economists and geographers—sought better models and theoretical formulations by which to explain spatial variations in land value. By the 1960s, it had already become clear that the assumption of a single dominant central business district in patterning land users' decision processes was inaccurate. Fifteen years earlier, it had been recognized that the city was a multicentered arena of location decisions (Harris and Ullman, 1945). The forces affecting land value were too complex to be accommodated by the assumption of proximity to a single nucleus (Yeates, 1965).

Thus a long line of scholars began to unravel the varying effects of the location of residence and jobs, housing market behavior, and racial discrimination on the spatial patterns of land value in urban areas (Kain, 1975). Many lines of inquiry would emerge along the way, including analysis of the logic of location decisions affecting specific land uses, especially industrial space (Cameron, 1973), commercial land (Berry, 1959, 1967), and public facilities (Dear, 1978; Teitz, 1968). Berry's classic analysis of the spatial organization of commercial activities still has much merit. In that study, Berry (1959) classified commercial activities into three spatial categories: specialized uses, ribbons (highway oriented), and nucleations. Studies of industrial location in the U.S. city have distinguished between old central city–oriented patterns of industrial clustering (such as in New York City's Garment District) and various more recent trends in decentralized clustering (industrial parks) or in random dispersal to either peripheral locations or strategic points of distribution (Cameron, 1973). In general, manufacturing locations have tended to decentralize to suburban locations (Muller, 1981). In the area of public facility location, it has been argued that the principles of efficiency and accessibility utilized to assess the locational benefits of private sector activities cannot be directly applied to the location of public facilities, since the measure of the distributive benefits varies with public goods (Dear, 1974).

The Social-Ecological Structuring of Space

An important current that has continued to run through intellectual discourse on U.S. cities deals with the theoretical significance of sociospatial segregation. This process is clearly tied to the distinct nature of North American culture that causes segmentation of urban space into neighborhoods and communities divided along class and racial lines. An important principle in the field of urban social ecology is that social groups occupy urban space through a process of competition. This competitive process produces the complex fabric of North American urban social areas, subdivided along the lines of socioeconomic status, family life cycle, and ethnicity (Berry and Horton, 1970; Hoyt, 1939; Murdie, 1969; Park et al., 1925; Shevky and Bell, 1955).

Classical theory in this area has shown that of the three major forces that subdivide North American cities, the most important seems to be socioeconomic status. U.S. cities remain highly segregated, despite advances in the legal and institutional processes affecting disadvantaged city dwellers. By and large, they continue to be mosaics of spatially and socially divided subareas. Inner-city ghettoes and working-class districts tend to surround the downtown areas. In social ecology studies, socioeconomic status tended to display a sectoral or wedgelike pattern in space. This trend continues in most U.S. metropolitan areas, with some modifications.

A second force affecting socially divided space has been that of family life cycle, or what is also referred to as the demographic factor. As residents move through the life cycle, their space needs vary; generally, these needs are translated in space into a concentric pattern around the inner city. Single-person or elderly households tend to locate closer to the center of the city, whereas family-producing households seek locations in the suburban areas. This pattern is often tempered by socioeconomic status, the more powerful force, but, nevertheless, has persisted in most U.S. cities.

Ethnicity has been a particularly important area of theoretical development in studying the spatial structure of U.S. cities. Owing to the late nineteenth- and early twentieth-century patterns of mass migration to the United States from Europe, followed by several waves of migrations of Third World minority groups in the middle and late twentieth century, the U.S. city has seen its spatial structure indisputably influenced by ethnic groups. Thus, considerable attention has been focused on such topics as the black ghetto (Rose, 1971), the suburbanization of blacks and other ethnic groups (Muller, 1976; Rose, 1976), and the spatial dynamics of other ethnic groups (Gans, 1962; Grebler, Moore, and Guzmán, 1970; Herzog, 1977). Ethnicity appears to exhibit an "enclave" spatial pattern. Ethnic groups cluster in ghettoes or ethnic territories opened up by early migrants settling in a port of entry, and followed by succeeding migrants concentrating in a zone of familiarity. Ethnicity remains an important force in the spatial segregation of social groups in U.S. metropolitan areas. The exploding ethnic landscapes of the Los Angeles metropolitan area offer an excellent example of the proliferation of this social-ecological process.

Intraurban Movement and Behavioral Systems

Another important body of urban spatial theory has addressed the various forms of behavior and movement that generate what are referred to as "activity systems." These are clearly a formidable cog in the machinery that defines urban spatial structure. One area of conceptual formulation is the study of residential mobility—the behavior of residents in choosing specific residential sites—something that scholars now regard as a highly complex subject, and one that is tied to both the demand and the supply cycles of the housing market, as well as to other social and economic forces indigenous to regional and national culture (Short, 1978).

Another behavioral subject is that of intraurban travel. Scholars have typically regarded three forms of intracity travel as significant: journey to work, journey to shop, and social (recreational) travel (Hartshorne, 1980; Stutz, 1976; Yeates and Garner, 1980). In the U.S. context, the dominance of automobile travel in the middle and late twentieth century and the gradual spatial decentralization of cities provide perhaps the most widely discussed pattern for urban mobility researchers. The journey to work represents the most important form of intraurban travel and has the greatest overall impact on spatial structure. With the widening ecology of the North American metropolis (Sanders, 1978), the longer journey to work has generated the most far-reaching impacts on urban spatial structure: distances traveled are greater and traffic congestion is more frequent, and questions about the long-term viability of fuel for automobiles and their corresponding negative impact on the physical environment (especially air quality) remain unanswered.

Politics, Planning, and Changing Spatial Structure

The political organization of urban space in U.S. cities has inspired some of the more important theoretical developments in the last two decades. Dissatisfied with the nature of urban spatial theory in the 1950s and 1960s, a growing contingent of scholars began to address "social justice" in the distribution of urban resources (Harvey, 1973), the inherent social contradictions and class conflict associated with the urban development process (Castells, 1977), the degree to which the urban setting was "manipulated" by powerful interest groups and institutions (Gale and Moore, 1975), and the fundamental contradictions of legitimate urban planning institutions and processes in capitalist cities (Dear and Scott, 1981). The study of urban space came to be regarded as something fundamentally political and ideological, replete with internal contradictions and problems linked to the nature of capitalist society.

The highly decentralized metropolis, with its many autonomous suburban towns, was regarded as an example of how social class contradictions shaped the form of the U.S. metropolis. Beginning in the late nineteenth century, elite social groups migrating to newly developed suburban communities organized politically to become autonomous governments, thus ensuring that their well-being would be institutionally buffered from that of inner city residents (Markussen, 1976). During the twentieth century, this arrangement has evolved into a pattern in which suburban towns possess more than enough resources to provide adequate services to their residents, but central cities do not, thereby producing what one author has termed "fiscal disparities" between central cities and suburbs (Cox, 1973). The existence of numerous autonomous political units within a single functionally integrated metropolitan region generates an atmosphere of political inefficiency and in-fighting, with individual towns looking out for their narrow interests rather than the broader needs of the larger metropolis they share. This problem has been labeled one of "metropolitan political fragmentation" (Soja, 1971). Finally, many writers also began to identify and empirically examine various types of conflict generated by the changing spatial organization of the city (Cox, 1973; Cox and Johnson, 1982; Herzog, 1983; Janelle and Millward, 1976).

Several points can be made about the nature of space in U.S. metropolitan areas. The most obvious one, expressed through a variety of conceptual frameworks, is that U.S. cities have a distinct spatial geometry—one that has become highly decentralized and dispersed in the present century. The nature of this spatial extensiveness and its implications reflect much of the research agenda in the scholarly study of U.S. urban space. The role of technology, politics, and social behavior has been examined within this context. The dominance of the automobile, the evolution of autonomous suburban governments, and the social desirability of suburban locations all have contributed to the process of decentralization and have been studied extensively. Equally numerous economic analyses have sought to understand the "rules" that govern the location decisions of land users in the dispersed metropolis. At the same time, functional questions, such as the longer journey to work or the decline of mass transit, have occupied other scholars.

With the gradual evolution of a spatially decentralized metropolis, much of the research on U.S. cities has focused on understanding the declining central city. Changes in land use, social composition, and functional importance, as well as questions about historic preservation, urban redevelopment, and ghettoes have concerned scholars seeking to understand and generate theory about U.S. cities.

The continued sociospatial segregation of social classes also has been an important area of inquiry in the study of U.S. urban space. Scholars have looked at this segmentation not only from the point of view of ecological models of competition but equally from that of critically evaluating institutions and processes that create an urban environment that is more advantageous to some than to others. Thus, the role of politics and socially based contradictions in generating inequalities in the urban environment has become a primary area of research in what is clearly an urban spatial setting of dramatic socioeconomic differentiation.

The Latin American Theoretical Context

Research on U.S. cities and their spatial structure is well documented and accessible. Numerous textbooks and anthologies address the subject directly. The study of urban spatial structure in Latin America, however, is far more diffuse. References to the forces affecting urban form south of the border appear far less frequently in the urban literature, and, for the most part, there are few comprehensive summaries of the subject. Some research on urbanization was carried out in the 1960s and is summarized in Hauser and Schnore (1965) and in Morse (1965). With only a few exceptions (Gilbert, 1982; Griffin and Ford, 1980; Portes and Walton, 1976), studies have not been updated, despite significant changes both in urban form and the processes of spatial transformation in recent decades. Despite some limitations in this literature base, however, a number of salient themes have emerged.

Centralization in Urban Form

A dominant theme in Latin American urban research has been the functional and social orientation of the urban morphology around the central plaza. Unlike the U.S. urban system, which evolved over a period of more than two hundred years, most Spanish American cities were built during less than one hundred years, principally in the sixteenth century, from 1520 to 1580 (Portes and Walton, 1976). During this period, systematic engineering plans for the design of colonial cities were devised in Spain. Some scholars believe that these plans were strongly influenced by the ideas of Greek and Roman urban architects and their leaders (Stanislawski, 1947). A series of Royal Ordinances were drawn up, specifying the precise details to be followed by the builders of new cities in colonial Latin America. In the "Royal Ordinance for the Laying Out of New Cities, Towns or Villages," the king of Spain gave specific instructions to colonial government officials about the exact location of the main plaza (in coastal and inland cities), its size (proportionate to the number of residents), shape, and the width and design of streets around it. In addition, precise orders were given as to the location of the main church, hospital, and other important public facilities (Nuttall, 1922).

These colonial cities tended to mirror what Sjoberg (1960) has termed the "pre-industrial city." That is, the elite social classes tended to cluster around the central plaza. The central plaza was designed to represent the religious and civic nucleus of the city. It symbolized the central role of the state and the church in Spanish colonial society. Around the central plaza were located the dominant social institutions: the church, the office of municipal government (*cabildo*), and the governor's palace. Within three blocks of the main plaza were located a number of other key social institutions, including the municipal jail, the public granary, the customs house, the royal tobacco monopoly, the royal treasury, and the town market (Swann, 1982).

It is not surprising, therefore, that the social geography of the Spanish colonial city exhibited the distance decay effects attributed to other preindustrial cities. As distance from the center of the city increased, a clear decline in socioeconomic status was exhibited. The upper classes tended to live near the center in walled cities of the preindustrial era, for reasons of military security and social status (Pirenne, 1952; Sjoberg, 1960); the elite of Spanish colonial society chose these locations for similar reasons, although Spanish colonial towns were not enclosed by walls. According to detailed civil and ecclesiastical censuses of Spanish colonial cities taken in the seventeenth and eighteenth centuries, the upper classes were clustered around the central business districts, and the urban poor were relegated to the periphery.

In these censuses, demographic, socioeconomic, and other data at the household level were recorded. A number of scholars have studied these data, and we now have precise reconstructions of the spatial structure of colonial cities in Spanish America (Robinson, 1975). Swann's (1982) detailed ecology of colonial Durango, for example, offers a spatial portrait of the town in the late eighteenth century. In general, housing problems were concentrated at the edge of town, and the high-income, problem-free zones located near downtown. Similar patterns have been discovered in studies of urban social ecology in other colonial Spanish cities. Furthermore, the same design strategies were used by Spain in colonizing other areas of the world, such as the Philippines.

The morphology of the Spanish colonial city has been called a "grid-pattern" design (Stanislawski, 1946). This refers to the rectangular nature of the master plan for colonial towns in the Spanish New World. With the central plaza serving as the spatial fulcrum of the town, a grid of rectangular streets was designed, with main streets running east and west, and north and south on a line contiguous with the edges of the main plaza. As stated in the Royal Ordinances issued by the king of Spain, "From the plaza the four principal streets are to diverge, one from the middle of each of its sides and two streets to meet at each of the corners. The four corners of the plaza are to face the four points of the compass, because thus the streets diverging from the plaza will not be directly exposed to the four principal winds, which would cause much inconvenience" (Nuttall, 1922). In many towns, smaller plazas with the same rectangular orientation were built around the main plaza.

The "grid-pattern town" was not invented by the Spanish. Its origins may even antedate the Greek and Roman empires. Scholars have observed examples dating back to the settlement of the Indus River Valley (Stanislawski, 1946). With respect to Latin America, one of the more comprehensive studies of cities done in the mid-1960s disputed the notion that centralized town structure was a product of Spanish colonial planning and the Laws of the Indies. Pre-Hispanic cities of the Inca, Mayan, and Aztec civilizations were observed to have displayed tendencies toward spatial centralization, as well (Schnore, 1965). Von Hagen's description of pre-Hispanic Cuzco, the capital city of the Inca empire, certainly gives evidence of this. Cuzco seemed to offer an architectural design in which the structure of Inca society was symbolized. As Von Hagen (1957, pp. 127–128) noted, "There was a grid-iron scheme for streets, converging out of two central plazas. . . . The principal buildings were located around the great plaza, and the towering Sun Temple occupied the most prominent part. . . . Out from the central plaza, called Huaycapata ('Joy Square'), spread the twelve wards of the city, divided roughly into four sections—the four principal directions or quarters of the world which gave the empire its name, Tawantinsuyu." The Inca state thus imposed order on the built environment by building cities in which the larger structure of the empire was symbolized through urban design.

Some scholars believe, however, that no clear evidence of grid-pattern designs existed before the Spanish conquest in the New World, and certainly not in Mexico. They use the descriptions of Spanish conquerers like Cortés, or of their historians (Bernal Díaz del Castillo), and note no mention of a grid pattern in pre-Hispanic Mexico City (Tenochtitlan) (Stanislawski, 1947).

Similar kinds of spatial ordering can be traced to Spanish colonial town planning both in Central America (New Spain) and South America (New Castile). It is clear that the Spanish colonial gridiron scheme possessed both functional and symbolic meaning. The location of the dominant institutions of the state (governor's palace, town council, etc.) around the central plaza emphasized the state's centralized control. It is well known that the plan of the Spanish monarchy was to construct a society in which the government of the king of Spain retained absolute control over the provincial governments. Power was centralized and absolute. The town councils reported to the regional governments (*audiencias*), which ultimately reported to the provincial governors, viceroys, and then to the king. The idea was to discourage political autonomy at the local level. Thus, the design of towns, in which all critical activities were performed in the locus of power at the physical center, enhanced the symbolic, centralized, hierarchical nature of Spanish colonial society. Even local government imposed the will of the state on town layout, investment in infrastructure, and the provision of services. These "police powers" were created to strengthen the position of the elite members of colonial society and to exclude and exploit marginal groups, particularly the indigenous population (Yujnovsky, 1975).

Sociospatial Polarization and the Role of the Elites

Scholarly treatment of the spatial structure of Latin American cities has also recognized the distinct spatial polarization of social classes, specifically, the important role of the elite social groups in dominating the direction of urban development. As the discussion above noted, the formation of the city in colonial Spanish America reflected the embodiment of the socioeconomic interests of the Spanish royal family. The physical city clearly mirrored these values by establishing the symbolic and functional presence of the state at the locational heart of the city—in and around the main plaza. Not only would key activities and land uses emanate from the center, but the central zone was only accessible to the elite social classes. The exclusion of native indigenous peoples from the Spanish new towns was made clear in the ordinances emanating from the crown in Madrid, with statements like "All settlers, with greatest possible haste, are to erect jointly some kind of palisade, or dig a ditch around the main plaza so that the Indians cannot do them harm" (Nuttall, 1922, p. 252).

Thus, the ecology of Latin American cities began with a set of institutionalized rules, directed by a mercantilist state, which implanted an imperial political system and its corresponding social hierarchy on the physical environment of the New World. Town planning encapsulated a form of social status that would quickly become embedded in the social space of the city. Indians were to be physically isolated outside the city, or segregated at the periphery, just as barbarian races had been kept outside the walls of cities in the Roman Empire.

Of course, as some scholars have shown, the social structure of Latin American cities eventually grew beyond the simple duality of rich versus poor, or Spanish versus Indian. Considerable miscegenation created multiple racial types, and there is strong evidence of differing degrees of occupational mobility for certain ethnic mixes. As a result, the mosaic of urban social structure in space became complicated by racial mixes and by the creation of more intricate socioeconomic classes (Beals, 1953; Borah, 1954; Mörner, 1967).

Nevertheless, an elite, propertied class emerged during the period of the "colonial city" (1530–1810). In this era, a strong, centralized state supported the sociospatial evolution of the city, and ownership of land became a symbol of social stature (Yujnovsky, 1975). Portes and Walton (1976) have argued that this essential orientation toward land ownership, elite prominence, and the economic exploitation of the poor masses was established during the colonial period and persists today. Yujnovsky confirms this by tracing the evolution of elite suburbs during the period of commercial capitalism, land speculation, and urban growth (1850–1930), followed by the modern period of "dependent financial and industrial capitalism." During the modern period, a dominant capitalist class linked to foreign interests emerged; governments continued to remain centralized at the federal level and to retain control over financial resources while social classes and housing markets became marked by severe disequilibrium. As he states (1975, p. 214): "The city is divided in two: an 'urbanized' part inhabited by the dominant upper strata of society, with a high level of infrastructure services, community facilities, and environmental quality in general; and another in which the dominated social groups are relegated to an inferior position, with lower accessibility, poorer living environments, and deficits of public services and utilities, as well as insecurity of tenure and instability on the land."

These observations have been verified in numerous analyses of Latin American urban spatial structure in the last three and a half decades. There is little question that there is spatial segmentation of social class in Spanish American cities. It has, however, been interpreted in several ways. Griffin and Ford (1980) have noted that socioeconomic elites dominate a disproportionately large area in Latin American city space—sometimes as much as one-quarter, or one-third of the total urban space. Elite residential sectors, they show, occupy a spatial wedge that, over time, emanates outward from the downtown, in a fashion similar to that of North American elite sectors. Other writers—such as Hansen (1934), writing about Mérida, Mexico; Leonard (1948), writing about La Paz, Bolivia; Caplow (1949), studying Guatemala City; or Hayner, who researched the evolution of Mexico City (1945) and Oaxaca (1944)—have noted that the pattern of centralization of the wealthy classes near the downtown began to break down at the turn of the century and was gradually replaced by a pattern similar to that in North America, in which fashionable suburbs on the edge of the city are developed. Sargent's (1974) study of the spatial evolution of Buenos Aires concludes that the Argentine capital displays a morphological transformation that resembles a North American city like Chicago more than it does Latin American cities. But Buenos Aires, with its European influences, may be an exception to urban spatial structure in Spanish America.

One study of the ecological structure of Guadalajara, Mexico, makes an important distinction between the suburbanization of the upper classes in Latin American and North American cities. The emigration of wealthy social groups to the outskirts of Guadalajara occurred because inner-city congestion, rising land costs, and the convenience of automobiles and telephones made suburban living a rational choice for people who had the resources to choose an ideal location within the city. But, unlike the U.S. cities, these elite enclaves did not evolve into independent suburban towns. Rather, they remained integrated with the city both socially and spatially. The authors surmise that wealthy Mexicans still view the urban life as "the good life," in contrast to the "crude, dull, somewhat dangerous life of the countryside" (Dotson and Dotson, 1954).

Thus although considerable peripheral growth of the upper classes has characterized the Latin American city of the contemporary era, the pattern diverges from that of the U.S. city. There are still both functional and political ties to the city itself. Amato (1969, 1970) has argued that the impact of elite residential location is more pervasive and ultimately skews the overall spatial configuration of the city. Where elites choose to live tends to attract other developments and infrastructure. Therefore, once elite neighborhoods are built, the entire development process may shift toward this axis. Amato finds this pattern more prevalent in medium-sized cities than in very large ones. It is very clear in both cases, however, that elite developments tend to attract important commercial expansion. In most Spanish American cities, the major commercial corridor of the city runs parallel to the elite residential spine, which typically extends gradually outward from the traditional central business district.

Marginal Settlements as a Sociospatial Force

In virtually every urban area, "marginal" settlements, in the form of shantytowns and squatter communities, are also important indigenous forces in Latin American cities. These "uncontrolled settlements" dominate the utilization of peripheral space in most Latin American metropolitan areas. Some scholars have written of the appearance of poor housing on the edges of Latin American cities as early as the pre-Columbian and colonial eras (Hardoy, 1982). However, the most significant period for large-scale growth of low-income settlements began in the 1950s, when the first waves of rural-urban migration in Latin America took place.

Urquidi (1975) has suggested two reasons why these marginal communities evolved. First, rural areas grew through natural increase, but were unable to attain a level of economic development capable of supporting inhabitants; this drove massive numbers of peasants toward the cities. Second, as a result of such great cityward migration, urban centers have been unable to absorb the incoming populations into the productive formal labor force, particularly in industry, leaving a large sector of underemployed and, consequently, an enormous population of urban dwellers without sufficient capital to afford the minimum levels of housing and neighborhood quality. Numerous other explanations for squatter community evolution have been offered in studies of Latin American urbanization. Among these are lack of sufficient land near the central city, extensive land supplies at the edge of urban areas, cheap intraurban transport, and the possibility of acquiring urban services at the periphery (Gilbert and Ward, 1985). Housing constructed in these zones is typically built by the residents themselves, with limited capital and innovative building techniques, and has been termed "self-help housing" (Gilbert, 1983; Ward, 1982). It is often located on land that is illegally occupied (Gilbert, 1981).

Thus, we find in Latin American cities in the last three decades the growth of new residential rings largely filled with migrants from rural towns and provincial cities who have swarmed into urban areas and created *asentamientos irregulares* (irregular settlements) as a response to inadequate housing opportunities. These communities typically consist of a mosaic of shacks and dwellings constructed with the most primitive of materials (including cardboard, scrap wood, and corrugated metal). Basic services such as piped water, sewerage, paved streets, and electricity are often lacking, although older squatter communities are eventually able to bring in water and electricity (Griffin and Ford, 1980).

Marginal settlements can actually be subdivided into several prototypical settlement types. Portes and Walton (1976) suggest three categories: (1) spontaneous settlements, formed illegally on unoccupied land and then subjected to gradual slow growth; (2) land invasions, established by the deliberate decisions of large numbers of homeless families; and (3) clandestine subdivisions, established by landowners who sell cheap parcels of land to poor families—low land prices are achieved by land speculators failing to meet the minimum government regulations covering land subdivision and provision of infrastructure. Cornelius (1975) distinguishes between squatter settlements and low-income subdivisions in Mexico City. Squatter settlements (*colonias proletarias* in Mexico) involve illegal invasions and occupation of land; low-income subdivisions (*fraccionamientos*) are settlements created legally by private land companies or individuals. Gilbert and Ward (1985) have found several distinct forms of occupancy on irregular land: illegal subdivisions, *ejido* subdivisions (Mexico), and invasions. These forms are dependent on the local landholding pattern, the price of land on the urban periphery, and the dominant political mood of the particular Latin American nations and of regions within those nations.

Several things seem clear in the scholarly literature on Latin American squatter communities. First, they have grown to dominate the physical landscape of cities over the last three decades. By some estimates, residents of squatter communities make up between 25 and 50 percent of the total population of major cities like Santiago, Chile; Caracas, Venezuela; Bogotá, Colombia; and Lima, Peru (Anthony, 1979, p. 4). Second, squatter communities physically occupy the peripheral lands of cities, principally because these lands are often either undesirable, or offer the least resistance to invasions by homeless families. Typical sites for land invasions are peripheral public lands rendered useless for sale or development because of their distance from the city center; their location on marshlands, steep river embankments, mountain slopes, or other irregular topography; their poor soil conditions; or their proximity to noxious facilities such as polluting industries, rail lines, or airports.

Squatter settlements represent the outcome of spatial and economic constraints imposed on migrants arriving in Latin American cities. Because of high unemployment and underemployment rates, these migrants find themselves unable to afford rental costs in most other parts of the developed city. They seek an alternative way of establishing permanent shelter; land invasions in marginal, undesirable areas at the urban fringe provide this alternative. As some scholars have noted, the legalization of land ownership is the highest priority for the majority of squatters (Portes and Walton, 1976).

Although squatter settlement growth has been one of the most important dimensions of Latin American urbanization in the post–World War II era, it has not occurred without controversy. During the 1950s, in a number of Latin American countries, the problems of urban poverty and land invasions were looked upon with disfavor, as reflected in various national publications by the use of such labels as *aberración social* (social aberration) or *cinturón de miseria* (misery belt) to describe these areas. Myths about the behavior of residents in these communities abounded—two particularly critical ones were the idea that violence and crime predominated, and that squatter communities were breeding grounds for Communist and neo-Marxist social movements (Collier, 1976). In fact, neither of these allegations proved true. Crime levels were no worse than in other parts of the cities, and resident political behavior tended to favor a moderate philosophy that emphasized working within the system, rather than overturning it (Cornelius, 1975). Ward (1986) has argued that in the case of Mexico, squatter settlements do represent a potential form of social tension, but one that the government can mediate through policies of land provision.

In the many case studies carried out in the 1960s and 1970s, it was discovered that squatter settlements could represent a positive social force in Latin American cities. They provided both an outlet for masses of rural peasants seeking permanent shelter and urban services, and a form of community organization for adapting to urban life (Mangin, 1967; Peattie, 1974; Perlman, 1976). Furthermore, the process of incrementally improving the physical structure of the house as resources became available represented one strategy of adaptation to urban living for the marginal poor. This method, called "progressive development" by one scholar (Turner, 1967), encourages self-management and is often preferable to the involvement of public bureaucracies in providing housing for the poor.

To summarize, the spatial structure of Latin American cities, although displaying some characteristics found in North American cities, has essentially been shaped by cultural and historical forces unique to the region. Utmost in importance has been the historically determined process of spatial centralization. The central business district established in the Spanish colonial era set important institutional, spatial, and political precedents for the symbolic and functional meaning of downtown. Despite social-ecological shifts in the nature of land-use structure, the downtown has retained importance as a repository for prestigious land uses and public facilities. In some cities, high-income residential districts still remain near the downtown. In other cities, these areas have filtered down to middle-income residents, as the rich migrate to suburban enclaves. But in all cases, the downtown still retains functional importance and is a locus of social movement, business decisions, and political concern, as well as a magnet for high land values.

Equally, though, Latin American cities have seen substantial ecological reordering in the present century, and the central business district no longer retains the complete dominance it had in the colonial era, nor even the importance it held in the early part of the twentieth century. Elite residential development has been an important force influencing urban structure. As elites have moved to suburban enclaves on the outskirts of the inner city, commercial development, office space, and other profitable land uses have tended to follow, often creating linear-shaped developments in a single direction. At the same time, the urban periphery has been overwhelmed with spontaneous, unregulated land invasions and the growth of squatter communities housing rural migrants. Thus, Latin American urban space has become highly polarized, with wealthy residents occupying high amenity pockets either near the downtown or in new suburban locations, while the poor settle in belts of shantytown communities surrounding the city in the least-desirable areas. The city becomes not only polarized social space, but a two-dimensional surface of infrastructure development—on the one hand, landscapes of industrial growth and modernization (highways, shopping centers, industrial parks), and on the other hand, vast subcities of squalor, with as much as 50 percent of the total population living in substandard housing, often lacking in basic services such as water, sewerage, and electricity.

Toward a Politics of Location and Urban Spatial Structure

It is no longer sufficient to speak of urban space in an objective manner, divorced from the social and political contexts of societies in which cities are housed. Of all the forces that constrain and shape urban form, politics, above all, cannot be ignored. As Lefebvre (1976, p. 32) has stated: "In these approaches towards politics and its intervention in the planning process, the postulate of space as an objective and neutral object was retained. . . . But it now appears that space is political. Space is not a scientific object removed from ideology or politics; it has always been political and strategic."

Thus, to fully explicate the nature of urban spatial form, one must accept the notion that urban space is highly politicized. This sort of thinking is widely accepted in the current scholarly literature. Two important sources of discourse originating in western Europe include theories of social organization and urban space (Castells, 1977), and of urban social movements (Pickvance, 1976). Another important dialogue on the politics of urban space has sought to evaluate the limitations of urban planning in Western, capitalist society (Dear and Scott, 1981). Such discussions have their roots in earlier concerns raised about the ability of urban theory to address the basic inequalities of distribution, and the resulting social injustices that plague cities (Harvey, 1973).

As Chapter 7 will make clear, the comparative politics of urban spatial structure has become fundamental to understanding the nature of U.S.–Mexico border cities. Of the important currents that run through the literature on urban spatial politics, several can be distinguished for both of the cultural contexts being examined here— North America and Latin America.

The North American Context

The political forces affecting the form of North American cities have several distinguishing features. First, public control over the shape of the city has been historically weak in the United States. Urban planning has never been a particularly strong institution. Some scholars attribute this to the nation's historical antiurban bias (dating back to Thomas Jefferson), and to the century-old pattern of granting greater legal precedence to private property rights over the public interest (Fainstein and Fainstein, 1978). During the nineteenth century, for example, private property and homeownership were emphasized at the expense of community-oriented planning (Warner, 1972). When compared with other Western nations, such as Great Britain, planning in the United States pales considerably. As one study notes, U.S. cities have no real "guardians" of the public interest, except for, by default, the courts (Clawson and Hall, 1973). At the turn of the century, as industrialization and urban growth were occurring simultaneously, no public sector tradition for managing city growth existed. Not until the 1920s did several decades of growth, massive land speculation, and essentially unplanned city expansion give way to formal government intervention in the land planning process (Reps, 1965).

A prominent force shaping the political organization of U.S. urban space emerged from the earlier condition of weak public sector control over urban growth. During the late nineteenth century, as industrial growth and immigration began to impose large-scale changes on the spatial structure of U.S. cities, decisions regarding residential location became far more critical than they were during the preindustrial era. The negative attributes of the inner city—industrial pollution, traffic congestion, overcrowding, and crime—generated an exodus by upper- and upper-middle-class families to the outskirts of the city. Initially, these suburban enclaves depended on the central city for the provision of water, sewerage, transportation, and other urban services. Thus many of these communities were annexed into the jurisdiction of the central city. But gradually, as more elite families migrated to the new suburban settlements, a move to establish local autonomous governments began. Municipal "home rule" was facilitated by state laws that permitted suburban towns to become incorporated and to assure their political and social separation from the ills of the central city. By establishing this politically motivated arrangement, governments institutionalized a spatially segregated metropolis; many observers feel that this is precisely what elite residents and their powerful allies in government wanted (Markussen, 1976; Walker, 1978, 1981). Not only did this process create sociospatial segregation, however, it also established the conditions leading to a proliferation of local governments in twentieth-century metropolitan regions, a condition that has been aptly labeled "metropolitan political fragmentation." Because the political organization of urban space is characterized by multiple jurisdictions sharing one metropolitan region, U.S. cities now have serious distributional inequalities in terms of the location of problems and the location of fiscal resources needed to solve those problems (Cox, 1973; Martin, 1965; Newton, 1975).

As a result of both weak city planning traditions and a politically fragmented metropolis, a third important characteristic of U.S. urban space, in a political sense, is the existence of a well-entrenched competitive bargaining process in contemporary urban development. In U.S. cities today, most changes in land use introduce conflicts of interest for parties affected by the outcome of the decision—these may include local residents, firms, interest groups, or other urban actors. The U.S. city has become an arena in which various interests compete for optimal locations or for optimal outcomes in land-use decisions. The stakes are indeed high, since housing is the most important investment for a majority of U.S. citizens, and since banking, finance, and real estate have become multi-billion-dollar industries in most parts of the United States, especially in areas with high growth rates.

This competitive bargaining process is viewed in the scholarly imagination as one of "locational conflict" (Cox, 1973, 1978; Cox and

Johnson, 1982). The thesis behind such an approach is that U.S. urban politics is distinctly geographical and spatial, since most interest groups in cities seek to maximize the positive externality effects around their home or business and to minimize the negative externality impacts. Again, enormous financial investments are at stake at one end of the socioeconomic spectrum; at the other end, property value—perhaps the most important financial issue for the average U.S. homeowner—is the greatest cause for participation in the local political process (Cox, 1978). The problem politically is that these conflicts are not managed fairly, as there is much ambiguity and even contradiction in the manner in which government intervenes (Castells, 1974; Goodman, 1971; Herzog, 1983). A clear manifestation is the disparity between resource demand (located in central cities) and resource supply (located in suburbs) (Cox, 1973).

The Latin American (Mexican) Context

Since Latin American cities are what most scholars would term "underdeveloped cities" (Urquidi, 1975), it is not surprising that many writers have taken a dim view of the role of politics in overcoming the problems and inequalities inherent in the urban structure of Latin American settlements. They tend to view the political process at the urban level in much the same light as at the national level—they observe that process to be controlled by an elite ruling class and manipulated in its interests to the disfavor of the urban poor. In cities, this process takes on the most visual and concrete form—what Portes and Walton (1976) term the "ecology of urban poverty": "The city thus becomes an arena where the long-term consequences of dependent capitalism turn dialectically upon itself. The growing scarcity of urban land casts into sharp relief the competition between the profit interests of the few and the basic need for shelter of the many. Massive urban migration has brought to light the intrinsic contradiction between the two functions and forces a change in the structure of capitalist land control."

The ecology of the Latin American city has both economic and political undercurrents and reflects the social-class polarization of society into an elite capitalist class linked to foreign interests, a growing middle class, and a large mass of urban poor. The resulting spatial relationships are symptomatic of these social cleavages, and it is the elite, in concert with government (the state), that has de facto control over the spatial structure of the city. For example, studies of Rio de Janeiro (Vetter and Brasileiro, 1978), Lima (Dietz, 1978), Monterrey (Bennett, 1987), and Guadalajara (Walton, 1978), among others, have shown that the wealthy urban classes tend to receive far more benefits from public sector intervention than do the poor. In Guadalajara, Mexico, for example, public works and infrastructure have responded more to the needs of the commercial and industrial bourgeoisie than to the needs of the poor. Transport developments have created increased access to commercial projects, and even the first line in the government-financed subway project was built to service the needs of the elite classes on the western side of the city (Walton, 1978). In a study of Mexico City, it has been shown that *ejido* lands on the outskirts of the metropolitan area, which under the Agrarian Reform Law could only be subdivided to provide housing for the urban poor, were in many cases (about 33 percent of all land subdivided between 1940 and 1975) subdivided to provide housing for the upper and upper middle classes (Garza and Schteingart, 1978).

In the last decade, studies of the role of government in Latin American cities have become more critical. No longer are state planning efforts automatically studied as forces of modernization and, therefore, healthy to Latin American cities. Observers have questioned the role of the state and its institutions in carrying out planning and development (Gilbert, 1982; Ward, 1986). Urban planning, for example, not only is limited by exclusive control by elite sectors, it is also debilitated by the historically weak role of local governments in most Latin American nations. Because so many nations have federal systems with highly centralized state structures, the central government has controlled the national budget, thereby seriously restricting the ability of cities to fund and control their destinies. The decision-making process is removed from the local arena to the centers of national power, where regional elites have far more influence than the urban poor and working class. In Peru in the 1970s, for example, urban planning was a low priority of the national government, which placed a premium on rural development (Dietz, 1978).

In Mexico, scholars have shown that local governments are situated at the bottom of the hierarchical system of public financing (Fagen and Tuohy, 1972; Ugalde, 1970). In fact, so great have been the fiscal austerity measures imposed by the federal bureaucracy on provincial cities in Mexico that many observers believe that important political movements are forming at the municipal level to counter this trend. These movements, labeled by some as part of the "urban reform" or decentralization process (Mori, 1982), seek to expand local government's access to public monies for use in addressing local infrastructure and other municipal investment priorities. Not coincidentally, this movement is paralleled by the recent pattern of increasing support for municipal officials in opposition parties, especially the Partido de Acción Nacional (PAN). Recent elections in the border states have demonstrated this emerging pattern of local voter support for opposition candidates.

In Mexico, criticism of the weak role of government goes beyond the problem of centralization of authority. Even in the national capital, researchers have been critical of the role of the state in urban planning. The state, it has been argued, has allowed the city to become an arena in which profit-seeking capital is allowed to determine the changing social ecology. Thus, only some areas of the city are reinforced by the state planning process and developed by private capital. Other areas are essentially abandoned by the state. The result is that social inequality and segregation within the spatial fabric of Mexican cities has worsened in the last three decades (Moreno Toscano, 1979; Mori, 1982). Segregation is fostered by inequalities in land allocation, which force the poor into the most inconvenient areas of the city, for example, zones with the poorest land characteristics (bad soils and flood potential), the fewest services, the worst access to transportation, and the greatest vulnerability to pollution sources (Gilbert and Ward, 1985).

The urban crisis has been exacerbated by the state. Space has become privatized, and the actions of government "planning" institutions have generally served to favor land speculation. Case studies of Mexico City, the seat of federal power, illustrate that even in places close to the locus of political authority, government intervention in urban development only serves to enhance the unequal sociospatial structure. Observers have pointed out at least three areas in which social movements against the government have arisen: land regulation, protests of land taxes, and lack of urban services (Moreno Toscano, 1979). They feel that the system of municipal governance needs to be reorganized and democratized and the chaotic ministry arrangement streamlined. On the other hand, these types of problems also serve to provide the state with a method for selectively intervening in a limited way to appease the public (through "planning" projects) and thus to create a symbolic image of social improvement without really altering policies that essentially are unfavorable to the poor masses (Ward, 1986).

Another important context for viewing the relationships between politics and the spatial structure of the Latin American city lies in the study of squatter settlements. Notwithstanding acknowledgment of the political dominance of elites, one still must consider squatter residents as a political force, real or potential. After all, the squatter settlements offer visible proof of the inability of the government to house the urban poor. Land invasions represent practical political responses to homelessness; therefore, residents of squatter communities represent a real or potential political voice. Ironically, as some researchers have discovered, once squatters gain legal title to land they may have acquired in an illegal manner (by invasion), they tend to behave conservatively in the arena of state and national politics (Cornelius, 1975). What most researchers have discovered is that in Latin America squatter settlements become a political force to the extent that they learn to use their votes in return for neighborhood demands. Put another way, they are successful to the extent that they channel their needs through political parties that are able to manipulate their votes in exchange for the promise of services (Perdomo and Nikken, 1982) or legalization of land (Collier, 1976). In some cases, land regularization is used by the elite incumbent political parties to win votes in the squatter neighborhoods and thus to withstand challenges from other power coalitions (Cornelius, 1975).

Summary: Urban Space along the U.S.–Mexico Border

As a prelude to the study of the formation of cities along the U.S.–Mexico border, this chapter has constructed a multistage theoretical framework. First, we assume that the formation of cities is the product of forces native to the production of urban space on each side of the border. Second, we ask to what extent U.S. border cities are a product of the forces that drive urban development in the United States and to what extent Mexican border cities are a product of that nation's urbanization process. We then examine these forces in both the U.S. and Mexican contexts. The latter is generalized to the larger cultural context of Latin America (as opposed to Mexico), principally because so much of the comparative urban literature has tended to take this view.

When we view urban space in its national/cultural context we clarify some important differences between the urban structures one finds in each nation. These differences range from rather obvious to more subtle ones. Of the former, it is clear that U.S. cities possess a far more dispersed social ecology than do Mexican cities. This can be attributed to differences in the historical importance of the city center and to the evolution of political institutions that allowed for peripheral growth and independent suburban governance in the United States. Equally, these contrasts are derived from the very different impact of transport technologies on cities in the two cultures. In the United States, widespread automobile ownership has contributed to a gradually widening ecological structure in cities. In Mexico, the automobile continues to be a luxury only the upper classes can afford in cities. The result is that by 1980, the average was 1.9 persons per automobile in the United States, whereas in Mexico the figure was 15.8 persons per automobile (Banamex, 1983, p. 261).

In Mexico, as in all of Latin America, central cities remain both symbolically and functionally vital to the organization of urban space, despite transformations in urban social ecology leading to elite suburbs and spatial decentralization. A second important difference between cities in the United States and Mexico is the content and magnitude of socioeconomic inequality embedded in urban space. Both Mexican and other Latin American cities continue to display an ecology of intense social polarization, with a large proportion of urban space devoted to squatter settlements where basic services are either poorly developed and maintained or completely lacking. Urban poverty on this scale simply does not exist in the United States.

When one turns to the arena of space and politics, the contrasts become more subtle. In both the United States and Mexico, there is significant sociospatial inequality within the urban social fabric. Yet the magnitude and the causes of that inequality must be distinguished. In the United States, inequalities in the use of urban space are the result of a competitive land-use/development bargaining process that produces "winners" and "losers." Many interest groups, ranging from private residents and landowners to commercial and industrial firms or politicians, have access to the competitive bargaining process. Typically, a political pattern has developed—private capital, often in concert with government, seeks to optimize profit from land determined to be valuable in the real estate market—either in suburban zones or near value-enhancing locations, such as parks and coastlines. Although the ecology of winners and losers may vary, a striking pattern resulting from competitive bargaining has been the continued disparity in land value between central city areas and suburbs.

In Mexico, spatial inequality is also the most salient characteristic of urban form; however, its causes and consequences differ markedly from the U.S. context. First, it is clear that control of urban space is limited to a far more restricted group of social actors—principally private capitalists and powerful elected officials and their circle of loyal followers, mainly at the state and federal levels. The competitive bargaining process that one finds in the United States is not nearly as extensive in Mexico. As many as one-third of the residents of most large cities do not even possess legal title to their land; thus much social energy in the political arena is devoted to land regularization and, after that, to gaining access to basic urban services such as water, sewerage, street paving, and lighting. The politics of urban development is not so much a question of debating the role of the state in developing particular areas of the city as it is a question of marginal social classes achieving legal land title and urban services that allow them to reach minimum housing and neighborhood quality standards.

Yet although one can point to differences between U.S. and Mexican cities and their spatial structure, the study of international border cities cannot end here. The location of these cities suggests the need for analysis that goes beyond a discussion of the national forces responsible for city structure on either side of the boundary. Clearly, social, spatial, and behavioral forces at work along the international border itself may influence the urban space surrounding it.

On the one hand, U.S. and Mexican cities are the product of their own national cultures; on the other hand, they share a strategic location with their neighboring urban settlements and increasingly are subject to social, economic, cultural, and even political forces that penetrate the international border. The effects of those forces on the structure of cities themselves and on the use of space remains, to some extent, unknown. As pointed out in Chapter 2, the growth of cities on international boundaries is only a very recent phenomenon in the larger historical sense, and thus no theoretical precedents exist with which to approach these questions. It remains, therefore, for scholars to examine empirical cases of binational border urban space to begin to understand how cities form along international boundaries, and what the implications of these formations will be for the future.

Comparative Morphology and Spatial Structure in the San Diego–Tijuana Border Zone

The intercourse between the Twin Cities is so constant and familiar that it is difficult to realize that they are dependencies of separate republics.
—William H. Chatfield (1893)

CHAPTER 4 DESCRIBED two distinct cultural contexts—U.S. and Mexican—in which theories of urban spatial dynamics have been generated. This chapter examines historical, economic, cultural, and regional forces that have contributed to the evolution of the spatial structure of a U.S. and a Mexican city joined at the international boundary. By placing a magnifying glass on the spatial dynamics of a case study border metropolis, we can begin to determine the impact of an international boundary on the urbanization process. With a combined population of nearly three million in 1988, the San Diego–Tijuana region offers an excellent laboratory for the study of the border urbanization process.

The Evolution of Urban Structure in Tijuana, Baja California, 1848–1950

Prior to the demarcation of a political boundary between the United States and Mexico in 1848, Tijuana was the largest of a string of small cattle-ranching villages dispersed across the valley of the Tijuana River in the Mexican territory of Upper (Alta) California. The most important social and institutional force affecting the region during this era was the mission system. Two religious organizations created separate, but often competing, systems of mission towns in the region: the Franciscans in Alta California, and the Dominicans in Lower (Baja) California. These organizations were the principal forces responsible for settlement and population distribution in northern Baja California up to the mid-nineteenth century (Piñera and Ortiz, 1983).

In 1846 the geopolitics of the region was shattered. A brief territorial war between the United States and Mexico resulted in the Treaty of Guadalupe Hidalgo (1848), in which the United States acquired vast amounts of new territory covering much of the present area of the southwestern United States (see Figure 1). The drawing of the international boundary at Tijuana following the war drew anxious attention from Mexico, which feared it might lose the fertile lands of the northern Baja California coast. In the end, the boundary line bisected the Valley of Tijuana, leaving the flattest lands within the United States. The hilly terrain south of the flood plain became part of Mexico. In the postwar negotiations, Mexico's access to the Pacific Ocean via the Baja California peninsula was saved.

The evolution of Tijuana to the end of the Second World War is very clearly connected to the city's border location. More specifically, its evolution is tied to the North American market economy. The history of Tijuana is, until recently, the story of a border town that became increasingly dependent on the dynamism of the southern California capitalist economy.

In the second half of the nineteenth century, the settlement of northern Baja California and the development of its resources and economy were far more influenced by the United States than by Mexico. Limited transport technology in the nineteenth century and the spatial concentration of resources, people, and political power in central Mexico meant that most Mexican border cities were politically, economically, and geographically isolated from the mainstream of Mexican life. In the meantime, U.S. influence, especially in the second half of the nineteenth century, continued to accelerate. The development of the cotton-growing economy in the Mexicali Valley was financed by U.S. capital, principally through the Colorado Land Company. The original development and subdivision of Ensenada was sponsored by a North American real estate company, the International Company, during the land boom of southern California in the 1880s (Piñera, 1983). Thus, the migration of capital and resources into southern California by the late nineteenth century signaled the beginning of large infusions of capital into Baja California, the subsequent exploitation of its resources, and the expansion of its principal settlements—Ensenada, Mexicali, and Tijuana. When the railroad reached

California in 1876, the rapid deployment of North American capital and entrepreneurship into Baja California was imminent.

In short, Tijuana's transformation from cattle ranch to urban settlement was fueled by the economic boom in southern California in the late nineteenth century and by the eventual spillover of capital and business ventures into Baja California. It was also facilitated by the Mexican president of this era, Porfirio Díaz, who advocated an open door policy for American capital invested in northern Mexico.

The initial growth of Tijuana as an urban settlement strongly supports these assertions. Tijuana languished as a small cattle-ranching settlement with no nucleus until the 1880s. In the 1880s, massive land speculation and a general boom in land subdivisions occurred just across the border in San Diego. Southern California towns like Coronado, Pacific Beach, Ocean Beach, La Jolla, and La Mesa grew during this era. In 1886 the International Company of Mexico (a U.S. real estate firm) built a settlement on Ensenada Bay. Influenced by these developments two wealthy Mexican families living in California realized that the region's land boom offered an opportunity to develop lands they owned in Tijuana. In 1889, the Arguello and Olvera families hired a Mexican engineer to design the first urban plan for the town of Tijuana, which at that time was called Zaragoza.

The first plan of Tijuana (1889) is significant in several respects (Figure 2). First, it located the main settlement adjacent to the boundary line and the customs house built in the early 1870s. This reinforces the notion that the town was oriented toward North America. Second, the plan was devised by Ricardo Orozco, a Mexican engineer who had worked for the U.S. real estate company that developed the town in Ensenada. Orozco was greatly influenced by U.S. design techniques of the era, which borrowed heavily from the European radial street pattern. The 1889 plan of Tijuana offered a design that combined diagonal streets with a series of central squares, the latter more reminiscent of the colonial gridiron plan used in the construction of cities in the interior of Mexico.

The use of a radial design pattern with diagonal streets was one key departure from the Spanish colonial design, which was essentially rectangular. Another was that from its inception Tijuana was not dominated by a single plaza. In fact, although the 1889 plan displayed a central plaza (Plaza Zaragoza) and a series of secondary squares, by 1921 the original central plaza had not become the

Figure 2. Plan of Tijuana, 1889

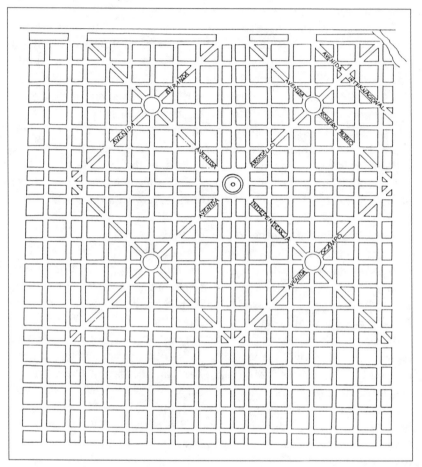

magnet for the location of key land uses (Figure 3). Instead, one of the secondary centers, the one closest to the international boundary line, attracted the largest cluster of residences, commercial activities, and important land uses. In addition, the prominent social institutions, such as the municipal palace and the church, did not locate directly on the central plaza, as in the Spanish colonial model, although they were situated nearby.

The early land-use configuration of Tijuana reflects not so much the city planning heritage of Spanish colonial engineers as the architectural influence of the real estate boom in southern California. The 1889 plan of Tijuana took some features of Spanish colonial design (plazas and rectangularism) and combined these with the European diagonal designs so popular in Baron Haussmann's plan of Paris and a number of town-planning designs being implemented in the western United States. Diagonal street patterns were also in vogue in other U.S. cities, such as Washington, D.C., and Indianapolis (Reps, 1965). The plan of Tijuana was a hybrid design typical of those being devised in towns throughout the Southwest.

The early plan of Tijuana did not reflect the values embedded in Spanish colonial society, which had so strongly influenced cities like Guadalajara, Puebla, and Mexico City. Instead, it embodied the economic values of a young Mexican border town, whose growth was highly vulnerable to forces north of the border. The tourist economy was the driving force behind location decisions made by households and investors in the early periods of Tijuana's growth. Between 1889 and 1921, the population of slightly more than one thousand inhabitants clustered in the northeastern corner of the space allocated for the urban plan—in an area just beyond the banks of the Tijuana River, only a few hundred yards from the international boundary.

At the turn of the century, the growth of Tijuana's northern neighbor, San Diego, would fuel the development of this border city. In 1898, as a result of military involvement in the Spanish-American War, San Diego was chosen as the site for a U.S. Naval base. Seven years later, when the monopoly of the government-regulated steamship lines was relaxed, thus allowing merchants to use cities like San Diego for ports, the city was opened as a major Pacific port. Both of these developments once again reinforced an emerging relationship between changes in the spatial structure of Tijuana and shifts in the U.S. economy. As San Diego expanded to accommodate its new economic activities as a port and naval base, a set of corresponding

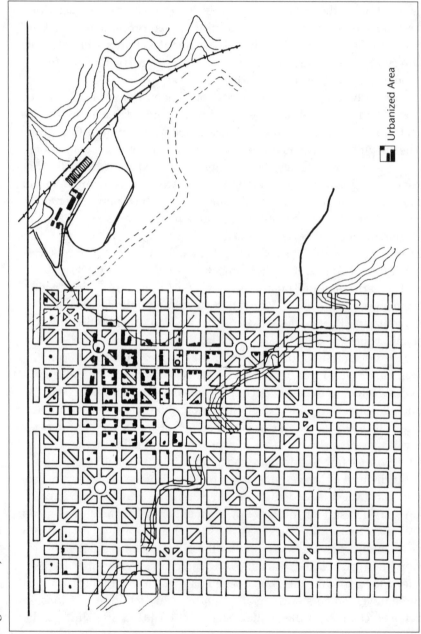

Figure 3. Tijuana, 1921

Urbanized Area

demands for services and goods was created across the border in Tijuana. These new activities in the Mexican border city would have a lasting impact on its morphology.

In the early decades of the twentieth century, Tijuana began to fulfill its legacy as a repository for recreational investments and the needs of North American capital. In 1906, U.S. businessman John Spreckels built a railroad line from Yuma, Arizona, to San Diego. The line crossed the Mexican border and connected Mexicali, Tecate, and Tijuana with San Diego. Two years later the Mexican government sanctioned gambling in Baja California. This initiated a flood of U.S. tourists into northern Mexico. The steady crescendo in the flow of North American tourists into Tijuana for recreation and gambling activities was given even greater impetus by the expansion of the reformist movement in California between 1900 and 1920. This movement sought to impose strict moral and religious standards on public behavior. As it gained momentum and political support on the U.S. side of the border, the development of tourist facilities south of the border spiraled upward.

Tijuana's spatial structure and physical landscape changed in accordance with social and economic developments north of the border. In 1916, the first racetrack in Tijuana was built just four hundred yards from the international border by a former boxing promoter from San Francisco. The builder not only constructed a new hippodrome, he improved roads leading to the facility and built a bridge across the Tijuana River.

Prohibition laws passed in the United States three years later marked the beginning of the "golden era of tourism" in Tijuana (Acevedo Cárdenas, Piñera, and Ortiz, 1985), a period that lasted from 1919 to 1929. During this time, Tijuana's landscape and structure were further transformed in a manner that reflected the city's increasing dependence on U.S. capital. The town witnessed the growth of industries, such as beer and wine production, tilted toward serving the growing clientele from the "dry" counties of California. Downtown Tijuana was gradually overrun with gambling houses, bars, cabarets, and other entertainment establishments. Cabarets such as the Foreign Club, Montecarlo, and Agua Caliente were built with U.S. capital and tended to employ only American workers, much to the dismay of Mexicans. During the same period, the U.S. government sought to stem the tide of tourism and alcohol consumption in Mexico by closing the border at 9:00 P.M. each night, but this only served to create a new demand for lodging in Tijuana and thus expanded the hotel industry of the town. On July 4, 1920, for example, some sixty-five thousand Americans and 12,654 automobiles crossed the border into Tijuana. The city's gasoline supply was rapidly depleted, and thousands of Americans spent the night in Tijuana. Some regard this as the beginning of the boom in the hotel industry in the city (Piñera, 1985).

By the late 1920s, Tijuana's social geography was polarized: the principal tourist-oriented zone was clustered along Revolution Street and the area between downtown and the racetrack; the Mexican residential area was located west of the main part of downtown. Lacking a traditional plaza, which had virtually disappeared in the 1920s as Tijuana became more oriented toward automobile use on linear streets, residents began to use a local park, Parque Teniente Guerrero, for public interaction (Piñera, 1986).

The U.S. Depression of 1929 further illustrates the degree to which Tijuana was driven by its ties to the United States. The Depression severely threatened the economic base of Tijuana, yet the city was able to survive because wealthy tourists from southern California continued to come. High unemployment in California led to the repatriation of nearly one-half million Mexicans during this era (Fuentes Romero, 1985). Many returned to live in border cities like Tijuana. Repatriated Mexican workers returning to Tijuana became an important force in the newly subdivided community of Colonia Libertad, an area lying directly along the border, near the old racetrack (Bustamante, 1985).

The building of Colonia Libertad displays, once again, the incorporation of U.S. influences into the built landscape and form of Tijuana. Colonia Libertad was the first neighborhood in Tijuana to use a system of major streets and service alleys in its street plan, a technique borrowed from the cities in California from which the repatriated Mexicans came. Even the name "Libertad" (Liberty), it is speculated, reflects North American influence—it is said that some of the settlers in this neighborhood were anarchists. The name reflected a symbolic interest in liberation from the forces of both the church and materialism. The slogan *"Ni iglesias, ni cantinas"* (Neither churches nor bars), used to describe the built landscape of this neighborhood in the early years of its formation, is instructive (Piñera, 1986).

Although President Lázaro Cárdenas tried to break Baja California's strong ties to the United States by ordering all gambling establishments closed in 1935, Tijuana was by then thoroughly infused with economic and cultural connections to the United States. These would be difficult bonds to undo, particularly since Mexico was a country struggling to modernize an underdeveloped economy. When the gambling casinos and bars in Tijuana closed down as a result of Cárdenas' decree, residents who had previously lived and worked in the United States began to look for employment in San Diego. Over the next decade, Colonia Libertad would develop and prosper as a result of money earned north of the border.

By World War II, dire shortages of labor in the U.S. border states unleashed one of the largest volumes of labor migration this continent had ever seen, a flow that has still not abated. In 1942, a treaty between the United States and Mexico formally created the Bracero Program, designed to allow Mexicans to cross the border legally in order to provide labor where needed in the United States. These migration flows would have a dramatic impact on Tijuana and other border cities, as thousands of rural peasants in Mexico came to the borderlands. Over time, those who worked periodically in the United States would settle in Tijuana.

By 1950, the city had grown to a population of 59,962, more than tripling its 1940 population of 16,486. The *braceros* returning to Tijuana reinvested their dollars into housing and business ventures; thus, the linkages with the U.S. economy persisted. However, in the post–World War II era, the attraction to the border would grow so much that those unable to sustain employment either north or south of the border would contribute to the formation of an enormous sector of marginal poor, giving the city a sociospatial formation similar to that of other large metropolitan areas in Latin America.

The Evolution of Spatial Structure in San Diego, California, 1769–1950

In 1769, the first mission of Alta California was established at San Diego. From 1769 to 1848, San Diego's physical growth was contained within the limits of Old Town (Figure 4), the settlement established during the period when San Diego remained under the jurisdiction of Mexico (Ford, 1984). During this era, a fort (*presidio*) was built at the confluence of the San Diego River and the bay, and a mission was moved farther inland along the San Diego River.

Figure 4. Port of San Diego, 1850

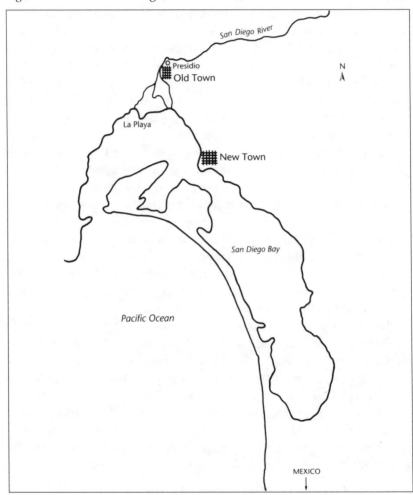

The mission towns of Alta California were rather remote settlements within the network of cities in colonial Mexico. Spain concentrated its resources and settlement efforts in areas that would generate more wealth for the crown—central Mexico, the coast, and the mining regions. Baja and Alta California were both too arid and too far from the core areas of development in colonial Mexico to be paid much attention.

San Diego was, thus, a modest mission town in the early nineteenth century. It has been aptly described during this era as "thin and precarious" (Lynch and Appleyard, 1974). The principal nucleus of settlers was located around the *presidio*, in an area that would later be called Old Town (Figure 4). The economic base of the town revolved around small-scale cattle ranching in the irrigated valleys of the region. By 1822, Old Town was a sparsely settled village of adobe huts, laid out according to the traditional rectangular gridiron plan.

Mexico achieved its independence from Spain in 1821. From 1821 to 1848, termed the "Mexican Period" by one scholar (Ford, 1984), the townscape began to change as a response to the transfer of jurisdiction from Spain to Mexico. Large buildings were constructed in Old Town by an emerging class of wealthy, landowning Mexicans. Beginning in 1831, the Mexican government moved to secularize the missions. An important social change involved the distribution of church-held lands to private citizens in good favor with the government. Some Mexican families became quite wealthy as a result of these land transfers, prompting at least one writer to describe the 1834–1846 period as the "golden age of Ranchos" (Camarrillo, 1979). In general, however, one must acknowledge that San Diego was a rather insignificant settlement before 1850. Its population at the time of the U.S.–Mexican War (1846) was only 350.

San Diego's transformation from rural village to regional metropolis began in the second half of the nineteenth century. What is significant about its growth in the late nineteenth and early twentieth centuries is that it quickly became fused to socioeconomic and political circumstances *north* of the border, as its ties with Mexico and with Baja California were gradually severed. Once the boundary line was drawn, separating San Diego from Mexico, the city quickly developed an economy and culture linked with the United States. These changes were also manifested in the evolution of a distinctly North American landscape and spatial structure that, within a few decades, would contrast sharply with its neighbor south of the border.

Following the Treaty of Guadalupe Hidalgo (1848), the new international boundary line artificially divided a natural ecological region—the Tijuana River Valley. There was some controversy as to where the line would actually fall, and Mexico was quite concerned about not losing fertile lands in the river valleys along the coast of northern Baja California. With the line drawn, San Diego became part of the United States and entered a period in which a transition from Mexican to North American statehood left a strong imprint on the physical character of the city.

During the period 1850–1880, San Diego evolved from mission and Mexican cattle-ranching settlement to a growing town linked to southern California, one of the important regions of expansion and economic development in the western United States. One important by-product of San Diego's transformation was the class conflict that emerged between Mexican landowners (Californios) and newly arrived Anglo settlers. This conflict had important geographical implications as San Diego's spatial structure changed in the middle of the nineteenth century. Anglo and Hispanic populations became polarized, initiating a sociospatial phenomenon that was re-created in the twentieth century (see Chapter 6).

When Anglo settlers arrived in San Diego in the 1850s, they found a class of elite Mexican property owners (*ricos*), as well as a smaller number of lower-class laborers (*cholos*). The usurpation of power from the Mexican landed class did not occur so much through violent racial clashes as through the gradual injection of an Anglo economy into the region, its steady superimposition over the Mexican economic base, and a shift in the racial mix toward an Anglo majority. Scholars have shown that members of the Mexican elite (Californios) were sympathetic to U.S. governance from the very beginning, since they had never been close to the distant federal government in Mexico City (García, 1975; Pitt, 1966). Still, Anglos quickly dominated political life in San Diego, even in 1850, when Mexicans still held a voting majority.

Mexican culture rapidly declined as more Anglo settlers arrived in the 1850s and 1860s. Cultural disintegration was greatly accelerated by the Mexicans' large-scale losses of property, on the one hand, and the penetration of Anglo capital into the region, on the other. Once the region passed into U.S. jurisdiction, the property rights of the Mexican Californios, who had received their property through land grants from the Mexican government, were called into question.

Mexican landowners were forced to engage in long-term litigation to retain title. At the same time, they began paying exorbitant litigation fees, high interest rates on loans, and unfair taxes. Many who defaulted on their tax bills lost their land in public auctions; others simply lost their land in contested ownership cases (Camarrillo, 1979).

Mexicans were slowly pushed out of a position of prominence in San Diego. While their properties were dwindling, many Californios suffered further because they had both sold off their cattle and speculated in mining ventures during the 1840s and 1850s. By the 1860s, when mining operations declined, the Californios did not have the cattle economy to fall back on. In the meantime, new forms of economic activity were being developed by Anglo investors—commerce and trade, whaling and fishing, agriculture. By the time rail connections with the Southwest were constructed in the 1880s, the decline of the Mexican population as a significant sociopolitical force was complete.

The imposition of Anglo culture on the San Diego region and the eclipse of the Mexican community had a distinct spatial expression. In 1850, the settled portions of San Diego hovered around the Presidio in Old Town, and a small area developed along the coast at La Playa (on the San Diego bay). Anglo entrepreneurs immediately sought to establish an alternative settlement to Old Town. Given the changes in the economic base and functions of San Diego, they felt that Old Town was no longer the optimal location for meeting the needs of the Anglo economy. Where the Spanish-Mexican mission of San Diego had functions that were religious, agricultural, or military-oriented, the Old Town location did not meet the objectives of a city that sought to become a trade center within the rapidly developing southwestern United States. Alonso Horton, a U.S. entrepreneur who came to San Diego in the 1860s, was said to have commented about Old Town: "I would not give you five dollars for a deed to the whole of it. I would not take it as a gift. It doesn't lie right. Never in the world can you have a city here" (Morgan and Blair, 1976, p. 15).

Anglo discontent with Old Town led to the investment in and subdivision of New Town in the flatlands on the bay. The transition from Old Town to New Town did not occur overnight. The first attempt to build at New Town in the early 1850s failed, but by 1870, Aionso Horton purchased 960 acres of land on the bay, subdivided lots, and quickly moved to sell "Horton's Addition" to the founding fathers of the city. After some resistance, key land users, including the banks, newspaper offices, hotels, and government, located in New Town. By the end of the 1870s, it was the primary settlement nucleus of San Diego. Old Town would fall into disuse. The eclipse of the Mexican community was nearly complete.

During the late nineteenth and first half of the twentieth centuries, San Diego established its role in the Southwest and in California. Its relationship to the regional and national economy would determine both its size and the spatial form of its growth. In the final decades of the nineteenth century, one very important regional issue was the question of where to build the western terminus of the transcontinental railroad. San Diego was intensely involved in attracting railroad entrepreneurs to make the final connection from Yuma. Ultimately, that connection was made to Los Angeles (in 1887); a direct line from Yuma to San Diego did not come until 1919. During those three decades Los Angeles became a city of over 500,000, but San Diego remained a more modest 74,361 (Harris, 1974).

Thus, regional linkages to the Southwest determined the growth and geometric form of San Diego in the late nineteenth and early twentieth centuries. This was a time of large-scale economic transformation in the Southwest, with the influx of railroads, industry, capital-intensive agriculture, and capitalist spirit. In San Diego, the boom of the 1880s led to the subdivision of new areas such as Coronado, La Jolla, Pacific Beach, and La Mesa. The principal expansion zones, however, remained tied to areas in and around downtown— the Gaslamp Quarter, Golden Hill, Hillcrest, and Balboa Park.

In the early twentieth century, San Diego celebrated its emergence as an important deepwater port. A naval base was established in the first decade of the century. In 1915, the Panama-Pacific Exposition promoted the city's growing stature as a port. A new wave of Hispanic-Mediterranean architecture swept over the city with the construction of the Prado in Balboa Park, the Santa Fe railroad station, and a number of residential structures in Kensington, Mission Hills, and around Balboa Park (Ford, 1984). The development of street car technology opened up trolley line communities such as North Park, East San Diego, Kensington, Hillcrest, and Normal Heights. Prior to the Second World War, the development of automobile technology would yield an early period of strip development along boulevards, although more substantial growth would not occur until the economy prospered in the aftermath of the war.

Contemporary Spatial Structure in San Diego and Tijuana

Several elements of the historical formation of settlement space in the Tijuana–San Diego region stand out. Although the region itself occupies a singular ecological space—the river valley and environs of the Tijuana River—the evolution of the two cities has remained acutely separate, despite proximity and historic events which caused overlap. Once the international political boundary was drawn in 1848, Tijuana and San Diego evolved under very different conditions.

Tijuana's growth was tied to the North American market economy. The city's spatial structure, land-use pattern, and built environment were transformed according to the rhythm of changes north of the border. From its inception as a town, the location of Tijuana's central business district a few hundred yards from the border reflected its northward orientation. The first city plan was drawn up during the California real estate boom of the 1880s, and reflected a vision of U.S. subdivision plans adapted to its Mexican setting. From 1890 to 1950, Tijuana's spatial transformation was rooted to its changing relationship with the United States. At various times, Tijuana was a repository for U.S. investments in tourism and recreational activities, as well as for the consumption of those services; later it became a medium for labor exchanges with employers in California, and still later for new economic exchanges that fed the needs of California's prospering and dynamic economy in the twentieth century. This pattern of economic dependency on the United States left a lasting imprint on Tijuana's spatial structure as the city entered the post–World War II era, a time when its largest growth would occur.

San Diego's growth from mission town to metropolis was quite different. Contrary to Tijuana, once the boundary line was drawn in 1848, the city needed only about two decades to discard and dismantle its ties to Mexico. During the period 1846–1870, the power of the Spanish-speaking elite (the Californios) subsided, and the city fell under the influence of an Anglo power structure, fueled by the important economic interests of the era—agriculture, banking, railroads, regional trade, and mining. The traditional Mexican settlement in Old Town was displaced as the nucleus of the city, and a new downtown, New Town, formed on the banks of the San Diego Bay. More important, San Diego became a town linked economically to the growing southwestern United States. It was through these linkages, solidified by the coming of the transcontinental railroad and through financial ties with important regional cities (San Francisco, Los Angeles, Yuma, and Salt Lake City), that San Diego became a city tied to the U.S. economy rather than to the border economy.

What remains, however, is to examine the spatial structure of Tijuana and San Diego from 1950 to the present. Both cities have grown into high-order metropolitan centers, and one needs to examine the forces influencing their growth and how these are manifested in changes in urban form and function.

Tijuana, 1950–Present

Tijuana's changing morphology and spatial organization from 1950 to the present reflect the transformation of the settlement from a small city isolated from national and international markets to a regional metropolis strongly integrated both into the Mexican national economy and the market economy of southern California (Castillo, 1986). Two forces—population growth and expansion of the city economic base—were responsible for the transformation of Tijuana's spatial structure.

From 1950 to 1980, the city's population grew to more than ten times its 1950 size, from 65,364 to over 700,000 inhabitants (Table 10). Growth rates during the 1950s, 1960s, and 1970s ranged from 7 to 11 percent annually, making the city one of the fastest-growing metropolitan areas on the continent. By 1985, over 45 percent of the total population of Baja California resided in Tijuana.

About two-thirds of this growth was the result of migration from the interior of Mexico. As Table 11 suggests, in-migrants to Tijuana came from widely dispersed regions in Mexico's interior, although a clear pattern skewed toward western states (Jalisco, Sinaloa, Michoacán, Sonora) is evident. By 1979, the place of origin of heads of households was quite diverse. Most important, only 15.02 percent of heads of households came from Baja California. Incredibly, more (19.31 percent) originated in the state of Jalisco (the most populous state in western Mexico) than in Tijuana itself (Instituto de Investigaciones Económicas y Sociales, 1980).

The formation of Tijuana's morphology by successive waves of in-migrants is important to an explanation of the city's spatial organization. Before 1950 (Figure 5), Tijuana's urbanized area remained

Table 10. Population Growth, Municipio de Tijuana

	Population of Tijuana	Annual Growth Rate (%)	As % of Total Population of Baja California
1900	350	—	4.6
1910	969	—	9.9
1921	1,228	—	5.2
1930	11,271	—	23.3
1940	21,977	6.9	27.8
1950	65,364	11.5	28.8
1960	165,690	9.7	31.8
1970	340,583	7.2	39.1
1980	709,340[a]	7.3	46.5
1985	867,719	5.6	46.5
1990[b]	1,129,000	5.6	—
2000[b]	1,815,000	4.8	—

Sources: Secretaría de Industria y Comercio, Dirección de Estudios, 1930, 1940, 1950, 1960, 1970; and Oficina del Gobernador, Estado de Baja California, 1984.

a. Population recorded in official federal census was 461,257, later widely disputed.
b. Estimated.

Table 11. State of Origin of Recent Immigrants to Tijuana, 1984

State of Origin	% of Total Number of Immigrants
Jalisco	23.2
Other	15.7
Sinaloa	13.0
Guanajuato	8.0
Michoacán	7.7
Sonora	7.6
Durango	5.8
México	4.7
Zacatecas	3.8
Distrito Federal	3.7
Nayarit	3.5
Chihuahua	3.3

Source: Instituto de Investigaciones Sociales, UABC, 1984.

Figure 5. Tijuana Growth Pattern, 1889–1984

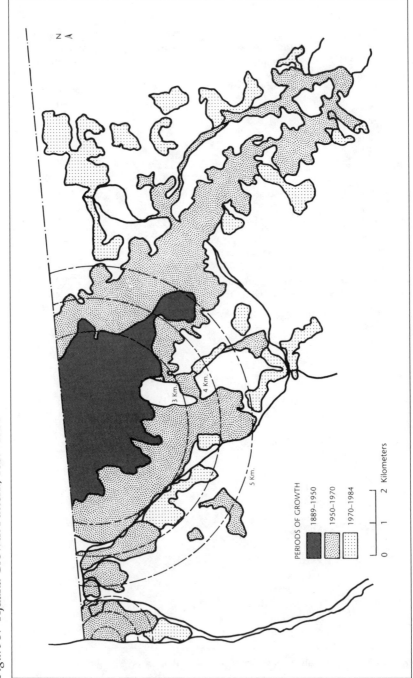

PERIODS OF GROWTH

■ 1889–1950
□ 1950–1970
▫ 1970–1984

0   1   2 Kilometers

Source: Ranfla and de la Torre, 1986.

within a zone concentrated around the traditional downtown. The edges of the 1950 urbanized area reached only to points about 4 kilometers (2.5 miles) from the city center. As successive waves of migrants arrived in the city during the next three decades, the process of growth was bipartite: (1) The majority of in-migrants who arrived without significant sources of income typically sought land in the least-desirable locations, normally places where land could be invaded and where property ownership could be established. This land was located outside the settled areas of the city, in unplatted canyons, hillsides, and other marginal areas, especially on the southwestern side of the city, in the hills east of Colonia Libertad, and in pockets of marginal land to the southeast. (2) Those in-migrants who were employed (professionals, businessmen, and so on) chose elite locations near the already urbanized zones of the city. This second category of in-migrants represented a very small proportion of the total numbers of migrants arriving during the period 1950 to 1980.

Thus, the spatial form of Tijuana was dictated by its massive expansion through the in-migration of predominantly low-income inhabitants of the interior states of Mexico (Griffin and Ford, 1980). Of the city's expansion from 65,000 to over 700,000 in thirty years, more than half of the residents moved into spontaneously settled "popular neighborhoods" (*colonias populares*). These irregular settlements grew for two reasons: (1) newly arriving residents typically could not afford the high rents on land in the serviced portions of the urbanized zones; (2) local government was not sufficiently organized, funded, or technically trained to absorb the large incoming population in a rational, orderly manner. Tijuana grew in a chaotic fashion. Spontaneous urbanizations housing the poor, newly arrived migrants evolved on the edges of the city, and the upper and upper middle classes occupied privately funded subdivisions in and around downtown (especially in the Chapultepec-Cacho-Hipódromo area), or in other high-valued areas (Playas, along the coast, for example).

A second force that fueled the spatial transformation of the city was the expansion and diversification of the economic base, particularly through greater integration into the U.S. economy and, more slowly, into the Mexican economy. From 1950 to 1980, the orientation of Tijuana's economy gradually moved from the primary and secondary sectors to the secondary and tertiary sectors. By 1982, nearly 60 percent of the city's economic base was devoted to tertiary activities. The most important among those included retail and wholesale trade, tourism, and services. The city also expanded its secondary sector from 23.8 percent in 1950 to more than 33 percent in 1982. That sector is still growing rapidly, principally because of the assembly-plant operations attracting U.S. and other foreign investment capital to the region. The *maquiladora* industry in Tijuana has had an explosive impact on employment from 1970 to 1988. Since 1970, employment has increased by 1,000 percent to more than thirty-eight thousand employees (Sinkin and Marks, 1988).

The modernization and diversification of Tijuana's economy has taken several forms, all of which have left their mark on the city's built environment and morphology. Tourism and trade have expanded as a result of government-sponsored projects. As early as the mid-1960s, the Mexican government, through the National Border Program (PRONAF), sought to beautify border cities as a way of increasing revenue from tourism. Highway projects, monuments, parks, and other new infrastructure contributed to an expansion of investments in tourism by the Mexican private sector, as well as capital ventures from U.S. companies. In Tijuana, the widening of Revolution Street, the redevelopment of downtown, and the development of the River Zone have all contributed to a growing tourism sector by creating tourist-oriented zones in the city. With the number of tourists entering Baja California surging to over twenty million per year by 1984, and with Tijuana controlling nearly three-quarters of that volume, this sector will continue to play a crucial role in the city's future.

These zones have typically overlapped commercial interests and allowed for an expansion of the city's commercial operations, including retail stores, office buildings, and the professional and technical services sector. Both the River Zone and the downtown now house new office buildings for this dynamic economic sector. An increasingly diverse array of commercial establishments is currently housed in Tijuana, with activities such as restaurants, hotels, retail stores, auto repair, construction, and services dominant.

The original PRONAF border development program called for the construction of industrial parks in the border cities (Dillman, 1970). In Tijuana an industrial park was built at Mesa de Otay in the 1970s. It houses many of the city's largest *maquiladoras* and a total of more than eighty factories. It has also become a growth pole for the city's eastward expansion. Several smaller industrial parks exist in the La Mesa area, and a second major park is planned for the El Florido satellite center on the road to Tecate east of the city. Not only have industrial parks been built, but the industrial sector has diversified, with growth in such areas as apparel, furniture production, sporting goods, transport, and electronics (Clement and Jenner, 1987).

The modernization of Tijuana's economy has had a number of important spatial impacts. As mentioned above, economic expansion has tended to create zones of high productivity in the city. Such zones include (1) the downtown, a zone of tourism, commercial activity, U.S.–oriented services, and business; (2) the River Zone, an area of heavy commercial activity, office space, government operations, and some tourism; and (3) the Agua Caliente/López Mateos Boulevard corridor, running parallel to the river, an area of high commercial concentration, automobile-oriented uses, and important city facilities, such as the municipal coliseum, the racetrack, hotels, and the new Agua Caliente office building and commercial complex. To some extent, these zones generate employment for the majority of the city's elite residents, who live nearby, and for a growing middle class, which resides in La Mesa, in some of the older neighborhoods around downtown, and, more recently, in the Mesa de Otay area. The expansion of Tijuana's economy has physically transformed some zones of the city and indirectly provided employment for both an elite class and a growing middle class, which occupies the zones between the elite locations and the squatter communities on the edge of the city.

In the post-1950 era, Tijuana has grown from a highly concentrated, pedestrian-scale city whose development was confined within a 3- to 4-kilometer (about 2-mile) radius, to a concentrically expanding metropolis, whose outer edge reaches 8 or 9 kilometers to the south and east, and more than 12 kilometers (7.5 miles) to the southeast (Figure 5). Tijuana's spatial decentralization can be attributed to the increase in per capita automobile ownership between 1950 and 1980, and to the government's support of improved intracity highway infrastructure. The increase in the number of automobiles can be explained by higher-than-average incomes and the proximity of an extensive used car and auto parts market in southern California. As a result, Baja California has the lowest inhabitant-per-automobile ratio (3.8 inhabitants per automobile) in Mexico, far lower than Mexico City (6.0) and Mexico as a whole (16.3) (Table 12).

In general, one can speak of two discrete periods in the city's spatial transformation after 1950: the period from 1950 to 1970, and

Table 12. Per Capita Income and Automobile Ownership for Selected States, Mexico, 1980–1981

State	1980 Population (thousands)	Total Registered Private Autos (1980)	Inhabitants per Auto (1980)	1981 per Capita Income (pesos)
Baja California	1,225	317,953	3.8	7,561
Baja California Sur	221	21,925	10.1	8,591
Chihuahua	1,934	177,768	10.8	2,813
Distrito Federal	9,373	1,557,727	6.0	5,482
Guanajuato	3,044	107,110	28.4	1,788
Jalisco	4,294	384,563	11.2	2,800
México	7,546	226,255	33.3	2,994
Michoacán	3,049	60,846	50.1	1,075
Nuevo León	2,463	177,286	13.8	4,960
Oaxaca	2,518	30,900	81.4	850
Puebla	3,280	120,098	27.3	1,583
San Luis Potosí	1,671	43,344	38.5	1,210
Sinaloa	1,880	47,436	39.6	2,432
Sonora	1,499	90,465	16.5	4,055
Tabasco	1,150	15,673	73.3	11,294
Tamaulipas	1,925	132,110	14.5	3,642
Veracruz	5,265	124,944	42.1	2,548
Yucatán	1,035	45,433	22.7	2,592
Zacatecas	1,145	15,509	73.8	1,450
National total	67,383	4,124,279	16.3	3,220

Source: Instituto Nacional de Estadística, Geografía e Información, 1982.

growth since 1970. During the former, Tijuana's influx of immigrants was channeled primarily into three zones: (1) along the highway to Tecate to the southeast, initially in the La Mesa area, and later in surrounding and outlying *colonias;* (2) in the hills and canyons to the southeast of the central business district—this is where a large proportion of the city's poorest squatter communities sprang up; and (3) along the coast in the Playas area.

Because much of this growth was spontaneous and unplanned, the government tried unsuccessfully to intervene and rationalize the city's expansion. For example, in 1961, Governor Esquival Méndez declared "urban district" boundaries for Tijuana, outside of which no urban subdivisions would be authorized. But since most of the city's spontaneous growth involved illegal land invasions, the government decree did little to prevent a continuation of chaotic development patterns. The government also built the La Misión–Tijuana aqueduct in an attempt to supply water to the city, but this would prove so inadequate by 1970, that the government would be forced to seek emergency supplies of its quota of Colorado River waters diverted through the United States (Cabrera Fernández, 1978). In 1962, the government also commissioned a master plan for the city, the Plan Regulador para la Ciudad de Tijuana, but the plan both underestimated growth and failed to clarify and assign responsibility for controlling growth to specific public agencies (Padilla, 1985). In general, the most striking feature in the city's expansion from 1950 to 1970 was the absolute dominance over the cityscape of the spontaneous irregular settlements, particularly in the southwestern zone of the city, where a number of monstrous "popular neighborhoods" (*colonias populares*), such as Colonia Obrera, Ciudad Jardín, El Rubí, and Francisco Villa, emerged.

From 1970 to the present, the continued growth of squatter settlements has been juxtaposed against an increase in government intervention to develop the touristic and other productive zones mentioned above. The result is a more polarized urban spatial structure than before. Government investments have upgraded the valuable lands in the downtown area, along the redeveloped River Zone corridor, and along the valuable coastal strip. A new area of development has also opened up during this period—the Mesa de Otay to the east of the city center. Two federal decrees have divided the land into a residential development zone and an industrial development area. Originally, government interest at the national level was to create an enormous residential-industrial growth pole; thus the area would have been called Ciudad Industrial (Industrial City). Over time, the industrial park plan was separated from the residential plan, and the Mesa became an important growth district for the city. However, workers in the industrial park's more than eighty factories did not necessarily live on the Mesa. In fact, workers experienced considerable difficulty in traveling to jobs on the Mesa de Otay, particularly those who use the inadequate mass transit system (Joulia Lagares, 1986). The Mesa de Otay continues to be a dynamic growth area with important facilities: the airport, two universities, technical schools, an industrial park, numerous residential developments for middle-class families, and a planned commercial development that will rival the River Zone shopping mall. In addition, the opening of the second border crossing into San Diego has enhanced the attractiveness of this area for future investments.

To achieve the redevelopment of the River Zone, the government displaced nearly five thousand families and spent millions of dollars to channelize the flood plain of the river (Herzog, 1985). This project represents the largest public development program in the city's history. At the same time, the continued growth of squatter settlements remains the greatest burden on the city's future well-being. By the early 1980s, estimates of the size of the squatter population ranged from 38 percent (Hiernaux, 1986) to 42.5 percent of total population (de la Rosa, 1985), or between 300,000 and 335,000. Estimates are that these settlements occupy nearly one-fourth of all the city's urbanized space (ibid., 1985), and probably closer to one-half of the residential territory in the city. Thus, by 1985, Tijuana, as it was beginning to re-structure itself into a diffuse spatial setting with a strong sectoral tendency from center to southeast, became even more polarized spatially than it was in 1950; this remains the dominant agenda for social and spatial planning into the twenty-first century.

San Diego, 1950–Present

The period of 1950 to the present covers nearly four decades in which San Diego has been transformed from a small city and center of naval operations to one of the nation's twenty largest metropolitan areas. The region's population increased from 556,808 in 1950 to over two million by 1985, a 274 percent increase (Table 13). These changes place San Diego in the same category as other Sunbelt metropolitan areas, such as Houston, Atlanta, and Phoenix, whose rates of growth were among the highest in the nation during the three decades following the Second World War (Perry and Watkins, 1977).

As in the case of other Sunbelt cities, much of San Diego's growth occurred as a result of in-migration from outside the city's boundaries. By the late 1970s, the predominant pattern was an increase in migration from the western region (northern and southern California, other western states), as well as a continued flow of migrants from eastern states. A decline in migration to San Diego from the central and southern regions of the United States also became clear by this time. Prior to 1970, proportionately more incoming migrants came from the South and Midwest (Central) regions (CIC Research, 1978).

Table 13. Population Growth, San Diego Region, 1930–2000

	Population	% Increase
1930	209,659	3.8
1940	289,348	3.8
1950	556,808	3.8
1960	1,033,011	3.8
1970	1,357,854	2.3
1975	1,559,505	2.3
1978	1,715,100	2.3
1985	2,082,800	2.3
1995[a]	2,473,500	2.3
2000[a]	2,647,200	2.3

Source: San Diego Association of Governments, 1981.

a. Projected.

Equally important in explaining San Diego's spatial change from 1950 to 1985 is the changing economic base of the city. Following World War II, San Diego's importance as a harbor continued to define its employment base, which was anchored by the largest naval base in the nation and by the marine corps training base at Camp Pendleton. The city began to build its industrial sector around these activities, a trend that began during the Second World War. Between 1950 and 1985, San Diego became an important center of aircraft and aerospace manufacturing, but also grew in several new sectors, including chemicals, apparel, and electrical and nonelectrical machinery. By the late 1970s, 15 percent of the city's employment base was concentrated in manufacturing. The region's economy began to diversify. Tourism, which attracts over one billion dollars to the area annually (Heiges, Stutz, and Pryde, 1984) constitutes 10 percent of the area's employment. High rates of construction (6 percent), and finance, insurance, and real estate (5 percent), can be attributed to the importance of land and property development to the region's economy. Trade, services, and education also display high employment figures, reflecting the region's continued growth over the last three decades (Overall Economic Development Program, 1979).

These employment figures have a very important application to the question of San Diego's spatial structure: between 1950 and 1985, the city essentially became a center of tourism, services, high-technology industry, and the property development business. These activities attracted a large number of well-salaried, highly educated white-collar workers. The result is that between 1950 and 1985, in-migrants to San Diego were predominantly middle- and middle-upper-class, white-collar professionals (with the exception of the military). One study of in-migrants showed that more than half had jobs on arrival in San Diego, with a substantial number employed in professional, technical, and managerial positions. The same study also showed that both before 1970 and between 1970 and 1978, about 50 percent of incoming migrants earned more than the median household income for San Diego; another one-fourth earned the same or slightly less than the median income (CIC Research, 1978). As a result, persons arriving in San Diego during the 1950s, 1960s, and 1970s earned sufficient income to demand owner-occupied housing. Equally, since households were demographically in the family-producing stage, their space needs dictated purchases of single-family homes large enough to accommodate a growing family. These demands had a direct impact on the gradual form of expansion the metropolitan region took between 1950 and 1985.

If one traces the spatial changes imposed on the San Diego region by growth from 1950 to the present (Figure 6), several observations can be made. In 1950, the regional population of slightly more than 500,000 was clustered around the traditional central business district lying on San Diego Bay and in a number of surrounding neighborhoods that had grown during the city's mass transit/trolley era. These mesa-top, streetcar neighborhoods included Old Town, North Park, Hillcrest, Kensington, Normal Heights, East San Diego, and Southeast San Diego. In addition, population concentrated in some older suburban communities, also linked by trolley to downtown, including the coastal towns of La Jolla and Ocean Beach, and south bay cities of Chula Vista and National City. The spatial form of the urban area conformed to the stellate pattern typical of the mass transit, pre-freeway era, with three wedgelike sectors of development: the Mission Valley corridor, the Southeast San Diego–south bay sector, and the coastal corridor. There were also smaller concentrations of population in two north county areas—Oceanside and Escondido—but population densities in north county during this era were rather low.

The principal growth occurring during the 1950–1960 era was generated by new automobile technology and changing patterns of neighborhood access created by newly constructed highway and

Figure 6. San Diego Growth Pattern, 1930–1975

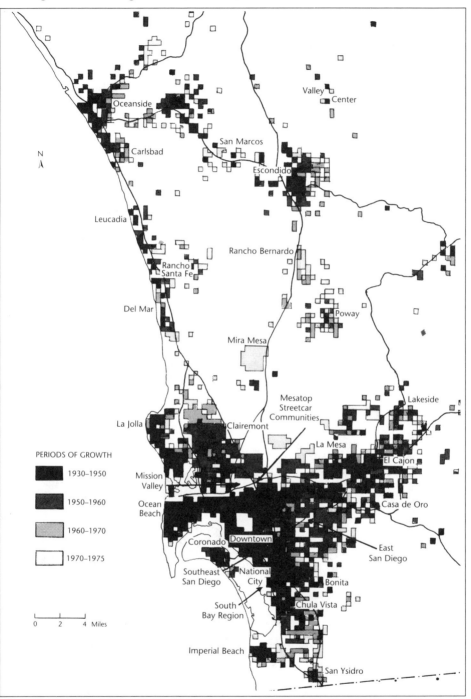

Source: Comprehensive Planning Organization, 1975.

Table 14. Total Population of San Diego Region, by Jurisdiction

Jurisdiction	1978	1985	1995	2000	% Change 1978–2000	% of Region 1978	% of Region 2000
Carlsbad	28,500	51,800	84,100	93,900	229.5	1.7	3.5
Chula Vista	78,400	90,000	113,400	118,400	51.0	4.6	4.5
Coronado	18,100	21,600	23,600	23,300	28.7	1.1	0.9
Del Mar	5,300	5,100	5,100	5,000	(5.7)	0.3	0.2
El Cajon	69,400	75,000	77,600	78,000	12.4	4.0	2.9
Escondido	56,700	73,700	83,600	84,500	49.0	3.3	3.2
Imperial Beach	20,500	23,500	26,000	28,200	37.6	1.2	1.1
La Mesa	49,900	53,600	56,500	56,800	13.8	2.9	2.1
Lemon Grove	20,200	22,700	23,600	24,100	19.3	1.2	0.9
National City	47,400	49,200	49,700	51,400	8.4	2.8	1.9
Oceanside	66,600	—	111,100	144,400	116.8	3.9	5.5
Poway	30,900	38,100	57,400	60,500	95.8	1.8	2.3
San Diego	806,000	939,100	1,043,800	1,078,200	33.8	47.0	40.7
San Marcos	14,800	25,100	34,900	35,200	137.8	0.9	1.3
Santee	36,100	45,700	57,100	58,600	62.3	2.1	2.2
Vista	33,000	42,200	50,200	51,400	55.8	1.9	1.9
Unincorporated	333,300	439,100	575,800	655,300	96.6	19.4	24.8
Total region	1,715,100	1,995,500	2,473,500	2,647,200	54.3%	100.0%	100.0%

Source: San Diego Association of Governments, 1981, p. 26.

Note: No exact population figure available for Oceanside in 1985.

road systems. One began to see the first evidence of a multinucleic urban region, with suburban towns creating their own industrial and commercial bases in competition with the traditional downtown. Cities like La Mesa, which nearly tripled in population from 1950 to 1960 (10,946 to 30,441), and El Cajon, which experienced nearly a 700 percent increase (from 5,600 to 37,618), are the best examples of the evolution of semiautonomous suburban cities during this period (see Table 14). In general, the largest growth during the period was to the east (El Cajon, La Mesa), where the wedge both widened and lengthened, and to the north, where the Oceanside and Escondido agglomerations became denser and expanded slightly. New growth centers along the coast in Carlsbad and Del Mar also appeared for the first time. The south bay wedge of Chula Vista–National City also expanded and became more densely settled, but to a lesser extent than the eastern and northern regions. Within the city of San Diego, there was increasing suburbanization to the north in the Clairemont Mesa–University City, and Linda Vista areas, and infilling in and around existing neighborhoods, including the State College area, East San Diego, and Southeast San Diego.

During the decade 1960–1970, infilling in the southern and eastern wedges continued. The stellate form of the pre-1950 era began to soften as the old mass transit communities were overshadowed by developments in suburban towns and infilled suburban growth. The urbanized portions of the city became more densely populated than before. From 1970 to 1980, the most striking spatial characteristic of the urban region was the phenomenal growth of north county. During the 1970s a number of towns in north county appeared for the first time, including San Marcos and Vista. Both Escondido and Oceanside expanded their populations to over fifty thousand inhabitants. North county exhibited sectoral growth along the principal transport corridors: Interstate 5 to the south and Interstates 78 and 76 to the east. Most important, for the first time, north county and the urbanized core of San Diego became integrated by developments along the Interstate 15 corridor (Mira Mesa, Poway, Rancho Bernardo) and the coastal, Interstate 5 route (Del Mar, Cardiff, Encinitas, Carlsbad). Along these linear arteries, the construction of elite "country estate" developments like Rancho Bernardo or wealthy suburban developments like La Costa began to create continuous corridors of urban development between once-rural north county and the nucleus of the San Diego urbanized area. During this period one sees the gradual widening of the ecology of the region to include rural settlements such as Lemon Grove, Spring Valley, and Bonita to the southwest, and Lakeside, Santee, and Poway to the northeast.

By 1980, San Diego's spatial form was highly dispersed and dictated by the intricate freeway networks that linked communities. Despite considerable infilling, the morphology of development remains somewhat sectoral. The highest densities (Figure 6) cluster within the downtown–Mission Valley–La Mesa–El Cajon corridor; the south bay corridor, which now reaches to the Mexican border; the Interstate 15 corridor, with a strong agglomeration at Escondido; the coastal corridor along Interstate 5; and the Interstate 78 corridor from Escondido to Oceanside. In general, the population is highly dispersed; projections for the year 2000 (Table 14) suggest that much of the growth will occur in north county towns like Carlsbad (229 percent increase projected from 1978 to 2000), Oceanside (116 percent increase), San Marcos (137 percent), and Poway (95 percent). The city has truly become a metropolitan "region"—multinucleated and sprawling. Downtown San Diego has completely lost its dominance in the region: the land surface accommodates a morphology of "urban villages," highly decentralized, autonomous communities spread out over the landscape of the region (Leinberger and Lockwood, 1986).

Comparative Spatial Structure in a Bicultural Border Metropolis

An important conclusion about spatial structure in Tijuana and San Diego can be drawn from the analysis above; that is, the political boundary not only separates the United States and Mexico jurisdictionally, but also sharply divides the urbanization processes that have led to the growth of large cities along the border. National culture is a critical determinant of urban spatial formation, even when two urban places share an international boundary. Although some boundaries serve to bring cultures together, the U.S.–Mexico boundary does not entirely perform such a function. The wealthy North and developing South clash at the meeting place of two contrasting societies. More generally, the cross-border relationships constitute a microcosm of bilateral relations.

One measure of the clash between U.S. and Mexican culture at the boundary can be found in both the divergent structures and the visual landscapes of border cities. Over time, cultures produce cities that reflect the underlying values, priorities, and meaning attached to location and urban form on each side of the border. Cultures also produce different architectural styles, although I have not attempted to analyze those here. Regional and national economic and political dynamics in each country are partly responsible for shaping different city morphologies. Thus, even in areas of high interdependence, such as a border region, neighboring cities reflect the pull of national politics and culture, which generate distinct built environments and spatial structures. Differences between the modern versions of Tijuana and San Diego vindicate these observations.

Tijuana in 1950 was a concentrically shaped urban nucleation, concentrated within a settled sphere three to four kilometers from the central business district. In many ways, it resembled the classic "pedestrian city" of the United States a century earlier. Although some of its compact structure is due to the historical importance of the downtown, two other explanations can be posed: first, economically, it is less expensive to provide neighborhood services in areas closer to the urbanized core; second, limited private automobile ownership made access by road impractical for the majority of residents, although this pattern has changed in the last decade. Still, it will take some time before the morphology is reshaped to accommodate the car.

Between 1950 and 1980, the city experienced a large-scale diversification of industry and the growth of an enormous tertiary economy. Massive population expansion took place. Population grew by 1,000 percent in three decades. By 1980, the boundaries of the urbanized portion of the region reached 12 to 14 kilometers (7.5 to 8.75 miles) to the southeast, with the principal growth concentrated in the coastal zone, the Mesa de Otay, the southeast (La Mesa; along the road to Tecate), and the periphery, especially in the southwestern quadrant of the urban area, where many of the squatter communities are located. Although its periphery is expanding considerably, Tijuana in the early 1980s still displays a relatively concentrated morphology, with important locations clustered in the central portion of the city, either downtown or along the one important development corridor represented by the River Zone, and its parallel commercial corridor along Aguas Calientes Boulevard, and along the highway to Tecate.

San Diego, on the other hand, displays a far more decentralized, sprawling spatial form. In physical area, the San Diego urbanized region is probably three to four times larger than the Tijuana region (see Figures 5 and 6). By 1970, most of Tijuana's development was concentrated within 3.75 miles of downtown; San Diego's growth, however, was heavily concentrated on the periphery. The urbanized area extended to the north as far as Oceanside (30 miles from downtown), to the south to San Ysidro (12 miles), and east to El Cajon (14 miles). From 1970 to 1985, although much of Tijuana's growth amounted to infilling within 7.5 miles of the city (Figure 5), San Diego's growth (Figure 6) was channeled toward exurban and rural towns such as Santee, Lakeside, Poway, Rancho Santa Fe, and Rancho Bernardo, all lying 18 to 20 miles from the central business district. San Diego was able to develop its periphery because of, first, an extensive streetcar system and, later, the construction of a wide-ranging freeway network, opening up suburban locations for housing to the north, east, and to a lesser extent, the south.

Thus one can clearly contrast the spatial scales of the two metropolitan areas. San Diego, by 1985, had become a sprawling, decentralized, metropolitan region of nearly two million inhabitants, served by an excellent freeway system. Tijuana counted over one million inhabitants by 1985, but its spatial form remained concentrated within a 7.5-mile radius of the city center. Equally, the Mexican border city's periphery was plagued by chaotic and unplanned squatter settlements. Where suburban expansion represented a planned "solution" for San Diego's above-average growth rate, peripheral expansion in Tijuana was an unplanned response to excessive in-migration and to inadequate housing opportunities and limited policy responses to growth.

The difference between "planning" in San Diego and in Tijuana revolves around the use of government to regulate and allocate land for development and to monitor servicing of developed land. In San Diego, all peripheral development was carefully regulated under the State of California Subdivision Map Act and the Environmental Quality Act. These state laws require developers to conform to specific guidelines in the subdivision of land, provision of services, and mitigation of environmental impacts. Equally, all land must conform to the city zoning standards. In Tijuana, much of the land developed on the urban periphery in the 1950–1980 period was in effect not governed by any specific public regulations. Housing was built on unserviced land, in flood-prone canyons, or on steep, sloping hillsides. No state intervention prevented these developments, even when, in some cases, they took place on public lands.

Comparisons of the use of land in the two cities are equally revealing. Table 15 shows that San Diego allocates nearly twice as much land for industry as does Tijuana. One possible inference is that Tijuana is several decades behind the average U.S. city in terms of establishing rational controls over urban space. It suffers from a shortage of land for large industrial tracts as well as from an

Table 15. Land-Use Breakdowns, Tijuana and San Diego

Land Use	% of Total Land
Tijuana (1984)	
Residential	17.0
Industrial	1.9
Commercial	2.7
Public[a]	2.0
Regional facilities/special uses[b]	9.7
Streets/public transport	10.5
Vacant (small parcels)	7.3
Vacant (large parcels)	12.7
Subdivisions under development	1.5
Subdivisions under negotiation	1.0
Areas unsuitable for development[c]	33.4
San Diego (1977)	
Residential	17.8
Industrial	3.5
Commercial	2.2
Public/Semipublic[d]	22.4
Streets and highways	11.8
Total developed	57.7
Agriculture and vacant	42.3

Sources: Secretaría de Desarrollo Urbano y Ecología (SEDUE), 1984; City of San Diego, 1979, p. 10.

a. Includes health and education facilities and local, state, and federal offices.
b. Includes airport, horse racetrack, country club, and military installations.
c. Includes canyons, riverbeds, steep hills, and ridges.
d. Includes local, state, and federal offices and facilities; public schools; parks; military installations; private schools; and churches.

abundance of industrial sites that are incompatible with surrounding land uses. In addition, the city of San Diego has more of its land devoted to streets and to public uses (parks, military), whereas Tijuana has a slightly higher percentage of land in commercial activities. Tijuana has more vacant and unusable land than San Diego, a topographic feature that has made land-use planning even more challenging. More than one-third of Tijuana's land is owned by the government, principally the federal and state government, indicating, as I discuss in Chapter 7, the dominant role of government in the urban development process.

The distribution of commercial, industrial, and other key land uses in the two cities suggests important differences. The location of industry, for example (Figures 7 and 8), contrasts the decentralized nature of San Diego's industrial parks with the more sectoral locational pattern of Tijuana's industrial sites (mainly in the River Zone/Aguas Calientes Boulevard corridor, or Mesa de Otay). These differences have been exacerbated by the contrasting degrees of intraurban mobility in the two cities. San Diego's freeway system is far larger and more developed than Tijuana's highway network (Figures 7 and 8). Not only does San Diego's freeway system extend outward to wider areas of influence, it can accommodate much larger volumes of traffic, is more sophisticated in design and materials used, and covers more miles of terrain. Unlike San Diego's extensive and modern six- to eight-lane freeways, Tijuana's highway network consists of two- and four-lane roads, many unfinished or in need of repairs. The highways intersect more regularly with collector roads and arterials and therefore do not allow for high-speed intraurban automobile travel to the extent that San Diego's freeways do.

Other important land-use patterns emerge (Figures 9 and 10). San Diego is a "recreational" and tourist-oriented city. Thus one finds far more open space and access to water and other amenities (bay, valleys, mountains). Second, one finds large amounts of land allocated for military uses and a systematic distribution of subregional commercial centers juxtaposed over the surface of the urban area.

Tijuana's land-use pattern contrasts dramatically. In Tijuana there is very little open space, or other recreational land uses. The city tends to have a much more mononucleic form—the downtown and the River Zone dominate in terms of the distribution of commercial uses. Large-scale commercial developments tend to be far more concentrated here than in San Diego. The River Zone represents the major focus for the location of important commercial, industrial, and public land uses. Although a secondary subcenter is being planned at the Mesa de Otay (with an industrial park, planned commercial center, and various educational facilities), and another in the future toward the southeast at El Florido, the present spatial structure remains highly concentrated. In fact, where San Diego has more than a dozen satellite centers of commercial, industrial, or office building development, Tijuana only has three—downtown, the River Zone, and the Mesa de Otay.

These contrasts become even more dramatic when one looks at the social ecologies of the two cities. For many years, scholars have conceived of urban social ecologies as reflections of the meanings different cultures attach to urban space. Higher-income residents in the city typically find the most prized locations, filtered within the locational tastes of their culture. Other income groups are sorted into neighborhoods on the basis of their socioeconomic and demographic levels; often ethnicity has been determined to play a role in the social geography of urban areas. That these sorting processes occur within a framework rationally tied to the larger city organization gives rise to the use of the term "ecology" to describe the social geography of urban areas.

In Tijuana (Figure 11), one sees a clear social stratification within the city into distinct, generalizable ecological zones. These generally tend to be differentiated by income across space in a fairly systematic manner. Higher-income families locate in neighborhoods near downtown and in the hills to the south, overlooking the River Zone. These communities are typically privately funded subdivisions with all urban services (water, electricity, sewerage, paved streets, and so on). A second zone of high-income residents is evolving along the coast, both in the Playas area and farther south toward Rosarito. Middle- and working-class families are clustered in neighborhoods adjacent to the wealthy zones, but arrayed in a concentric ring slightly farther from the downtown. This concentric pattern, which some observers believe is tied to processes that create similar spatial structures in other Latin American cities (Griffin and Ford, 1980), has been slightly modified in the last decade. Recent state-sponsored housing construction programs are interrupting the pattern by encouraging the growth of middle-class housing projects on the edge of the urbanized district, in such places as Mesa de Otay, Cerro de Colorado, and the Alamar River zone, as well as in the Playas de Tijuana area.

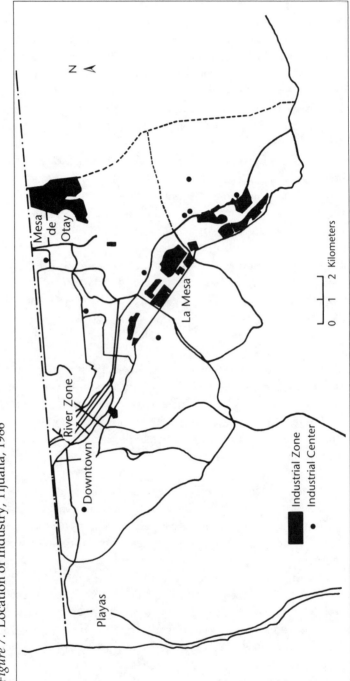

Figure 7. Location of Industry, Tijuana, 1986

Figure 8. Location of Industry, San Diego County, 1986

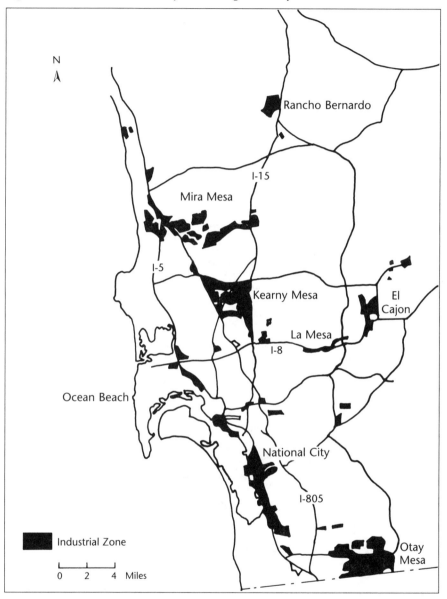

Figure 9. Land-Use Structure, Tijuana

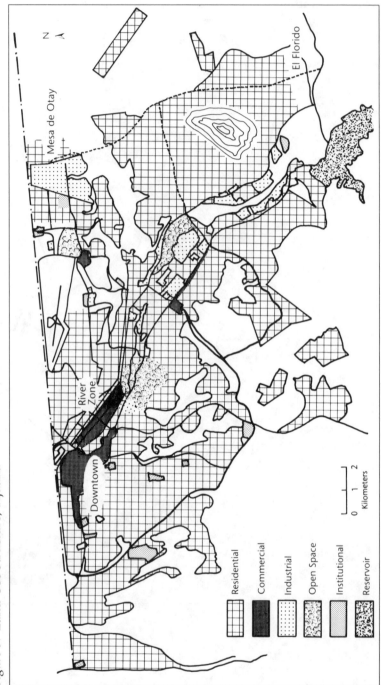

Figure 10. Land-Use Structure, City of San Diego

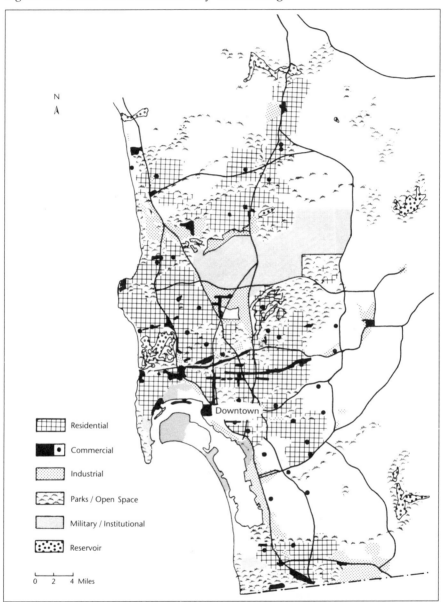

N

Residential

Commercial

Industrial

Parks / Open Space

Military / Institutional

Reservoir

0   2   4   Miles

Downtown

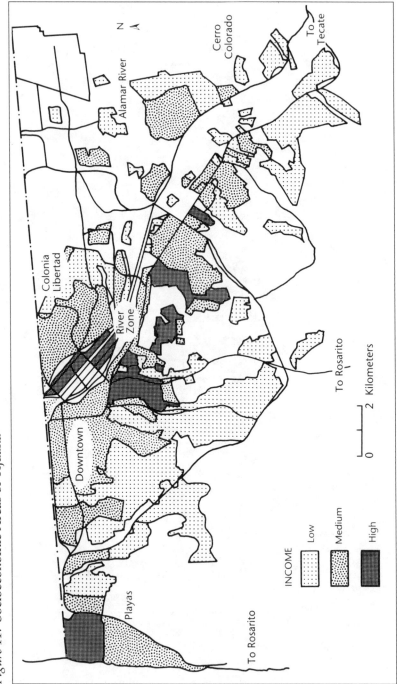

Figure 11. Socioeconomic Areas of Tijuana

Figure 12. Socioeconomic Areas of San Diego

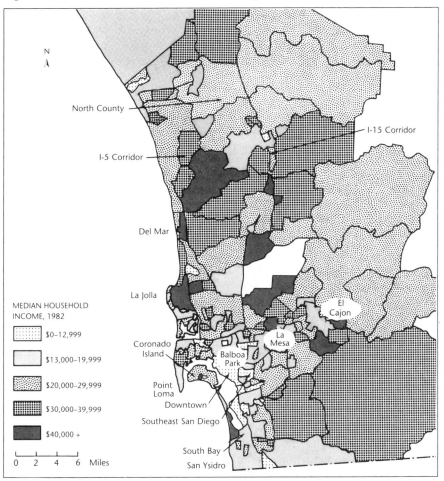

The poorest residents have generally been clustered in areas of topographic inconvenience (hills, canyons, flood plains) farthest from the downtown. These zones lie outside the middle-class neighborhoods, particularly to the southwest and south central parts of the city, as well as in the canyons east of Colonia Libertad, and in areas along the road to Tecate.

San Diego's social ecology is different (Figure 12). Here, it is not the downtown that dictates the location of socially prestigious neighborhoods, but rather the coast, northern locations, and environmental amenities (bay, canyons, hills, open space, parks, view corridors). In general, the ecological ordering of social areas tends to be sectoral rather than concentric, as in Tijuana. Wedges of higher-income residents locate along the coast from Point Loma to La Jolla and Del Mar, or along the Interstate 5 corridor in north county. Other high-income pockets are found near Balboa Park, along the Interstate 15 corridor, and in south bay. A few prestigious residential enclaves are found on the eastern periphery as well, and on Coronado Island. Social exclusivity in remote suburban locations appears to disrupt the "ecological" notion of a metropolis of functionally integrated residential areas. Suburban or even rural privacy dominates the elite locational mosaic in San Diego.

The poorest areas in the San Diego region display sectoral spatial patterns as well. The largest sector of low-income residents runs from downtown San Diego to Southeast San Diego, San Ysidro, and parts of surrounding areas. A second wedge runs from downtown through mid-city and East San Diego into La Mesa. Other enclaves can be found spread around the county, especially in the older central cities (Oceanside, Escondido, El Cajon), and in some renter-occupied enclaves in older beach communities. Middle-income areas tend to dominate the suburban zones built in the 1950s and 1960s, both to the north and east of downtown.

Perhaps the most striking contrasts of all emerge from comparisons of the social geography of the two border cities. In Tijuana, strategic locations are established by the historical value attached to the downtown and the elite spine running to the southeast along the river. High-status locations concentrate along that spine and around the central business district. Only recently have high-status neighborhoods emerged along the coast in the Playas zone. In general, residential ecology orients toward the traditional central business district and its recent companion business district—the River Zone. Elite dwellings continue to be built around these development districts, and real estate values here have skyrocketed in the last decade.

In this Mexican city, social class varies inversely with distance from the CBD and River Zone. One exception to this spatial principle is that marginal housing can also appear in canyons or on other harsh land surfaces that the wealthy or middle classes do not occupy. Thus, one finds pockets of low-income housing tucked into elite neighborhoods near the center of the city. The region's precipitous topography (canyons, hills) creates this pattern. In general, in Tijuana one finds a rather traditional, compact morphology seeking to adapt to a massive rural-urban migration pattern that has enveloped the city. This clash has resulted in the kind of chaotic land pattern typical of many Third World cities—including settlements in semihabitable places, at the very edge of the urban area, or in inaccessible canyons and flood plains, thereby creating zones of marginally serviced residential neighborhoods.

San Diego's residential ecology offers a dramatic contrast. Its CBD has an effect almost directly opposite to that of Tijuana's. San Diego's CBD and its commercial spine (El Cajon Boulevard and University Avenue running to the east) are low-status locations—some of the lower-income areas of the city lie near them (see Figure 12). There is a direct correlation between distance from the city center and social prestige. In San Diego, residential locations derive value not only from their proximity or distance from the CBD, but from a range of locational attributes that enhance or detract from exclusivity, privacy, environmental beauty, and refuge from the high-density elements of the city. There appears to be a high correlation between residential wealth and semirustic, rural locales. Some of the wealthiest areas of the city lie in highly remote settings on the outer edge of the urbanized region or in areas of great physical beauty (Point Loma, La Jolla, and Coronado Island, for example).

Although one can compare the social ecologies of the two cities with illuminating results, it may also be useful to consider their orientation toward each other. In Tijuana, the wealthy live near the downtown and therefore near the international boundary, which is a few hundred yards from the central business district. In San Diego, the wealthy tend to live away from the border, with most elite neighborhoods increasingly clustering toward the northern sectors of the city. Ironically, as one study describing San Diego in the early 1970s noted: "The natural gradient may be west to east, but the *social* gradient is clearly north to south. This social slope is becoming steeper and public actions tend to steepen it. South of the border are the extensive slums, and the pattern runs right up to the north county. For prestige, a home buyer will locate as far 'upstream' as he can afford" (Lynch and Appleyard, 1974). The seeming orientation of San Diego's social ecology away from the Mexican border raises the question: To what extent is there a functional overlap between the ecological and spatial forms of neighboring U.S. and Mexican border cities like Tijuana and San Diego? The next two chapters attempt to shed some light on this question and its political implications.

6 Dimensions of Transboundary Urban Space

Few economies and societies are as tangled together as those of the United States and Mexico.
— David Ronfeldt and Caesar Sereseres (1983)

To what extent does an international boundary separate the urbanization processes and the city forms that evolve around it? In the previous chapter, an analysis of the spatial structures of two border cities—Tijuana, Mexico, and San Diego, California—uncovered rather striking differences between the morphologies of the two settlements. Yet the evolution of spatial structure did not unfold in an entirely independent manner. The two cities influenced each other. Tijuana's evolution was very strongly tied to the U.S. economy and to a growing interconnection with San Diego. San Diego's growth was perhaps more subtly influenced by Mexico, yet in the post–World War II era, those influences became more direct. Despite the differences between the two border cities, there is evidence to suggest that a new ecological form is evolving—a kind of transboundary urbanized region within which a set of social, economic, and ecological linkages connects households, firms, interest groups, and businesses across the political boundary. This functional geographic area might be termed "transboundary urban space." In this chapter, we examine the dimensions of such a geographical notion, both conceptually and empirically.

Cities, Interdependence, and the Borderlands "Social System"

The idea of transboundary social formation is certainly not surprising to anyone who has studied the U.S.–Mexico border region. Although nineteenth-century historians characterized the boundary zone as a sparsely populated area of transition between two nations, the twentieth century has brought far-reaching changes to the region. Demographic shifts in both the United States and Mexico have transformed the boundary corridor into a field of confrontation of social, political, and economic forces native to the two nations. The border zone has become a place unto itself. It has developed a measure of autonomy, economic dynamism, and its own rules. With a steady migration stream feeding the population of northern Mexican border cities and several generations of Mexican Americans entrenched north of the border, the region has cultivated a unique "social system" (Alvarez, 1984). This system fuses family structures, culture, social interaction, and factors of production over time and across the boundary. One of its important by-products has been the bicultural built environment along the border.

Historians recognize the inherent cross-border social linkages tied to the evolution of the border region. Mexican citizens living north of the boundary line established by the Treaty of Guadalupe Hidalgo (1848) became part of a new nation-state. The subsequent history of the U.S. Southwest, however, is intimately tied to social and cultural connections with Mexico (McWilliams, 1968; Meinig, 1971).

Since the drawing of the international boundary, the process that has had perhaps the strongest integrating effect in the borderlands has been that of Mexican labor migration to the U.S. Southwest (Galarza, 1964; Gamio, 1930). The migration process can be thought of as one manifestation of an emerging transboundary social system that has its roots in the demand for Mexican labor in the U.S. Southwest starting at the turn of the century.

What is clear about this social system is that it evolved out of a regional demand for labor and a corresponding regionalized supply of labor at distinct moments in a time continuum. Demand and supply became systematically interconnected as the borderlands matured economically, moving from a marginal, unsettled region in the mid-nineteenth century, to an increasingly populated and economically productive zone slightly more than a century later. Cross-border migration became a vital social force in the economic development of the Southwest—Mexican labor was essential to the building of infrastructure, food production, manufacturing, and, more recently, to the provision of services for the rapidly growing population of the borderlands.

By no means was the borderlands social system equitable, however. Scholars have shown that the migration cycles feeding into the expanding southwestern economy, beginning in the late nineteenth century, were strongly tied to fluctuating economic and political circumstances north of the border (Bustamante, 1978). Events in the United States like World War I, the Depression, World War II, and the postwar boom generated direct impacts on the volume of Mexican labor migration permitted into the Southwest and on the institutional structures created north of the border to manage this migration flow. The creation of the U.S. border patrol in the 1920s, or of "Operation Wetback" in the 1950s, reflect moments when the U.S. need for Mexican labor subsided. On the other hand, during periods of high demand for Mexican labor, an opposite institutional response, such as the signing of a treaty with Mexico to create a "Bracero" program during the Second World War, are observed. In short, the migration process itself reflects the socioeconomic polarization that is basic to the formation of the borderland region.

The drawing of the border divided an industrializing nation in the process of expanding its frontier from an underdeveloped one that would need three-quarters of a century to generate a social revolution, and the rest of the following century to construct a democratic society capable of building a strong economy around its resource base. The economic disparity between the two sides of the border played a key role in defining the nature of the social system connected with the growth of the borderlands. The migration process was one part of the fabric of unequal socioeconomic relations between the United States and Mexico. U.S. capital established virtually absolute domain over the production process in the borderlands, both north and south of the border. Mexican immigrant workers became the dependent servants of capital (Fernández, 1977). Along the border, Mexican interests were consistently subordinated to U.S. economic power (Castellanos, 1981; Rico, 1983). In some cases, as in the development of cotton production in the Mexicali Valley or the construction of the port of Ensenada, U.S. capital penetrated directly into Mexico. Even on the U.S. side of the border, social inequality toward citizens of Mexican descent dominated, as historical analyses of Mexican Americans in the Southwest have shown (Camarrillo, 1979; Romo, 1982).

Within this global context of unequal U.S.–Mexican relations, the boundary zone has carved out a distinct role: it has become a medium for economic and social interaction. As the U.S. Southwest matured into a dynamic economic region, Mexican border cities evolved into important interim destinations for migrant workers. Later, during periods of mass deportations out of the United States, they served as points of return and temporary residence for expelled workers seeking to reenter the United States. Martínez (1977) has referred to these two important functions as "springboard/receptacle" functions. They represent part of the reason for the demographic transformation of the borderlands. For nearly a century, the transboundary movement of Mexican laborers has unfolded, gradually leaving large clusters of temporary and permanent residents in cities on the Mexican side of the border. North of the border, a Mexican American population and its ethnic heritage has gradually become entrenched.

The growth of paired urban centers, or "twin cities," at the U.S.–Mexico border is an outcome of the century-old social system that evolved in the borderlands. The cross-border interconnections between pairs of settlements was recognized early in the evolutionary history of the modern border zone (McWilliams, 1968). Increasingly, studies of border cities have emphasized the transborder nature of their social formation. Among these have been analyses of Ciudad Juárez (Martínez, 1978), El Paso (García, 1981), and Tijuana (Piñera, 1985; Price, 1973).

More intriguing, however, has been the question of symbiosis associated with these paired urban places. Researchers studying such border city complexes as Brownsville-Matamoros (Gildersleeve, 1978), Laredo–Nuevo Laredo (Sloan and West, 1976, 1977), El Paso–Ciudad Juárez (D'Antonio and Form, 1965; McConville, 1965), and San Diego–Tijuana (Duemling, 1981; Herzog, 1985) have identified a pattern of transborder interdependence that is cultural, economic, and even spatial (Dillman, 1983). Price's study of Tijuana (1973) spoke of "international symbiosis," or the interdependence of two or more cultural systems.

Yet the notion of interdependence can be both complex and misleading. From a political-economic perspective, it is rather clear that a simple notion of "symbiosis" or "interdependence" must be questioned in light of the vast inequalities that separate U.S. and Mexican border cities. Some Mexican scholars, for example, regard the idea of "interdependence" as more rhetoric than reality, since the truth is that on most levels U.S. domination along the border is apparent

(Rico, 1983). Studies of Mexican border cities have shown that in the areas of tourism, twin plants, and commerce, there is not an environment of mutual benefit, but of Mexican subordination to U.S. consumer values (Castellanos, 1981). The large population of Mexican border cities can, in part, be attributed to concentrations of Mexican workers performing the function of a "reserve army of labor" at the disposal of U.S. industries and agriculture at the appropriate moments of high demand (Fernández, 1977, p. 116).

If U.S. and Mexican border cities have evolved in an environment of heightened transborder exchange, this cannot be viewed as anything but the highly unequal political and economic relationship that underlies the border zone. A dependency theory perspective quickly underscores the polemical nature of border relations and the delicate political environment within which border transactions occur. Yet there are those who still believe that it is necessary to engage in what one border scholar has termed a "positive analysis of U.S.–Mexico relations at the regional and urban scale" (Graizbord, 1983, p. 6). Important forms of transboundary interaction remain to be understood. In fact, a unique transboundary social geography is evolving around the international boundary line. As another border scholar has noted: "Economic, social and cultural relations between the twin cities have been more marked by increasing symbiosis than by the confrontation of differing systems" (Hansen, 1981, p. 156). Whether or not the border connection between U.S. and Mexican cities has been marked by confrontation or cooperation, what remains is a need to understand the nature of the sociospatial system that encloses these settlements.

Transborder Urban Space

Urban growth along international boundaries tends to produce a unique ecological structure—what we might call the "transfrontier metropolis." The transfrontier metropolis is an urbanized region formed by a U.S. settlement to the north of the boundary, and a Mexican settlement to the south. The urbanized area is fused into a single functional spatial domain that transcends the international border. This zone of transnational settlement space is functionally unified by common daily activity systems (work, shopping, school, social trips), shared natural resources and environmental features (air, water, flora, fauna), and product and labor markets that overlap the political boundary. Within this configuration, social and economic space are interrupted by the political border. The international boundary line sharply divides formal political jurisdiction over space. The line highlights the role of the state in border urban space. It accentuates north and south. Within the functionally integrated, transboundary urban spatial formation lie two culturally defined cities, Mexican and American. These cities retain the elements of their nationally derived ecological structure in terms of density, social geography, road configurations, centrality, and so on. The transfrontier metropolis thus embraces two opposing forces—the traditional cities, as defined by national culture, and the integrated metropolis, defined by evolving social, cultural, and economic processes that connect the United States and Mexico across the border on a daily basis.

A growing network of activity systems integrates settlements on either side of the border. These include legal and illegal labor migration from residential origins in Mexico to employment locations on the U.S. side of the border; shopping trips to U.S. commercial sites; shopping trips to Mexican commercial locations; trips to Mexican entertainment, tourist, and other service locations; social, family, and other recreational trips north and south of the border; Mexican children attending school north of the border. These activity systems have created a form of human spatial organization that transcends the political boundary. There is also a transboundary natural ecosystem. In most twin-city border settings, elements of the natural habitat, such as air, water, land formations, flora and fauna, function without regard for the politically defined international border. Air, water, and sewage flow freely between many twin-city metropolitan areas along the border today.

The importance of the physical environment as an element of transborder space must be emphasized. Beginning in 1848, the drawing of the international boundary between the United States and Mexico imposed an artificial line over a singular physiogeographical landscape. Two of the most important treaties between the United States and Mexico, one in 1884, the second in 1944, recognized the inherent problems of drawing a border across this land, especially when it affected the flow and distribution of valuable water from the region's major river systems, the Colorado, Rio Grande, and Tijuana rivers (Bevans, 1972). As more and more population filtered into the border zone in the second half of the twentieth century, maintenance of the delicate ecology of the region became even more complex.

Urban growth and the economic development of the border zone have magnified the reciprocal nature of border physical environment problems (Bath, 1986; House, 1982). Both the quantity and quality of water are in jeopardy because of the international character of the hydrological systems operating around the boundary. The supply of surface waters has been a major source of controversy; more recently, access to groundwater aquifers has generated new legal problems concerning national rights of accessibility. Cross-border flooding, industrial pollution, sewage spills and salinization of irrigation waters are other problems native to the border environment.

Water is perhaps the most crucial transborder physical resource. But there are other physiogeographical elements that integrate U.S. and Mexican settlements. Most border cities share both an airshed and a geological setting (valleys, mesas, riverbeds, and so forth). Climatic conditions and the circulation of air are not affected by the artificial boundary. Border inhabitants essentially face the same air quality needs. Where air pollution threatens residents of one side of the boundary (as in the copper-smelting region of southern Arizona, northern Sonora, or the twin cities of El Paso–Juárez and Tijuana–San Diego), it clearly poses a similar threat to those immediately across the border. Equally, disposal of solid wastes and dumping of hazardous and toxic substances pose problems for residents on either side of the boundary in an area that is densely settled. The location of potentially hazardous, polluting land uses, such as nuclear power plants, also generates an impact north and south of the boundary. In short, environmental health in U.S.–Mexico border cities is inextricably tied to the natural ecological setting the two national cultures share.

Taken together, cross-border social interaction—the daily movement of people in transborder space—combined with transboundary ecological linkages (hydrology, air, land formations) create a singular "ecosystem" that overrides the political boundary. The use of the term "ecosystem" recognizes that, despite the international boundary, or perhaps even because of it, there is substantial reciprocity in the sociogeographical milieu of transborder cities. This reciprocity is most distinctly expressed in space. The growth of cities along the border can be viewed as a humanly constructed built environment (houses, factories, commercial developments, roads, sewer systems, and the like) that reflects the inherent cross-border ties evolving over the last few decades. The emergence of interconnected border settlements is one of the most important by-products of twentieth-century demographic change in the borderlands. The organization of an increasingly unified transborder spatial system along the boundary gives rise to a research agenda vital to unraveling the meaning of the new geographic formation I have termed "transborder urban space."

Transborder urban space is a product of history. It is the result of decades of institutionalized economic interdependence, fueled by Mexican labor migration. It has become increasingly visible as a result of changes in the degree to which the political boundary blocks off intraurban movements. Transborder urban space is anchored by the marketplace. At the border, one must make a clear distinction between "economic space," which refers to spatial business systems that transcend the boundary line, and "political space," which defines behavioral systems locationally bounded by national political borders (Graizbord, 1983). The marketplace is unquestionably the driving force behind population growth and the development of the borderlands. At one time, as I noted earlier, border scholars were skeptical about the economic development potential of international boundary areas. Yet, as Chapter 3 points out, economic opportunity—in the form of trade, tourism development, industrial growth, services, real estate, and land development—is responsible for much of the economic growth that led to the evolution of the borderlands urban system.

One might even argue that the border has created economic opportunity that would not exist in its absence. This flies in the face of traditional thinking about border economies. For example, it is known that the attitude of the Mexican government early in the twentieth century was to leave the border undeveloped, since "the philosophy that reigned was to create a desert between both countries, thereby affording the interior and the capital some protection from the clutches of the American manifest destiny" (Enríquez, 1973, p. 90). The same attitude prevailed on the U.S. side of the border in the late nineteenth and first half of the twentieth centuries. That is why writers such as Christaller, Losch, and Hoover were skeptical about the economic growth potential of boundary areas. Because many of these writers came from an intellectual tradition of international trade theory, locational theory, and regional science, they viewed the border zone as simply another region, albeit encumbered with an international boundary. Thus, as Hansen (1981, pp. 19–34) has suggested, many of these writers predicted that economic activities would be repelled by the boundary. Their analysis, however, failed to incorporate cultural, historical, geographical, and ecological variables, as does much of regional science more generally. They viewed the boundary regions in terms of rigid sets of tradeoffs between labor, capital and product mobility, and open or closed borders (Beckmann, 1984).

The skepticism of regional science toward the economic development potential of border regions has not been borne out in the U.S.–Mexico boundary zone. Productivity is enhanced by the border. As Reynolds (1984) has argued, for example, Mexican migration to the Southwest border area has become integrated into the global production process of the region and is responsible for competitive and stable pricing of consumer products north of the border. Bustamante, in a more polemical sense, has long argued that Mexican labor is essential to U.S. production, as illustrated by the cyclical demand for labor tuned to U.S. economic (and political) trends. He uses the term "commodity migrants" to describe Mexican migratory movements as social behavior in the context of global capitalist relations of production, in which there is "self transportation of labor as a commodity to where the capital owner demands it" (Bustamante, 1978, p. 185). Thus, the movement of Mexican workers across the border into U.S. cities is not so much a social aberration as a component of an emerging spatial system of economic relationships in which capital, labor, and products flow north and south of the border according to the rationale of the marketplace.

Although economic space is the organizing mechanism of "transborder urban space," it has led to highly inequitable distributions of wealth around the boundary. The history of the formation of Mexican cities along the northern border is one of gradual attachment to the United States through dependent economic ties, creating what one observer has termed "dependent space" on the Mexican side of the border (Revel Mouroz, 1984). If there has been economic osmosis, it has occurred through a gradual spread of U.S. capital, via the North American consumption model, and a steady increase in Mexican investors' ties to U.S. business and capital north of the border. One study of the Mexican border region has shown that this dependency has reached the proportions of a crisis, as both the trade and assembly-plant sectors allow for a pernicious drain of capital out of Mexico into the United States (Tamayo and Fernández, 1983).

Despite the inequalities inherent in the emergence of transborder economic space and expressed in the built landscape of cities, which are the material expression of economic and spatial relations, there is an emerging transboundary spatial system. The existence of paired settlements along the nearly two thousand–mile international boundary is no simple accident of geography—it is the result of strongly articulated socioeconomic relationships expressed in space. Both human and physiogeographical systems operate on a cross-border basis. How these relationships affect the border built environment, the humanly constructed landscape that is superimposed on the natural environment over time, remains an unanswered question. To what extent is the built environment of border settlements becoming a transboundary phenomenon? How do land-use and urban development decisions near the international boundary take into account the neighboring national jurisdiction and city?

Empirical Dimensions of Transborder Urban Space: The Tijuana–San Diego Region

The Transboundary Marketplace

Urban space is often shaped by the forces of the private market. On the U.S.–Mexico international boundary, this process unfolds with an interesting twist: the workings of capital are filtered through two disparate economic systems. San Diego, California, and Tijuana, Mexico, provide one example of the confrontation of highly unequal urban economies within a functionally integrated space. To begin with, Tijuana is far more dependent on San Diego than San Diego is on it. It is also a much poorer city. A white-collar professional in Tijuana earns on the average perhaps $3,000 per year, whereas in San Diego the same occupation pays ten times that salary. Tijuana's economy is still more tied to agriculture and manufacturing than is San Diego's, although both cities also devote a great deal of labor to three sectors: trade (including tourism), services, and construction.

Despite differences in levels of income and in urban economic structure, there is no question that a transboundary marketplace is evolving in the San Diego–Tijuana region. Since 1960, Tijuana has had the fastest-growing urban economy in Baja California. In 1960, it held 31.5 percent of the state's economically active population; by 1980, that figure had grown to 40.3 percent (Ramírez Acosta and

Castillo, 1985). For the three sectors most responsible for that tremendous growth—industry, trade, and services—the principal causes of the expansion are linked to Tijuana's integration with both San Diego and southern California. In the industrial sector, Tijuana's growth is mainly explained by the arrival of the twin plant–assembly program in the late 1960s. Tijuana's strategic location near the port of entry into southern California and near high-technology resources in San Diego County, has allowed the city to expand its assembly-plant economy to a point where it now is responsible for employing 65.6 percent of Baja California's *maquiladora* workers.

The second sector, trade, is also strongly linked to San Diego. Tijuana exports an enormous supply of consumer goods to North Americans, maintaining a competitive edge over U.S. merchants simply through lower prices. Ironically, as one border scholar has noted, at the same time, Tijuana does not necessarily produce some basic consumer items for its own inhabitants, and its residents therefore purchase them in San Diego, thus creating an unhealthy drain of capital out of Mexico (Hiernaux, 1986). In the area of services, Tijuana derives a large proportion of its revenues from sales of tourist, entertainment, and personal services to North American consumers.

Although San Diego is clearly not as dependent on Tijuana for its economic growth and stability, it nevertheless has developed stronger economic linkages with its neighboring city over the past two decades. There are three principal areas in which San Diego's marketplace extends into Tijuana. First, San Diego extends its labor market into Tijuana through the legal and illegal hiring of at least fifty thousand Mexican workers on a regular basis. These workers provide the primary labor input for agriculture in San Diego County (Ramírez Acosta and Castillo, 1985) and are also important in providing labor in domestic services, hotel and restaurant service, gardening, construction, and manufacturing. Second, entrepreneurs in San Diego make important financial investments in tourism and other activities south of the border. It is difficult to measure these financial flows, or their counterparts from Mexican investors, because of the lack of data and the clandestine nature of these kinds of border transactions. Third, San Diego benefits from its proximity to Tijuana by capturing the market of Mexican middle- and upper-class consumers who purchase certain goods in San Diego County. Sales of commercial products to Mexican nationals in the late 1970s were estimated between two hundred and three hundred million dollars in San Diego County (Economic Research Bureau, 1985; Regional Economic Research, 1981). These sales dropped dramatically following the devaluation of the peso in 1982.

The Transborder Consumer Market

A transborder consumer market is possible when goods and services can be easily exchanged over the political boundary and when there are large enough threshold populations to make retail and wholesale trade a profitable venture. Population was one of the concerns of classical location theorists like Christaller and Losch, who wrote decades before sizable cities were located on international borders. Classical location theorists doubted that a dynamic consumer market was feasible in what were then sparsely populated boundary zones.

The U.S.–Mexico border zone today displays large enough consumer markets to emerge as one of the leading retail development regions in either nation. Also, despite periodic setbacks, there has generally been a positive climate for economic relations across the boundary since the late nineteenth century. President Porfirio Díaz, beginning in the 1880s, encouraged expanded trade with the United States and allowed the penetration of North American capital into northern Mexico. In 1885, a *zona libre* (free zone) was created. It permitted duty-free movement of goods within twenty kilometers (twelve miles) of the border in Mexico. Over the next seventy-five years, different forms of duty-free zones or frontier enclaves were created and removed according to the political attractiveness of a more open border for U.S. consumers. The Mexican frontier zone became highly sensitive to and dependent on the economy on the U.S. side.

Following the termination of the *bracero* farmworker program in the late 1950s, Mexican border cities experienced their highest unemployment levels in decades. Waves of Mexican farmworkers deported from the United States combined with masses of poor rural migrants from the interior to create a population explosion and social unrest. In 1961, partly because of these social pressures, the Mexican government created the Programa Nacional Fronterizo (National Border Program), which was essentially a regional development project that sought to regenerate the border cities, diversify their economies, and provide physical improvements. Once again, the government defined the frontier territory as a zone within twenty kilometers of the boundary and sought to create policies to stimulate the Mexican economy and interrupt the flow of capital into the United States.

A second important Mexican policy initiative began in the early 1970s. In an effort to halt the exodus of Mexican capital to the north, the government created the "Artículos Ganchos" (a *gancho* is a hook) program, which allowed duty-free import into the Mexican frontier zone of commodities usually purchased on the U.S. side (for example, clothing, shoes, records, and appliances). The idea was that if goods were sold at equal or lower prices in Mexico, the money would be retained there. But in fact, the Artículos Ganchos program simply reinforced the imports-oriented consumer behavior patterns of Mexican border residents while discouraging local production of these items (Urquidi and Méndez Villareal, 1978).

The government also tried to encourage the construction of shopping centers in the Mexican border cities by granting business investors subsidies on 100 percent of import duties on consumer goods and equipment needed to run the stores; in 1978, the government even decreed that 49 percent of the investment could come from U.S. interests. Still, only a few shopping centers were built in cities along the two thousand–mile border before 1980. More recently, Mexican investors, hoping to profit from the reduction in the price of goods caused by the declining peso, have begun to invest in shopping centers along the border.

In general, the retail behavior of Mexican border residents has been tied to the U.S. economy and to U.S. goods. This reinforces the work of scholars who have emphasized the historical basis for creating "dependent space" on the Mexican frontier (Revel Mouroz, 1984). Recent studies in Mexico express grave concern about the retention of capital on the Mexican border, even when that capital is earned in dollars (on the U.S. side) or in U.S.–sponsored *maquiladora* plants. The fact is that there has been an enormous flow of dollars and pesos from the Mexican frontier into the United States. One of the most comprehensive studies of this phenomenon estimated a loss of between $600 million and $740 million in 1972 (Tamayo and Fernández, 1983). Had the peso not been devalued since 1982, by today, perhaps as much as $1 billion might be spent annually on retail purchases north of the border. Obviously, with less buying power since 1982, Mexicans are spending less north of the border. Still, there is a considerable flow of money from Mexico into the United States—

more than $50 million in retail sales in San Diego in one year following the devaluation (Economic Research Bureau, 1985).

In general, Mexicans tend to buy manufactured goods such as clothing, consumer durables (washing machines, refrigerators), electrical goods, appliances, cars, and food (poultry, eggs, salt, bread, milk, margarine) in the United States (North, 1970). Obviously, a major factor affecting Mexican consumer behavior has been the strength of Mexican purchasing power. In the 1960s, the peso remained stable at 12.5 to one dollar, but in 1976, the first of a series of devaluations seriously weakened Mexican purchasing power along the border (Mungaray and Moctezuma, 1984). The impact on the United States was felt immediately. In 1976, one study showed that in San Ysidro, California (south San Diego County), the 1976 devaluation led to a 63 percent reduction in wholesale trade and a 40 percent reduction in retail sales (Stoddard and West, 1977). A study of the second major devaluation, in 1982, shows similar results for San Diego County (Economic Research Bureau, 1985). The percentage of sales of retail goods to Mexican nationals in selected regional shopping centers in San Diego County went from 7.5 percent in 1979 to only 4.4 percent of total sales in 1983. While total retail sales increased in the county from about $800 million to over $1 billion in 1983, sales to Mexican nationals fell from a high in 1981 of about $100 million to a low in 1983 of one-half that amount, or about $51 million. The peso devaluation of 1982 had an immediate effect on Mexican shopping behavior in San Diego. Following a 73.5 percent increase in Mexican spending between 1979 and 1981, the period 1981–1982 saw a decrease of 33.7 percent in Mexican retail purchases, and 1982–1983 witnessed a decrease of 23.7 percent.

One should not underestimate the general signal that Mexico's economic crisis is sending out along the border. The pattern of continued peso devaluation threatens dramatically to transform Mexican retail consumption behavior near the boundary, as Mexican spending power declines. The implications for the U.S. economy, U.S.–Mexico relations, and the structure of cities must be closely monitored.

Mexican Consumers and Space

Despite the vulnerability of Mexican shoppers in the United States to fluctuations in their own economy, Mexican consumer behavior in San Diego County operates within a rational spatial framework. Aggregate retail spending displays a "distance decay" effect, as illustrated in Figure 13. Given the distribution of large-scale shopping centers in San Diego County, Mexicans represent the largest percentage of overall sales at retail centers closest to the border. Mexican retail consumption (as a percentage of total retail earnings) falls off as one moves away from the border. The actual pattern, however, is not purely a function of distance; it is also a function of consumer knowledge. In 1981 Mexican consumers spent in discrete San Diego locations, principally the south bay malls, Mission/Fashion Valley, and La Jolla. Mexicans tend to patronize the most popular malls in south county, Mission Valley, and La Jolla, but do not equally patronize other popular locations in either east county or north county. They show specialized knowledge and spatial preference for specific locations. These patterns of consumer behavior are consistent over time between 1979 and 1983 (Economic Research Bureau, 1985).

Equally interesting are patterns derived from a 1983 survey I supervised of Mexican shoppers crossing the border at San Ysidro into San Diego County. Table 16 summarizes the mobility patterns of Mexican consumers in the sample population. Here we see the spatial logic of the Mexican consumer, grouped according to types of purchases (purpose of trip), distance traveled, and mode of transportation. We observe a very rational spatial organization of shopping behavior, disaggregated into three categories: (1) pedestrian, short-distance trips (these trips are taken mainly to purchase low-order goods, principally food, and represented 39.7 percent of the sample population of Mexican consumers entering San Diego in 1983); (2) mixed pedestrian/auto (about 50 percent of each), medium-long range (7–8 kilometers) trips (which involve the purchase of higher-order goods such as clothing and articles for the home, and represented 26.5 percent of all shopping trips in the sample); and (3) long-range, automobile trips. This last category represented 33.8 percent of all trips in the sample, and involved trips of more than 9 kilometers, and the purchase of major electrical appliances or business-related items. (The large percentage of "business purchases" may in fact have included clandestine mass purchases of U.S. goods for small retail operations in Mexico.)

What the data in this sample show is that there is a clear spatial ordering of Mexican consumer behavior in San Diego. Figure 14 illustrates this rational spatial pattern. On both the origin and destination sides of the border, there is a distance bias in the frequency of

Table 16. Average Shopping Distance (to the U.S.) and Mode of Travel, by Type of Purchase, Tijuana Consumers

Type of Purchase	No. of Persons	% of Total	Distance, Home to Border (km.)	Mode of Travel to Border (%)		Distance, Border to Store (km.)	Mode of Travel in U.S.[a]				
				Walk	Auto		Walk	Trolley	City Bus	Bus	Auto
Food	87	39.7	2.6	71.9	28.1	2.6	43.8	13.5	7.9	3.4	0.0
Clothing	42	19.2	3.9	57.1	42.9	7.4	9.5	26.2	14.3	2.4	4.8
Domestic articles	16	7.3	4.8	50.0	50.0	8.2	5.1	33.3	2.1	0.1	1.2
Major electronic appliances	14	6.4	5.4	23.1	76.9	9.8	6.7	15.4	0.0	0.0	1.0
Other (business purchases)	60	27.4	4.9	11.4	88.6	9.9	3.7	3.9	0.5	0.1	3.1
Total	219	100.0									

Source: Survey of Mexican border crossers directed by author, San Ysidro, 1983.

a. Breakdown of percentages of people who walked to border; discrepancies in ratios attributed to no-response cases.

Figure 13. Mexican Retail Consumption in San Diego County, by Shopping Centers, 1981

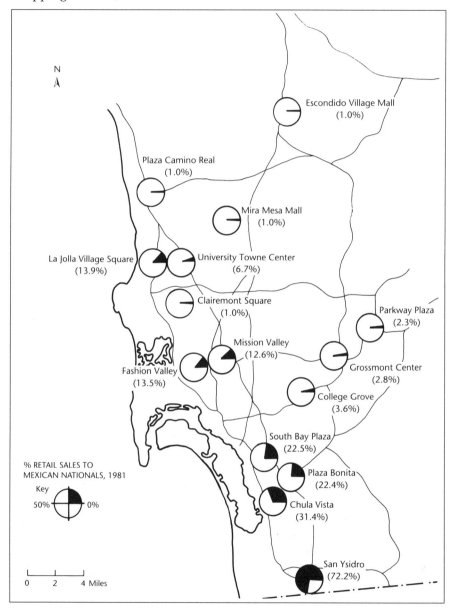

Figure 14. Transborder Shopping Trips, Northbound

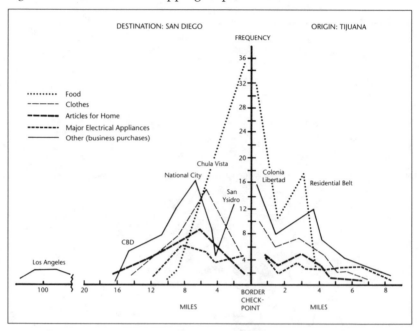

consumer movement, although in Tijuana it tends to be less pronounced for higher-order goods. In San Diego County, there is also a systematic spatial pattern for Mexican shopping behavior, a pattern that is ordered by product type. Food purchases display the steepest slope—consumer purchases fall off sharply with distance from the border. Clothing purchases peak at the six-mile point and then begin a steady decline; articles for the home display a similar pattern. Electrical appliance purchases are steady through the South Bay area from zero to four miles from the boundary, increase between four and eight miles and then fall off sharply. Business purchases are high in San Ysidro, fall off between San Ysidro and South Bay, and rise between Chula Vista and downtown San Diego.

These spatial dynamics reinforce the notion that Mexican consumer activity in San Diego is not a fragmented or whimsical process; it is a well-established practice in which San Diego becomes an extension, albeit irregular, of the spatial fields of behavior for Mexican consumers in Tijuana. For lower-order goods, such as food and clothing, Tijuana consumers utilize a variety of transit modes on the U.S. side of the border (see Table 16). In our survey, those who crossed the border to purchase food generally walked to their shopping destination (43.8 percent out of the 71.9 percent who crossed on foot). They mainly shopped in grocery stores in San Ysidro. Others used the light rail transit system (the trolley) to reach shopping destinations (13.5 percent), or traveled by bus (7.9 percent) within about 2.6 kilometers of the border. Pedestrians also made more clothing purchases than did automobile passengers. There is a much wider range of transit options in San Diego for clothes shopping than for food shopping; thus, of the 57.1 percent of the sample population of shoppers who crossed the border on foot, travel to clothing stores was made by trolley (26.2 percent), by bus (14.3 percent), on foot (9.5 percent), and in other ways to areas averaging 7.4 kilometers from the border. Tijuana shoppers, this suggests, know where they wish to make purchases, and how they can get there. They behave in much the same way as retail consumers in any city—they trade off distance and the inconveniences of changing modes of transit to get access to goods they perceive as necessary for consumption. The spatial segmentation of Mexican consumers by product type follows many of the principles of central place theory for urban market behavior. Tijuana residents are willing to travel farther for higher-order goods, which they purchase less frequently. Purchases of food or clothing involve more regular trips, often by foot, and closer to the border.

These movement patterns are part of a network of linkages that connect households, firms, and other points on both sides of the boundary. Each day thousands of work, shopping, recreational, business, social, and other trips are made between San Diego and Tijuana. Table 17 offers a snapshot of the distribution of trips by type for a sample of 856 border crossers in June 1983.

A 1977 study estimated that about 106,000 people cross the border between San Diego and Tijuana each day (Metropolitan Transit Development Board, 1977). Table 18 breaks those movements down by category, using Immigration and Naturalization Service (INS) statistics and other estimates. We see that there is a larger flow from Mexico into the United States (over 60 percent of the daily flow heads north). Clearly, not all of these trips are between an origin in Tijuana and a final destination in San Diego. Another study of border crossers, however, estimated that on a typical weekday, about 52,258 people crossed the border going north, and of that group, two-thirds of the northbound trips had a destination within ten miles of the border (Comprehensive Planning Organization, 1978). Although this

Table 17. Trips from Tijuana to San Diego by Purpose, Tijuana
Residents

Purpose of Trip	Number of Trips	%
Home	8	1
Work	378	44
School	18	2
Recreation	31	3
Shopping	213	25
Social	90	11
Business	78	9
Other	40	5
Total	856	100

Source: Survey of Mexican border crossers directed by author, 1983.

Table 18. Daily Travel Profile of San Ysidro Border Crossing, 1976

Traveler	Person Trips (One Way)	% of Total Trips
Into U.S.		
Mexican national		
visitor/tourist	52,500	49.5
Green card commuter	10,000	9.5
U.S. citizen commuter	5,000	4.7
Into Mexico		
U.S. citizen resident	34,500	32.5
Other nationality	4,000	3.8
Total	106,000	100.0

Source: Metropolitan Transit Development Board, 1977, p. 12.

information is a decade old, we can draw some important inferences
from it. Of the 67,500 average daily trips into San Diego County by
Mexican visitors or commuters, or Mexicans with U.S. citizenship
(Table 18), about 44,500 are to destinations within the San Diego urban area. The numbers probably vary slightly on weekends, with the
spatial field of origins and destinations extending slightly farther
from the border. Of the daily trips by U.S. citizens into Mexico
(34,500), some of these may not originate in San Diego nor terminate

in Tijuana. However, a study of tourism in the region in 1974 estimated that about 70 percent of San Diego's tourist attraction visitors come from the city or county of San Diego (Little, 1974). Thus, based on trends in the 1970s, we can probably assume that three-quarters of the daily flow of U.S. citizens into Mexico comes from the San Diego County metropolitan area. Destinations may cluster either in Tijuana or nearby Rosarito and Ensenada.

Table 18, in effect, suggests that the magnitude of activity systems linking Tijuana and San Diego is considerable. The numbers have probably grown since the mid-1970s. The estimate of 15,000 commuter workers traveling daily to San Diego is extremely low (some unofficial estimates place the figure at 25,000 to 30,000). Still the figure is impressive. Of the 52,500 visitors from Mexico, probably 30,000 or so are border residents taking a work-related, social, recreational, or business trip. Perhaps 25,000 to 30,000 San Diegans travel to Tijuana for recreational, business, shopping, or social purposes. These numbers give some sense of the human flow leading to a spatial organization that supersedes the political boundary. In a more global sense Figure 15 offers high and low estimates of the annual one-way border crossings between Tijuana and San Diego. By 1995, this figure suggests, between 60 million and 75 million people will cross the border at Tijuana–San Diego each year, making this the largest international border metropolitan region in the world.

Figure 15. Annual One-Way Border Crossings, Tijuana–San Diego

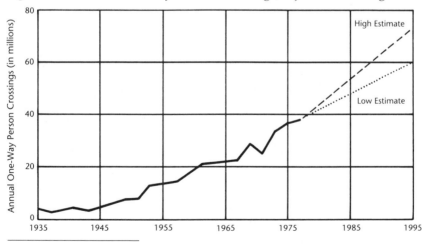

Source: Metropolitan Transit Development Board, 1977.

Mexican Commuter Workers

Another important dimension of U.S.–Mexico transboundary social space is the phenomenon of cross-border labor markets. Although much has been written about the global spillover of undocumented Mexican workers into the United States, little research has been carried out on the legal movement of Mexican workers to daily employment locations north of the border. Overshadowed by the much larger flows of illegal workers from the interior of Mexico into the southwestern United States, "frontier workers" represent an important component of U.S.–Mexico border transfrontier social geography. They reflect a regionalized response to the social context of production in the border zone: lower standards of living south of the border, and greater availability of jobs at higher wages to the north. One response to this socioeconomic polarity is the commuter worker phenomenon: a set of workers whose place of residence (Mexico) is separated from their place of work (United States) by an international border.

But this phenomenon is not entirely limited to the U.S.–Mexico border region. Any place in the world in which some difference in economic development or employment structure is combined with dense settlement patterns near an international border is just as likely to produce a frontier worker pattern. Such is clearly the case in western Europe, where, by the mid-1970s, 250,000 workers commuted across international boundaries daily along the Swiss, French, Dutch, German, Belgian, Italian, and other national borders (Ricq, 1982).

The process of daily transfrontier labor migration occurs within a complex political-institutional context along the United States–Mexico border. To commute legally to work, a resident of a Mexican border city technically needs either proof of lawful permanent residence in the United States (what is often referred to as a "green card") or a nonimmigrant visa for temporary entry into the United States. These are the only categories of non–U.S. citizen border crossers from Mexico legally permitted to work according to the U.S. Immigration and Naturalization Service (INS). A third category of border crossers can enter the United States legally—these are border residents, Mexican citizens who reside permanently in a Mexican border city and possess a nonresident border crossing identification card (the so-called white card) approved by the INS. This document permits entry into the United States for a maximum of seventy-two hours within twenty-five miles of the boundary. More than one million Mexicans along the border possess these cards, and thousands await approval by the INS (Hansen, 1981).

Of the Mexicans with border crossing privileges, thousands are working illegally on the U.S. side. Although no official statistics exist on this problem, it is generally acknowledged that this pattern occurs, since INS officials admit that they do not have the resources to monitor Mexicans unlawfully using the temporary visitor/border card to enter the United States for work. Once Mexican citizens cross the border with the white card, there is no INS mechanism in place to regulate their activities beyond the international checkpoint. Clearly, such a monitoring process would be extremely expensive to implement. Furthermore, even if caught, these Mexicans would likely hide their identity and claim to have crossed illegally; they could then be declared as "entered without inspection" (EWI), and voluntarily return to Mexico without a penalty, thus preserving the precious border crossing card (ibid., p. 90).

The political-institutional context of the border allows commuter workers the opportunity to regularly enter the United States legally. This opportunity, growing out of the symbiotic relationships that have evolved around the border, has led to the formation of a social class of border crossers who use the crossing privilege to earn income. The "international journey to work," although violating official U.S. immigration policy, is an important part of the de facto functional relationships connecting people and economic activities on either side of the border.

I supervised a survey of commuter workers in the Tijuana–San Diego region in 1983. There are several constraints on doing such a survey. First, interviews are conducted while commuters are waiting in long lines to cross the border and are reluctant to give out information that they think the U.S. or Mexican government might use against them. Second, some "commuter workers" use a nonwork border crossing card to work on the U.S. side illegally—these workers do not want to participate in a survey for obvious reasons. Nevertheless, the survey I organized produced the well-articulated origin-destination pattern illustrated in Figure 16. The patterns are not altogether unlike those for other U.S. metropolitan areas. The difference, of course, is that the origins lie on one side of an international boundary, the destinations on the other. The dispersal of origin and destination points suggests that this labor market phenomenon is not

Figure 16. Commuter Workers in Tijuana–San Diego: Origin-Destination Patterns by Employment Category

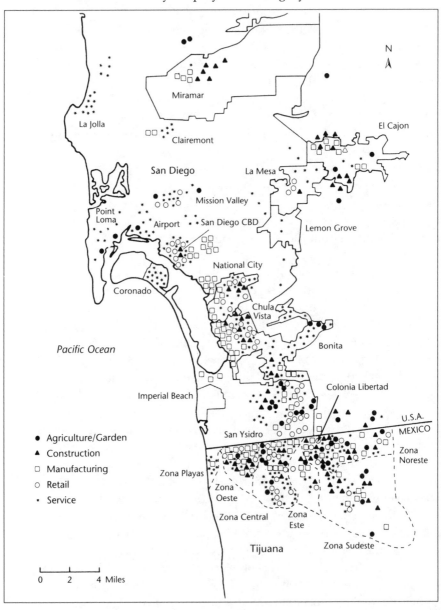

N

La Jolla

Miramar

El Cajon

Clairemont

San Diego

La Mesa

Mission Valley

Point Loma

Airport • San Diego CBD

Lemon Grove

National City

Coronado

Chula Vista

Pacific Ocean

Bonita

Imperial Beach

Colonia Libertad

U.S.A.
MEXICO

San Ysidro

Zona Noreste

● Agriculture/Garden

Zona Playas

▲ Construction

□ Manufacturing

Zona Oeste

○ Retail

• Service

Zona Central

Zona Este

Tijuana

Zona Sudeste

0   2   4 Miles

restricted to a few specialized submarkets, but penetrates the larger employment structure of San Diego County.

Table 19 presents occupational structures for two sample populations of Mexican commuters to San Diego. We see that Mexican commuter workers primarily occupy the tertiary sector (more than 50 percent in trade and services in 1983) and manufacturing, but also work in agriculture and construction.

One should not forget, of course, that a second major category of Mexican workers in San Diego County exists alongside the commuter

Table 19. Occupations Reported by Mexican Commuter Workers, 1980 and 1983

Occupation Category in U.S.	Number	%
1980		
Agriculture	25	12.0
Construction	27	13.0
Manufacturing	61	29.3
Trade (wholesale, retail)	33	15.9
Services	39	18.8
Other	23	11.0
Total	208	100.0
1983		
Agriculture	30	6.9
Construction	58	13.3
Manufacturing	107	24.5
Retail/trade	35	8.0
Services	196	45.0
Hotel/motel	43	9.9
Personal	14	3.2
Auto repair	47	10.8
Private household	25	5.7
Gardening	50	11.5
Other	17	3.9
Other	10	2.3
Total	436	100.0

Sources: 1980: Community Research Associates, 1980, p. 168; 1983: Survey of Mexican border crossers directed by author, San Ysidro, 1983.

workers—that is, undocumented Mexican immigrant workers. Of an estimated 20,920 illegal workers in San Diego County in 1980, the majority were employed in tertiary activities (retail trade and services), and construction (Community Research Associates, 1980). These numbers are comparable to the figures for Mexican commuters. Both classes of workers are concentrated in the tertiary or service activities and in construction. The data and our previous observations suggest also that there may be some overlap between the two categories. Illegal commuter workers may pass information about jobs along to their social contacts south of the border, creating a stream of illegal workers to those jobs in the United States. Although no hard data on this phenomenon exist, it is considered likely because of the obvious parallels between the illegal migrant and illegal commuter worker experience, as well as the San Diego County data.

Origin patterns for Tijuana's commuter workers (Figure 16) reveal one important feature of the commuting process—commuter workers tend to originate in areas very close to the CBD, particularly on the western and eastern flanks of the central city. Both of these origin zones are established middle- and working-class neighborhoods. It is not surprising that a large percentage of the pool of commuter workers originates here. Many of these residents have lived in Tijuana for more than a decade and are likely to have established networks of contacts north of the border. They are also more likely to have acquired the valuable resident border crossing card.

One of the principal origin areas for Mexican commuter workers is Colonia Libertad (Figure 16). One of the oldest neighborhoods in the city, this *colonia* was mainly built by repatriated Mexican workers deported from California in the 1930s. Residents of the neighborhood began to work illegally in San Diego in the late 1930s, when the closing of gambling casinos and other U.S.–financed activities eliminated many employment opportunities south of the border. Colonia Libertad residents have a history of cross-boundary commuting and have acquired considerable expertise in finding transboundary employment. In addition, Colonia Libertad is located directly on the boundary line and close to the San Ysidro crossing. Residents have intimate knowledge of and familiarity with the border crossing.

The origin data for Tijuana commuter workers suggest a strong correlation between location in working-class neighborhoods south of the border and the propensity to cross the border legally to work on a regular basis. There is a distinct absence of significant origin points in the primary squatter settlement zones in Tijuana, areas principally on the edge of the city, or in inaccessible canyons and flood plains. Residents of these neighborhoods are generally more recent arrivals to the city, and thus less likely candidates for border crossing cards. Equally, they probably do not have the connections to find employment in San Diego. It is possible, however, that the squatter settlements are origin zones for illegal border workers.

The locational patterns for worker-destination sites in San Diego County are more spatially dispersed than origin points in Tijuana. A number of explanations for this can be offered. First, there is a clustering of destinations in the south bay communities of San Ysidro, National City, and Chula Vista. Thus, the subregion between downtown San Diego and the border houses the majority of commuter workers, creating a kind of specialized commuter labor submarket for Mexican workers. This submarket has both a spatial and a functional logic. Spatially, it is closest to the Mexican border and therefore geographically accessible to daily commuters, allowing some conservation of income and time in transport costs. Functionally, it is tied to the trolley and bus systems that serve the south bay area corridor between downtown San Diego and San Ysidro. Other spatial concentrations of workers appear in downtown San Diego, Mission Valley, and La Jolla.

There are also interesting and important spatial concentrations of workers by occupational categories. In fact, when destinations are disaggregated by employment category, a clear pattern of subregional labor market segmentation of Mexican commuter workers emerges. These spatially segmented labor submarkets appear in at least six occupational categories: automobile repair, entertainment/ hotel industry, agriculture, landscaping, construction, and manufacturing.

Automobile repair jobs tend to cluster in Chula Vista, National City, and south San Diego. These jobs include mechanical and upholstery repair, as well as body work and painting. This labor market reflects a spillover of skills from Tijuana into the United States. Automobile repair and recycling have become one of the principal trades of downtown Tijuana, and an important service exported to U.S. consumers. A transboundary service industry appears to have evolved. Mexican American entrepreneurs in south bay cities provide inexpensive services to the San Diego metropolitan area, just as in Tijuana. That a substantial number of Mexican workers commute to these jobs is therefore not terribly surprising—it simply illustrates another form of economic and social collaboration between the two cities.

Another clustering of jobs occurs in the entertainment and hotel service sector. Given that the hotel industry is so vital to San Diego's tourist economy, it is not surprising that a large number of service workers from Mexico are destined for jobs here. One of the most important commuter worker groups is that of Mexican women employed as maids in hotels. In the sample data mapped in Figure 16, two destination areas for these workers stand out: San Diego Bay and Mission Valley, both prime tourist activity zones in the metropolitan area. Other service jobs such as household domestic workers are concentrated in wealthy neighborhoods such as Point Loma, La Jolla, and Bonita.

Still another segmented labor submarket can be found in agriculture. San Diego County, with its four thousand–square miles of terrain, usually ranks among the nation's ten most productive counties in terms of aggregate agricultural revenues. Most agricultural laborers tend to cluster in the south bay area, in zones where truck farming predominates. The other important agriculture production area is north county. Interestingly, few legal commuters listed this as their destination. One might attribute this to the distance decay effect—perhaps a commuter trip of thirty miles one way might dissuade legal Mexican commuters. A more compelling explanation is that north county employs a large number of *undocumented* Mexican workers at extremely low wages (Nalven and Frederickson, 1982), and therefore commuter workers cannot compete for jobs there.

In the category of landscaping, Mexican commuters work in north county, principally because this is where the largest number of new housing tracts are located. A similar pattern exists for residential construction jobs. These jobs cluster at the edge of the city, particularly to the north and east, where much of the new housing development is located.

In the manufacturing sector, work locations clustered in the south bay region and downtown, two important industrial districts. These districts house some of San Diego's important heavy industries (shipbuilding, canneries, chemicals, food and fish processing). A demand for the least-desirable, unskilled, low-paying jobs, such as manual assembly, cannery work, and laundry work, exists at these sites. Once again, the data suggest the evolution of a social and ecological equilibrium between San Diego and Tijuana, articulated through the gradual formation of a balance between the transboundary supply and demand for labor.

Manufacturing and Transborder Territorial Linkages

Industrial growth has been perhaps the most important catalyst in the rapid transformation of the economic base and demographic structure of U.S.–Mexico borderland areas in the last two decades. Prior to 1960, as noted earlier, the U.S.–Mexico border was not considered a strategic location for important economic activities. Manufacturing, which had been traditionally confined to the northeastern U.S. manufacturing belt or to a few other urban industrial zones, many near large metropolitan regions, did not seem to be an activity that would be attracted to the remote U.S.–Mexico international frontier region.

Yet the early 1960s saw the beginning of worldwide changes in the organization of production. Innovative manufacturing forms and changing technologies allowed for the increased separability of different stages in the production process. One result was the diminishing importance of "nonlabor" factors, such as transportation, in the production calculus (Storper and Walker, 1984). Industrial entrepreneurs saw the strategic value of isolating labor-intensive operations within the overall manufacturing process (Grunwald and Flamm, 1985). This approach became even more important as new high-technology industries began to dominate the world capitalist production system. Corporations realized that the assembly phase of production was labor-intensive, and that it might be possible to lower production costs by seeking cheap labor in foreign countries.

Thus began, in the early 1960s, a wave of investment by U.S. industries in "offshore" production facilities in Puerto Rico, Korea, Taiwan, the Philippines, and Singapore. Despite the uncertainties associated with political instability in many of these nations, U.S. firms viewed cheap labor as the only strategy available to remain competitive with the rest of the world in certain product markets (House, 1982). Two U.S. Tariff Code provisions—806.30 and 807.00—were established through the Tariff Classification Act of 1962 to allow for the duty-free entry of North American components assembled outside U.S. boundaries. U.S. firms would only pay tariffs on the "value added" to their assembled product.

In 1965, recognizing that U.S. firms were relocating labor-intensive operations overseas, the Mexican government established the Border Industrialization Program (BIP), a policy initiative aimed at attracting U.S. assembly plant operations to Mexico. Full implementation of the legislation did not occur until 1971. Mexican law allowed duty-free import of all necessary machinery, equipment, and raw materials, as well as components needed to engage in offshore production. All products had to be exported from Mexico, and 90 percent of the labor force had to be Mexican nationals. There were also provisions concerning minimum wages and conditions of work. Thus began the *maquiladora* program, the title derived from the Spanish word *maquila*, which traditionally referred to the portion of flour retained by the miller as payment for grinding a client's grain (ibid., p. 216).

Between 1969 and 1983, the *maquiladora* program began to dominate the overseas location decisions of U.S. firms. Whereas in the early 1960s Hong Kong and Taiwan attracted five times as many offshore facilities as Mexico, by 1983 Mexico exported more than twenty times the value added in duty-free components as Hong Kong, and more than twice as much as its nearest competitor, Malaysia. By the early 1980s, the assembly-plant program was earning about one-half billion dollars in annual foreign exchange for Mexico (Grunwald and Flamm, 1985, p. 143).

The Territorial Impact of Maquiladoras. The growth of the manufacturing sector at one point was considered crucial to the evolution of a strong economic base in most cities in the industrialized world. In fact, for several decades, theories of urban economics revolved around "basic" or export-oriented economic activities. These activities generated surplus income for the city from sources outside of its boundaries. The classic analogy between cities and nations—and the need to export more than was imported—was an intellectual cornerstone of urban economics during the 1950s and 1960s. The urban economy has recently become more service-oriented. Nevertheless, manufacturing still plays a key role in structuring both the economy and the spatial form of the city, since employment patterns determine to some degree how land is developed and used.

When one examines U.S.–Mexico border cities, therefore, an important question should be posed: To what extent do *maquiladoras* influence the spatial organization and structure of urban areas along the border? This seems to necessitate a further question: Can the assembly plant–style of industrial growth serve as a permanent force in shaping land uses and economic activities on the border? Two concerns emerge out of these questions: first, the extent to which *maquiladoras* create positive economic impacts in the transboundary metropolis; and second, the type of regional economic development *maquiladoras* bring to Mexico.

Other writers have attempted to address these issues. From the beginning of the U.S.–Mexico assembly plant program, the term "twin plants" has been used to describe the coproduction system that was envisioned for the border area. The idea was that a capital-intensive facility would locate north of the border, and its counterpart, a labor-intensive plant, would locate in the Mexican border city. Thus, a symbiotic relationship was envisioned for *maquiladora* complexes locating along the border. The U.S. plant would produce the inputs to be assembled across the border in Mexico. The finished products would then be shipped back to the U.S. side, where distribution would take place. It was assumed that both countries would benefit from this process, and that there would be a natural transborder economic exchange process that would strengthen the border economy. In fact, in most border cities, particularly in Texas, U.S.–owned *maquiladoras* are supplied by plants located away from the border, principally in the northeastern U.S. manufacturing belt (Grunwald and Flamm, 1985; House, 1982). In the California border zone, the U.S. firms supplying the assembly parts are located mainly in Orange County, the Silicon Valley, or other places away from the border. The incentives for locating assembly plants in Mexico—principally cheap transport costs to U.S. markets, cheap labor, and reduced executive relocation costs (*maquila* executives can work in Mexico, but reside in the United States) (Clement and Jenner, 1987; House, 1982)—do not apparently spill over to U.S. parent company relocation decisions. There appears to be no major incentive to engage in wholesale relocations of large U.S. parent companies, although smaller distribution, warehousing, and "staging" plants are often located along the border. Thus, in some ways the concept of the "twin plant" is a myth—a majority of assembly plants do not have counterparts north of the border.

In a larger sense, we can raise the question, to what extent do *maquiladoras* generate long-term linkages that become embedded in transfrontier urban space and therefore permanently restructure that space? One study of Ciudad Juárez postulated a relationship between state-based infrastructure for industrial development and changing residential ecological structure (Christopherson, 1983). The long-term impacts of *maquiladoras* are clearly tied to their ability to generate regional economic linkages of a dynamic nature. It becomes important to distinguish between assembly-plant zones as "export enclaves" (Suárez Villa, 1984)—cheap labor platforms managed by transnational corporations and divorced from more integrated ties into the local economy—and assembly-plant locations tied to more permanent economic development zones—for example, areas with genuine backward and forward linkages, well-trained managers native to Mexico, genuine technology transfers, positive working conditions, and equitable distribution of costs and benefits among host country and foreign investors (Sklair, 1987). Although these questions have yet to be empirically tested across the entire two thousand–mile boundary, some light can be shed on them as we return to our case study area, the Tijuana–San Diego region.

Maquiladoras and Spatial Linkages in Tijuana–San Diego. In the last two decades *maquiladoras* have become one of the centerpieces of the Tijuana economy. By 1985, the twin-plant program accounted for nearly two hundred factories and 25,697 jobs (Clement and Jenner, 1987). In 1982, the manufacturing sector employed slightly more than a third of the city's total labor force, most of this in assembly work. In general, assembly plants represent perhaps the most important new economic sector in the overall growth of the state of Baja California. Tijuana has about 64 percent of all the *maquiladoras* in the state.

Table 20 shows the location of staging plants and parent firms for *maquiladoras* in Tijuana. The distinction between "parent plants" and "staging plants" is an important one. Although large amounts of U.S. capital are invested in assembly plants, they are not always invested in U.S.–owned plants. Instead of forming direct subsidiary companies in Mexico, U.S. firms sometimes subcontract to Mexican firms to carry out the assembly work, or form temporary arrangements, called "shelter plans," in which Mexican companies perform assembly work until U.S. firms are ready to establish their own subsidiary. This is important because it has an impact on the kind of facilities, if any, located on the U.S. side of the border. Mexican subcontracting firms may not attract a U.S. parent plant, but rather a staging plant, which usually supplies only minor inputs into the production process or simply engages in distribution and information processing. In some

Table 20. Location of Staging Plants and Parent Firms for
Maquiladoras in Tijuana

	San Diego	Southern Calif.	Rest of Calif.	Rest of U.S.	Foreign
Staging plant/ distribution office	30	2	—	—	—
Parent firm	58	62	11	38	3
Total	88	64	11	38	3
% of grand total	43.1	31.4	5.4	18.6	1.5

Source: Mexico Communications, 1986.

cases, staging plants turn out to be little more than a single office manned by one worker, a communications link with the "real" parent plant located away from the border. In Table 20, we see that the *maquiladoras* in Tijuana do seem to be significantly linked both to San Diego (43.1 percent of all U.S. companion firms) and southern California (31.4 percent of all firms). Yet, the linkages to San Diego may be misleading, since most of the staging plants are probably very small operations tied to a fully operational firm beyond the border, and many of the parent plants are also quite small.

As Table 21 suggests, these linkages are product-based as well as territorially-based. Tijuana assembly plants in the electronics and apparel categories are linked with U.S. firms in southern California; *maquiladoras* that produce electronic goods or other industrial commodities, such as furniture, lamps, medical supplies, and sports equipment, are linked with U.S. firms in San Diego. This suggests some degree of specialization in the transboundary coproduction linkages.

Several other elements affect the way *maquiladora* systems create transboundary linkages. The assembly plants create localized impacts. For example, assembly-plant sitings on the northern Mexican border usually lead to the location of special facilities on the U.S. side to service the Mexican assembly plants. These include staging, assembly, and distribution facilities. In California these kinds of facilities created 1,274 jobs and $11.5 million in lease-rent expenditures in 1985 (Clement and Jenner, 1987, p. 71). In addition, some *maquiladora* workers choose to live north of the border and spend their income in the United States. In fact, in the 1970s, it was estimated that 60 to 75

Table 21. Tijuana's Assembly Plants, Attributes by Location of Parent Firms

	San Diego	Southern Calif.	Rest of Calif.	Rest of U.S.	Foreign
Total firms	88	64	11	38	3
Product categories[a]					
Electronics	22	18	3	11	2
Other manuf.	27	10	3	11	—
Apparel	4	23	—	1	—
Wood/cork	9	6	1	1	—
Other metal	13	5	—	2	—
Machinery	2	—	—	2	1
Food	1	—	2	1	—
Leather/shoes	2	1	1	—	—
Firms with 100% Mexican ownership	37	30	5	9	0
Large *maquiladoras* (more than 250 employees)	8	12	2	9	3

Source: Mexico Communications, 1986.

a. Not all firms reported product categories.

percent of all wages earned along the border were spent in the United States (Bustamante, 1975), although by the 1980s this amount has probably shrunk to well below 50 percent. Many *maquiladora* operating costs are expended north of the border, including supplies, services, and the hosting of business visitors. In California, this figure reached between $35 million and $50 million in one year (1985).

Despite the financial impacts *maquiladoras* impose on both sides of the border, the question of their long-term viability as a leading border region source of income remains. On the matter of economic viability and territorial permanence, there seem to be two schools of thought. On the positive side, it is clear from recent data that U.S. firms remain very interested in Mexico as a location for assembly plants. Despite the "footloose" nature of offshore plants, Mexico's attraction is its proximity to markets, cheap transport costs, and relatively cheap, nonunionized labor. In southern California, we see the emergence of specialized cross-boundary industrial alliances that hint at permanence. We also see significant benefits to the U.S. border economy in Mexican retail spending, support facility expenditures north of the boundary, and special facilities.

On the negative side, *maquiladoras* have not actually diversified economically—they are still dominated by electronics, apparel, and small manufacturing. There are severe inequalities in the structure of production and management (Hiernaux, 1986); large producers control too much of the overall employment generated; women are the principal workers and are often exploited (Fernández Kelly, 1983). There are few backward linkages to inputs coming from Mexico, or forward linkages to markets in Mexico. The backward linkages have not materialized because of deficiencies in quality control, unmet delivery schedules, insufficient production capacity, and high prices (Grunwald and Flamm, 1985, p. 164). Forward linkages do not seem to occur because the Mexican government has shown little interest in allowing the *maquilas* to compete with national industries. Ironically, then, the Mexican government is perpetuating the "export enclave" mentality. Despite their successes, the *maquilas* remain an example of how dependent space is created along the border—land uses unfold in a way that enhances Mexico's dependence on the United States without creating clear long-term alternatives to the current system. The linkages in space remain, but they become empty artifacts if not backed up with policies that allow Mexico to overcome its dependence on the United States as the industrial partner; to date, these policies have been slow to materialize, even as the number of *maquiladora* plants grows.

Transfrontier Social Space: Mexican Americans in San Diego

Daily spatial activity systems, such as commuter worker flows or journey-to-shop cycles, represent one dimension of transfrontier urban space. Spatially defined externalities in industrial production reflect another. A third important dimension of transboundary space is of concern here: social space. Clearly, the living space around the boundary has been influenced by common historical, economic, demographic, and geographic forces. These translate into a unique social fabric on the urbanized border, with both a Mexican settlement and a North American settlement strongly influenced by Mexican culture. On the U.S. side of the border, the process of Mexican

American settlement and assimilation represents an important dimension of the formation of transboundary social space. An important attribute of a border metropolis like Tijuana–San Diego is the existence of a regional class of Mexican migrants who have gradually been assimilated into U.S. urban society. Over time, Mexican immigrants have established legal, long-term residence in U.S. border cities like San Diego, raised families, purchased housing, and entered the permanent urban labor force.

The spatial and ecological role of Mexican Americans in the San Diego region offers another measure of the unique sociospatial system that operates in transboundary urban areas. Mexican immigration, over nearly a century, has left a substantial population of permanent residents in San Diego County. This raises the question: What kind of spatial-ecological impact has the Mexican American community had on the San Diego metropolis, and how does this fit into the perspective of a transfrontier border metropolis?

A number of general observations about the ecological and spatial impact of Mexican Americans in U.S. cities can be ventured. Like other racial groups in the United States, Mexican Americans established ethnic enclaves. Immigrants concentrated spatially in reception zones made accessible by low rents or the possibility of multifamily occupancy. Where they settled depended on the nature of the urban area and their reasons for migrating to it. In some cities, like El Paso, they clustered in shacks near the railroad yards, where they found unskilled jobs (García, 1981); in others, like Santa Barbara and Los Angeles (Camarrillo, 1979) or Albuquerque, they settled in the central city, near the Mexican plaza in the historic *pueblos* built by Spanish colonists; in still other towns (Fresno) they found residence in labor camps or agricultural enclaves at the edge of the city (Grebler, Moore, and Guzmán, 1970).

Segregation has probably had the greatest impact on Mexican American urban social space. Romo, in his study of Los Angeles' Chicano community in the early twentieth century, pointed out that, although proximity to jobs and affordable housing were factors affecting Mexican American residential location in the 1920s and 1930s, Anglo discrimination was an equally potent force in maintaining the original barrio location near the old plaza in downtown and in spawning the formation of new enclaves in East Los Angeles across the river (Romo, 1982). Restrictive covenants and other institutional and social forces served to keep Mexican Americans out of predominantly Anglo neighborhoods. At the same time, limited upward social and occupational mobility restricted the geographical choices of Mexican American residential locations, thus preserving the pattern of spatial segregation.

Social scientists have attempted to explain the Mexican American residential ecological experience, but with mixed results. Despite their steadily increasing presence in the urban social fabric of many southwestern U.S. cities, Mexican Americans seem to have remained both economically and spatially excluded from better occupational and housing opportunities (Herzog, 1977, 1986). One explanation has been the "internal colonialism model," which sees the subordination of Mexican Americans as part of a more global system of U.S. exploitation of Third World cultures and minorities (Barrera, Muñoz, and Ornelas, 1972). A second explanation argues, first, that capitalist society creates dual housing and labor markets, and, second, that Mexican American inequality is tied to the interdependent nature of the world political system (Morrissey, 1982).

Much of the above is useful as a context for explaining the spatial-ecological experience of Mexican Americans in San Diego. The earliest settlement enclave of Mexican Americans was in the original downtown, or Old Town, section of the city. Following the decision to move San Diego's central business district to New Town on the bay in the 1860s, Old Town's Mexican American population stagnated to a small, isolated minority. The displacement of the Mexican *pueblo* in Old Town by an Anglo-oriented central business district in a different location is symbolic of the territorial political experience of San Diego's Mexican American population more generally. The Californios, who had been prominent landowners and important citizens in Mexican San Diego before the 1850s, quickly lost their social standing and political power in the decades following the Treaty of Guadalupe Hidalgo.

Between 1860 and 1900, San Diego became an Anglo town, and its economy and built landscape reflected the power of the Anglo business and political community (see Chapter 5). If some Mexican/Hispanic architecture—such as the Mediterranean-like residences in the neighborhoods of Kensington and Mission Hills—adorned the cityscape, this was not a signal of any sort of resurgence in the political or economic position of Mexican Americans. Beginning with the Panama-Pacific Exposition held in San Francisco in 1915, a Spanish-style landscape started to filter into the urban architecture of the city.

One scholar has called this architecture, which dominated in the 1920s, the "Mission Revival" style (Ford, 1984). This period saw a revival in construction of Spanish colonial houses, streets lined with palm trees and exotic Mediterranean vegetation, and public buildings (such as the Santa Fe railroad depot) designed in the Spanish colonial style. It is ironic that this architecture emerged in a period when, as a social group, Mexican Americans had the least social and economic clout in the city. The Hispanic architecture is not symbolic of any great leap in social well-being and prestige for Mexican Americans— quite the opposite. That Old Town would become a thriving tourist area in the post–World War II period has little meaning for Mexican Americans, few of whom reap significant profits from this tourist enclave. The use of the Mexican colonial theme to extract profits for a non-Mexican social class is common to the Southwest; it is what McWilliams (1968) has called the "fantasy heritage" of the region.

In general, one can best understand the social geography of Mexican Americans in San Diego by viewing their experience through the politics of location and landscape. The location of any ethnic group in urban space is a product of territorial politics: competition for access to desired residential location and to the power to control what happens to those locations once they are settled by members of that ethnic group. The built landscape of ethnic neighborhoods reflects the outcome of numerous confrontations with government and other interest groups over land-use decisions affecting the ethnic area.

Harvey (1978, p. 9) has defined the "built environment" as "the totality of physical structures: houses, roads, factories, offices, sewerage systems, parks, cultural institutions, educational facilities, and so on." He has stated that "capitalist society must of necessity create a physical landscape—a mass of humanly constructed physical resources—in its own image, broadly appropriate to the purposes of production and reproduction." The social ecology of the San Diego Mexican American community reflects Harvey's view of the political economy of the urban built environment. Mexican Americans are highly segmented in space. This pattern can be traced to a long period of history in which Mexican Americans have been unable to gain political control over their residential territory. Historical variables have played a role in this process. For much of the latter portion of the nineteenth and the early twentieth centuries, San Diego lacked the economic base to attract a large and permanent Mexican population. It became merely a way station for Mexican migrants. By 1930, the city of San Diego had only about nine thousand Mexican Americans (Table 22), whereas Los Angeles, 120 miles to the north, had almost one hundred thousand Mexican American inhabitants.

This difference in ethnic population size is explained by the development of a manufacturing economy in Los Angeles in the early decades of the twentieth century, bolstered by connection to the transcontinental rail system. Nearly two decades before San Diego, Los Angeles became the railroad terminus of the West Coast. It was able to build a strong industrial base while San Diego's economy remained limited to nonindustrial activities, such as tourism. Unskilled Mexican labor was drawn toward Los Angeles, and by 1970, the proportion of employed Mexican Americans working in manufacturing in Los Angeles (37.1 percent) was nearly double that in San Diego (20.8 percent) (U.S. Bureau of the Census, 1970). Los Angeles, for more than six decades (1900 to 1970), was the principal destination of large waves of undocumented Mexican immigrants crossing into the United States. San Diego did not have the industrial base to retain a large portion of this immigrant flow. Its Mexican American population remained small, despite the proximity to Mexico. This certainly hampered the Hispanic community's efforts to establish political control over its residential neighborhoods.

The location of San Diego's Mexican American enclaves offers some clues about the settlement experience of immigrants during the twentieth century. By mid-century, Mexican immigrants had

Table 22. Evolution of San Diego's Mexican American Population

	Mexican American Population	% of Population	Total City Population
1910	1,222	3.1	39,578
1920	2,741	3.7	74,361
1930	9,266	6.3	147,995
1950	15,490	4.6	334,387
1960	38,043	6.6	573,224
1970	88,600	12.7	696,769
1980	130,613	14.9	875,538

Source: U.S. Census of Population and Housing, Census Tracts, San Diego, California, 1910–1980.

Note: The 1940 census did not record Mexican American population for San Diego.

established essentially two settlement enclaves in the San Diego urbanized area (Figure 17): along the industrial waterfront south of downtown (Barrio Logan), and in the south bay area near the border crossing (San Ysidro). Although the San Diego region grew mainly toward the north and east between 1950 and 1980, the Mexican American population grew essentially toward the south. As Figure 17 illustrates, by 1980, the principal Mexican American settlement areas were located in a corridor running between downtown, the old waterfront barrio, and the Mexican border. National City and Chula Vista, as well as parts of southeast San Diego, had become the primary areas of Mexican American residential occupancy. Table 23 further corroborates this point. In 1950, nearly 70 percent of the entire Spanish-surnamed population of San Diego resided within the city of San Diego in Barrio Logan and San Ysidro. As the Hispanic population spread to other areas of San Diego County between 1950 and 1980, there was a tendency for it to cluster in the south bay cities of Chula Vista and National City (nearly 14 percent of total Hispanic population by 1980) or in unincorporated areas of the county adjacent to the south bay (captured under the category "other" in Table 23). What is striking in Table 23 is that, despite the fact that the two fastest growing subregions of the city were in east county (El Cajon and La Mesa) and north county (Oceanside and Escondido), a disproportionately small number of Mexican Americans moved to these areas between 1950 and 1980.

This residential location process was hardly accidental, of course. Limited occupational mobility and lower per capita income restricted the housing choices of Mexican American families. San Diego social space is marked by considerable segregation of Hispanics and Anglos. Equally, Mexican Americans have been unable to maintain political control over the built environment, even in the city's most heavily Hispanic territories. If one looks at the politics of space in the two original Mexican settlement zones, Barrio Logan and San Ysidro, this phenomenon is most vividly illustrated.

Barrio Logan.   Barrio Logan is the historical nucleus of twentieth-century Mexican American settlement in the San Diego region. In the 1920s, this waterfront area, then called Logan Heights, evolved into the main reception zone for Mexican immigrants arriving in the San Diego area. Located about one mile south of the central business

Figure 17. Hispanic Population, San Diego, 1980

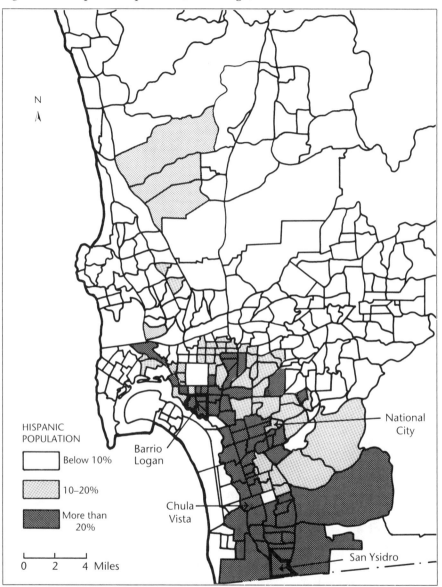

Table 23. Distribution of Mexican American Population in the San Diego Region, 1950–1980

City	1950	1960	1970	1980
San Diego	9,243	38,043	88,600	130,613
% of total	67.89	58.70	50.86	47.45
Chula Vista	711	1,882	10,886	19,624
% of total	5.22	2.90	6.25	7.13
El Cajon	—	1,011	3,924	5,862
% of total		1.56	2.25	2.13
La Mesa	304	621	2,770	3,177
% of total	2.23	0.96	1.59	1.15
National City	1,854	4,150	11,393	18,708
% of total	13.62	6.40	6.54	6.80
Oceanside	—	—	6,256	14,118
% of total			3.59	5.13
Escondido	—	—	4,687	9,378
% of total			2.69	3.41
Spring Valley	—	—	3,894	5,367
% of total			2.24	1.95
Other	1,502	19,103	41,799	68,430
% of total	11.03	29.48	23.99	24.86
Total surname pop. in region	13,614	64,810	174,209	275,277

Source: U.S. Bureau of the Census, 1950–1980.

Note: Population for census tracts with at least 250 Spanish-surnamed persons.

district, it became an important site for heavy industries locating along the waterfront after World War I. As industries moved into the neighborhood in the 1920s, high-status residents began to migrate out of the area into more desirable locations such as Mission Hills, Kensington, and East San Diego (Norris, 1983). Much like the original Mexican enclaves in other southwestern cities of the period, Logan Heights attracted Mexican Americans because of its proximity to industry. However, the availability of low-cost rental housing probably played an even more important role in allowing this Mexican American enclave to grow (Ford and Griffin, 1981), although another factor was undoubtedly the discrimination against this ethnic group in surrounding neighborhoods during the 1930s and 1940s (Harris, 1974).

By 1950, Logan Heights had evolved into a prototypical low-income, inner city "ghetto." It displayed both large concentrations of poor ethnic minorities (blacks and Mexican Americans) and an unusually high concentration of noxious industrial land uses. As more ethnic minorities filtered into the area by the 1960s, two distinct neighborhoods formed—Barrio Logan along the western edge near the waterfront, and Logan Heights to the east. Barrio Logan became the dominant Mexican American neighborhood of the city, although by the 1960s the Chicano population was also rapidly diffusing into the south bay and adjacent areas, mainly because the size of the population exceeded the amount of land and housing available within the traditional barrio.

Barrio Logan offers a revealing case study of the relationship between the Mexican American community and "the state" (government). The evolving border social system reflects a continuum of Mexican immigration: settlement in northern Mexican border towns, Anglo settlement north of the border, and, finally, Mexican American settlement on the U.S. side. Each phase of social evolution implied new geographic arrangements, and new forms of transboundary social relations. In the final phases, Mexican American neighborhoods, spatial enclaves of assimilating Mexicans, attempted to establish some territorial domain within the essentially Anglo power structure of U.S. border cities. Barrio Logan, the core of Mexican American settlement in San Diego, offers some clues on how these political-economic relationships evolved in space.

One writer's observations of Barrio Logan are revealing:

El Barrio de la Logan: entre verde y seco. . . . At the Corner of Crosby and Logan, the world is a monster machine. Concrete whips up, down, back and forth, east and west, north and south. Trucks and buses shoot and grumble past, overhead, underneath. Cars whine up the access ramps to the Coronado Bridge and throttle down the other side. . . . Whitish dust over everything, the detritus of the dream dissolving overhead. A humid depredation of a breeze, the stench from the canneries, along the waterfront. Big graffito: "Chicano Park. For Everybody." Someday this desolate grotto will have a place in history next to a meadow at Runnymeade, or the Boston Harbor, or Wounded Knee or Telegraph Avenue, or a vineyard in Delano, or to a sudden awesome stretch of dry sand at the bottom of the Red Sea (Coffelt, 1973).

The relationship between Barrio Logan's Mexican American community and the state, principally the city of San Diego, the Unified Port District, and several other local public jurisdictions, has been highly contentious over the last three decades. The community, until the late 1970s, was essentially unable to negotiate land-use decisions favorable to the preservation of the residential environment. What became clear early on was that both the city of San Diego and other public agencies favored the gradual conversion of the waterfront district to an industrial zone. Beginning in the 1930s, much of the barrio land was rezoned by the city for industrial use, thus allowing heavy industries like shipbuilding plants, kelp-processing plants, chemical storage companies, and other noxious industrial tenants to occupy land adjacent to Mexican American residences. This led to an open policy, in the 1950s and 1960s, of allowing rezoning and incompatible land-use configurations in the neighborhood. In the worst cases, noxious land uses such as junkyards, metal-processing firms, and waste-recycling plants were located near residences or schools. By the early 1970s, Barrio Logan had become a typical urban ghetto—epitomized by a patchwork of mixed land uses with heavy industrial sites located adjacent to residential sites or schools, pothole-filled streets, high noise and air pollution levels, a deteriorating housing stock, and high crime rates. The expansion of waterfront industrial locations physically cut off the bay from the residential sector.

State actions tended to exacerbate the deteriorating residential environmental quality of the Barrio Logan neighborhood. Two policy decisions made collectively by the city of San Diego and the state of California (Department of Transportation) were particularly damaging to the area. Both involved location decisions for the interstate freeway system. In the early 1960s, it was decided that Interstate 5 would be routed along a configuration that would cut diagonally through the heart of Logan Heights, effectively bisecting the community. The freeway, built in 1964, destroyed the spatial sense of community that had evolved over the previous four decades. Only a few years later, a second state action brought even greater social and spatial disintegration to the neighborhood. The city had debated replacing the ferry service to Coronado Island with a permanent bridge. When it finally decided to build the bridge, the connecting freeway interchange, I-75, was sited so that it sliced directly through Barrio Logan, perpendicular to I-5, thus creating a second physical barrier to community cohesion. Fifteen hundred people were displaced by the bridge and its feeder ramps. A series of unsightly pillars interrupted the visual landscape of the neighborhood; noise and traffic congestion increased substantially, and property values decreased. One of the many ironies emerging in this period is that these policy actions made it almost impossible for residents to move out of the area. While property values were plummeting in Barrio Logan, they were increasing dramatically elsewhere in the city, as the high demand for housing created a real estate boom in San Diego County. Longtime Mexican American residents of the neighborhood could not earn enough from sale of their homes in Barrio Logan to afford housing in comparable neighborhoods. They became economically trapped in a neighborhood that the state wished to convert to more profitable (industrial) functions.

Barrio Logan epitomizes the struggle between capital and labor over control of the built environment of the city. In a capitalist urban society, the built environment is a reflection of competition between a class of laborers seeking to create and protect urban space for consumption and protection and a class of profit-seeking entrepreneurs (capitalists) who view urban space as a territory for maximizing income through investments (Harvey, 1978). These seemingly abstract constructs are brought to life in the case of Barrio Logan. "Capital" consists of the waterfront industrial land users like the Navy, which employs fifty thousand people at the nearby naval base, and real estate and property interests, which would like to see the Barrio Logan area, because of its prime waterfront location, converted to a permanent industrial and institutional (military) land-use district. Capital sees the "barrio" or residential character of the land as an obsolete use. The role of the state (government) has been slanted in favor of the capitalist interests. Not only have state actions historically reinforced the deterioration of the community, but one government agency, the Unified Port District, has clearly operated against the Chicano community's interests by failing to support the acquisition of an adequate bay front park for the community. Up to the late 1970s, the city of San Diego did little to prevent the proliferation of noxious land uses in the community.

At the other end of the land-use bargaining spectrum lies the Chicano community ("labor"), which sees Barrio Logan as a historically grounded, legitimate living space—the oldest remaining Mexican

American neighborhood in the San Diego region. The interests of the Chicano community are varied: cultural and territorial pride, loyalty, and an inability to find affordable housing elsewhere. When the community realized that the state of California was planning to locate a police facility under the Coronado Bridge in the early 1970s, it organized a massive protest and eventually occupied the proposed site. In the end, the neighborhood was successful in negotiating an alternative land use for the site—a community park called Chicano Park, which today is adorned with a kiosk and numerous murals, creating a symbolic Mexican American landscape and a source of territorial pride. However, the victory is at best a hollow one. Despite Chicano Park and its magnificent murals, and the recent Community Plan, which calls for zoning strategies aimed at buffering industrial and residential uses, Barrio Logan remains a disadvantaged ethnic ghetto. Noxious land uses and heavy industry dominate the cityscape. Traffic congestion and freeway/industrial noise pollution are worse than ever. The pressure to develop industry along the waterfront continues as San Diego expands its economic base. Housing quality and the neighborhood ambience continue to decline.

San Ysidro. San Ysidro is located on the international border at the crossing into Tijuana. Although it is situated fifteen miles south of downtown San Diego, it lies within the jurisdiction of the city of San Diego. This was achieved through a clever 1957 maneuver in which a narrow strip of land running under San Diego Bay from downtown to San Ysidro was purchased by the city, thereby allowing it to comply with California law requiring that a local government have jurisdiction over property adjacent to the land it would annex.

In 1987, San Ysidro's population numbered 21,700, of which 81 percent was Hispanic and 52 percent foreign born (mainly Mexican). The enormous Mexican American population is not surprising; in many ways, San Ysidro is socially, economically, and even functionally connected to Tijuana. It represents a component of the border social system, a classic "border town" tied equally to two neighboring cultures. San Ysidro's ties to Tijuana really began during the "Golden Age" of tourism in Tijuana, 1920 to 1929. In 1919, prohibition laws were passed in the United States. One reaction in southern California was a sudden exodus of tourists into Baja California, where alcoholic beverages could be openly consumed. San Ysidro was quickly pulled into the economic orbit of Tijuana, and became an important functional cog in the built environment during the "boom" decade of tourism.

During the 1920s, the city of Tijuana became a recreational center for U.S. tourists. As North American entrepreneurs invested dollars in the construction of gambling casinos, bars, horse racetracks, and alcoholic beverage plants, connections between San Diego and Tijuana strengthened. Numerous forms of transit evolved to allow Americans access to Tijuana—railroad connections to San Diego and Los Angeles, boat connections with the port of San Diego, Greyhound bus routes, and of course, private automobiles. U.S. casino owners even built roads or bridges in Tijuana to enhance access to their investments. In addition, they brought in their own employees from San Diego. The combination of North American entrepreneurs and workers south of the border led to the demand for a U.S. "bedroom community" near Tijuana. San Ysidro, of course, was the logical choice: it allowed workers and investors to live on the U.S. side of the border, but within an easy daily commute of the tourist zone of downtown Tijuana. Given the added costs of transport in the 1920s, it is thus no surprise that San Ysidro quickly became an important enclave for Americans tied to Tijuana. During the height of the 1920s' tourism surge in Tijuana, a "tent city" sprang up in San Ysidro as the town literally became a bedroom community for owners and workers (Baker, 1980).

San Ysidro became even more dependent on Tijuana over time. Following the Depression and gradual withdrawal of U.S. business from Tijuana tourist enterprises, the housing boom in San Ysidro subsided. In 1933, the Mexican government nationalized most foreign-owned properties, thus driving out the remaining U.S. capital investments. San Ysidro reverted back to its earlier rural isolation. That would not last long, however. During the post–World War II era, urbanization and economic development enveloped southern California, and in the San Diego–Tijuana region, an international community began to evolve.

The San Ysidro community is a model of how one type of borderland settlement—a community of culture contact and ethnic preservation—becomes the interface between two countries. Over time, the community has emerged as an important port of entry for Mexican immigrants seeking work in the United States, and, because of its proximity to Mexico, it has evolved into a permanent enclave for Mexican Americans. Much like Barrio Logan, however, San

Ysidro's history in the twentieth century reveals that Chicanos have been unable to marshal political power to negotiate land-use decisions favorable to the maintenance of an adequate quality of life.

The post–World War II period has ushered in four decades of land-use decisions that are mainly unfavorable to the Mexican American population of San Ysidro. In the early 1950s, the U.S. Border Patrol located the detention facility for illegal aliens in San Ysidro, just to the northwest of the core of the town. This initiated a process in which San Ysidro became the institutional base for various federal agencies (INS, Border Patrol, Customs) responsible for guarding the border. By the 1970s, the disproportionate number of police vehicles and federal agents patrolling the area had created an atmosphere of a police state, certainly alienating to Chicano residents. As one observer stated: "It [San Ysidro] can resemble a place under martial law—where Border Patrol jeeps and vans, police cars, U.S. Customs vehicles and Highway patrol cars can be seen, while Border Patrol helicopters churn noisily overhead and at night aim their spotlights on homes and backyards where Mexican nationals may be hiding" (Montemayor, 1979).

In 1957, the city of San Diego successfully annexed the San Ysidro community. In San Ysidro, the Anglo elite saw an opportunity to reap the profits to be earned on properties around an international border crossing and along the south bay waterfront. They were also concerned that if they did not annex the lands, they might be annexed by one of the other south bay cities (Chula Vista or Imperial Beach), and thus the potential revenues to the city of San Diego would be forever lost (Baker, 1980). The San Ysidro community's interest (both Anglo and Hispanic) in annexing in 1957 was derived from its fear that it would be unable to afford the high costs of providing water from the Colorado River to its residents.

The community would quickly come to regret its decision. In the decade following annexation, Mexican Americans became strongly polarized and alienated from the Anglo elite that controlled city government in San Diego. During that period, their unemployment rate was consistently two or more times higher than the average rate for the city as a whole. They became dependent on the city for resources, but frustrated when, rather than getting positive responses, they witnessed the gradual destruction of the village atmosphere of their community through a series of unfavorable land-use decisions made by the city's elected officials. So unhappy were they about their relationship to San Diego that by 1973 a large segment of the community initiated a drive to de-annex. The lack of local representation, poor social service provision, and unfavorable land-use decisions were cited as the major reasons for applying to the Local Agency Formation Commission (LAFCO) for de-annexation. The lack of financial resources needed to sustain the de-annexation drive caused its eventual failure; however, the antipathy toward the city remained. A 1980 study of the community labeled it a "metropolitan colony" in which economic resources were drained by the larger city, cheap labor was exploited, little political power at the community level existed, and the principal ethnic minority group had become culturally alienated and politically disenfranchised (Baker, 1980).

In the late 1960s, local and national urban programs played a role in San Ysidro's growth and densification. San Ysidro was designated a Model Cities neighborhood, and through federal funds a proliferation of multifamily housing construction began. The intent to revitalize San Ysidro never materialized, however. Instead, the majority of multifamily residential projects ended up housing residents who were predominantly of lower-income background (American Institute of Architects, 1987). San Ysidro's population over the next decade doubled. The influx of new families contributed to a lack of identity within the community. In the 1970s and early 1980s, the city Housing Commission built public housing projects for non-Hispanic populations, principally blacks and Filipinos. In addition, private sector investors, taking advantage of the low land prices in San Ysidro, built low- and moderate-income housing. This has led observers to note that, by the early 1980s, San Ysidro had "become the dumping ground for low income housing" (Jefferson, 1986).

There were also land-use decisions that were harmful to the physical coherence of the neighborhood. In 1970, the city approved a cluster of 790 new homes that disrupted the grid pattern of the old settlement core through a cul-de-sac street pattern that formed "inward facing neighborhoods with their backs toward the older San Ysidro" (Baker, 1980). In the late 1960s and early 1970s, two interstate freeway corridors would wreak havoc on the design of San Ysidro. Interstate 5 (1967) skirted the southern rim of the community, creating a false and disruptive edge. Interstate 805 (1975) was even more destructive—the main freeway and the network of entrance/exit ramps dramatically split the community in half and created what observers describe as a "total break in the street fabric" (American Institute of

Architects, 1987). The light rail transit system (trolley) completed in 1981 had been hailed as a mechanism for increasing tourism in San Ysidro, but this never materialized. Instead, it became another intrusive land use that served to physically fragment the community and add to the congestion and land-use chaos that had been evolving for several decades.

One can see that, much like Barrio Logan, San Ysidro has been a territory in which the forces of capital, in concert with state actions, have sought to establish dominion for the maximization of profit and the accumulation of capital. At the same time, labor, principally in the form of the Mexican American community, has sought to establish an environment for consumption of housing, reproduction, and cultural enrichment. The built landscape of San Ysidro today suggests that Mexican Americans have been the losers. The villagelike atmosphere has essentially been overrun with freeways, a trolley, and recent commercial developments around the old settlement core. At the same time, the Chicano population, although representing a political majority in the community, has been unable to assert any control over the planning and land-use decisions affecting the neighborhood. San Ysidro is gradually being converted into a repository for rent- or capital-seeking land uses. Its commercial economy has been usurped by large-scale corporations, mainly from outside the community, that moved into commercial space between 1976 and 1983 (Williams-Kuebelback and Associates, 1986).

Summary

Para conseguir dinero
Yo me pasé la frontera
Iba dispuesto a la chamba
*Saliera lo que saliera.**
—"La bracera"

In this chapter, we have examined the concept of the borderland social system at the micro-geographic level of aggregation. The twin cities that hug the international boundary enclose specialized and

---

* "To get some money / I crossed the border / I was ready for work / Whatever might turn up."

unique social-geographic forms and processes. As the above *corrido* (Herrera-Sobek, 1984) suggests, a driving force of this social geography has been labor migration. The massive inflow of labor, although destined primarily for the United States, left its mark on the boundary area. On the Mexican side, the migration flow was partly responsible for the high growth rates of northern border cities. Mexican cities served as jumping-off points for migrants headed into the United States. Many stayed permanently in the Mexican border cities, returned via deportation, or returned when enough income had been earned to come back to Mexico.

In a global sense, the forces of the market have been largely responsible for the creation of functional economic space around the boundary and a rational human spatial organization linking discrete origin and destination points on either side. This spatial organization is quite dramatic in the case examined here—the Tijuana–San Diego region. Tijuana's economy is so strongly tied to capital, raw material, and product inputs from California that closing of the border would very likely diminish its gross product by at least one-half. San Diego does not display the same hypersensitivity to Tijuana's economy, but nevertheless looks to Baja California for clues as to future economic opportunities (San Diego Chamber of Commerce, 1978). Thus, the functional economic space defined by the Tijuana–San Diego region is highly uneven, despite escalating cross-border linkages.

Analysis of cross-border ties between Tijuana and San Diego reveals that much of the connectivity is generated by economically motivated trips across the boundary. The dominant transboundary travel categories are work, shopping/consumption, and business-related trips. It is clear from studying these movements that there are significant differences between the north-to-south and the south-to-north flows. The distribution of linkages favors those oriented toward the north. Of the average daily movement of about 106,000 persons across the Tijuana–San Diego border, more than 65 percent of these person trips are from south to north. Furthermore, if one looks at the types of trips, disaggregated by their importance to the economic well-being of the traveler, a wide divergence between Mexican trips north and U.S. trips south of the border is observed. Of the approximately seventy thousand Mexicans who legally cross each day from Tijuana to San Diego, between twenty thousand and thirty thousand are headed for work. Of the remaining Mexican border crossers, a large proportion are shoppers purchasing commodities vital to their households (or small businesses)—food, clothing, household goods. Of the Americans traveling south to Tijuana, a vast number engage in consumption of entertainment services, in tourist and other leisure-oriented activities. These trips are far less vital to the economic well-being of American border crossers. Thus, the spatial system within which U.S. and Mexican exchanges are united in the Tijuana–San Diego metropolitan area is a highly asymmetrical one, linking a city in a postindustrial nation with one in a developing nation. The motives and needs of border crossers within the emerging borderline spatial system must be clarified at all times. The inequalities are social and economic, and they manifest themselves spatially and politically.

Yet there are still important transboundary functional linkages in this twin city social environment. Mexican commuter worker patterns reveal a series of well-articulated labor sub-markets clearly outlined in space, by origin in Tijuana as well as by destination. Colonia Libertad in Tijuana, for example, is a community that sends disproportionately large numbers of commuter workers to San Diego. Nonwork transboundary trips tend to favor three principal destination communities: San Ysidro, Chula Vista, and National City, all south bay communities. This suggests a correlation between areas that Tijuana residents travel to and areas with a large Mexican American population (see Figure 17). From this, one can infer that strong ties exist between Mexican Americans and Tijuana residents. The south bay area of San Diego may be as strongly linked to Tijuana as it is to the rest of San Diego. In Tijuana–San Diego, social linkages do not end at the political border; they fade. As one moves north, the degree of interaction decreases. In some ways, I-94, the interstate freeway running from east to west toward downtown, serves more to divide Hispanic and non-Hispanic San Diego than does the international border.

Not only is the south bay area strongly integrated with Mexico, its Mexican American community has not been successful in establishing its own political power base, nor in translating its numerical supremacy into territorial control. Mexican American neighborhoods like Barrio Logan and San Ysidro are ethnic enclaves that have been unable to secure favorable land-use and planning decisions from city government. San Ysidro is in many ways more tied to Mexico by culture than to San Diego by political loyalty. San Ysidro absorbs 34 percent of the total border crossings between Tijuana and San Diego, in both directions, either as an origin or a destination (County of San Diego, 1978). It also handles an enormous amount of unaccounted-for capital (about $200 million a year), generated through its contacts with Mexico (Soble, 1985). It is an illustrative example of how the border social system operates to create communities that lie on one side of the border, but are economically, culturally, and functionally tied to the other side. Even politicians and other representatives of the state are unsure about the proper role for this border settlement— should it be an exchange district with Mexico, a stable neighborhood for Chicanos, a service zone for Tijuana residents, a reception area for workers and travelers entering San Diego, or a capital-generating community for private investors and government? Can it be all of these things at the same time (American Institute of Architects, 1987)? This dilemma underscores the complexity of the social system operating at the boundary and, among other things, puts a strain on land-use decisions near the border, as we shall see in Chapter 7.

7 The Politics of Space in a Transfrontier Urban Ecosystem

All boundaries are by their nature artificial and can only be viewed as an invention of the human mind. Lines may be a topographical convenience, they are not natural facts. Nature abhors lines.
—Paul G. Lapradelle (1928)

In Chapter 6, economic and sociospatial dimensions of border urbanization were outlined. Despite the asymmetrical properties of social formation in the border settlement system, there are systematic linkages connecting residents on either side of the boundary. Taken together, these linkages form the basis of an emerging spatial system that is transfrontier in nature. This chapter examines transfrontier linkages in the context of a functional "ecosystem." It then explores the political implications of such an ecosystem when it is interrupted by an international boundary. Empirical data are once again drawn from the case of the Tijuana–San Diego metropolitan area.

The use of the ecosystem concept takes into account the discussion in Chapter 4 of comparative urban space and spatial politics. An ecosystem embodies both two-dimensional space (land) and the functional elements of the physical environment (air, water, and so on). The politics of an ecosystem along the boundary encompass both questions of land-use planning (space) and environmental regulation. Along the border, there is an interplay between the two that is vital to understanding the nature of the transfrontier metropolis.

The Transborder Urban Ecosystem

International political boundaries continue to provide formal spatial closure in a world system of sovereign states. Yet as we saw in the previous chapter, some boundary regions, such as the U.S.–Mexico

frontier zone, have evolved under a condition of extensive transborder economic, social, and cultural integration. In these highly integrated regions, when the life cycle of any one urbanized boundary
area is examined in detail, a new transboundary social geography
emerges. In Chapter 6 we observed that numerous forces drive
Mexicans northward—work, shopping, business, and family-related
trips. Equally, a regular flow of North Americans toward Mexico has
been documented. We can also argue that the social geography of
bicultural cities like Tijuana–San Diego, forged over decades of
in-migration, consists of more than linkages of daily activity systems;
it involves the territorial adjustment of social groups like Mexican
Americans, through the gradual establishment of residential enclaves.

   This cross-border social system is one facet of the human geography of urbanized boundary zones. Figure 18 offers a conceptual
model of what might be termed the "transboundary urban ecosystem." It is expressed as a geographical system composed of three subsystems: the natural environment, the human or social environment,
and the built environment. The model attempts to capture the behavioral components of an urbanized area, in this case one lying on an
international jurisdictional boundary. However, the model's components are generic to all human settlements.

   The model in Figure 18, of course, simplifies a much more complex
process and could ignite some debate about the meaning of "ecosystem." From a physical geographic perspective, an ecosystem can be
thought of as a system of elements—energy from the sun, earth materials, air, and water—that combine with plant and animal organisms
to sustain life on the earth. In urban places, the notion of "ecology"
has been used to characterize human settlement patterns and social
interaction (e.g., the Chicago school of urban social ecology). Thus, if
one broadens the meaning of "ecosystem" to include social-ecological
elements as well as physical ones, a generalized model such as the
one in Figure 18 can be constructed.

   If one imagines a U.S. city on one side of a political boundary and
a Mexican city on the other, the model can be operationalized. The
natural environment consists of physical geographic features native
to the region: land surfaces (terrain, soils, vegetation), atmospheric
conditions (air), hydrological systems (water), and geologic or land
formations. A more detailed view of the urban physical environment
could, of course, be imagined. In such a view, the elements of the
physical environment not only interact, but some elements exist in

Figure 18. Transboundary Urban Ecosystem Model

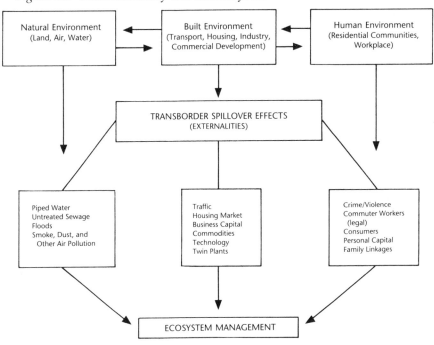

positive or negative feedback relationships with each other, either upsetting the balance of nature, or generating a steady-state equilibrium (Detwyler and Marcus, 1972).

The very obvious point is that the natural environment of a city (or complex of cities) operates according to principles that are widely divorced from the political geography of the human landscape. Hydrological processes, such as sewage outfall or the flooding of a river plain, are not constrained by the political border. Similarly, atmospheric conditions such as smog, or land surface features like slope and soil conditions, do not behave within a logic that recognizes the international political boundary. Equally, land formations such as mountains, mesas, and canyons, or geological processes like faults and earthquakes, are not influenced by the existence of an artificial legal boundary. In short, the physical environment exists independently of the political boundary, whether that boundary is local, state, or national.

The human or social environment does not exist in complete isolation from the international political boundary. Yet as the previous chapter illustrated quite clearly, there are dimensions of human geography at the border that run counter to its traditional barrierlike functions. The border is losing its historical role as a strict edge to the nation-state; it is becoming more porous. Much of that porousness derives from the fact that both production and consumption are no longer restricted within the boundaries of nation-states. People move across national boundaries to work, consume, engage in business transactions, or invest. Nation-states have only limited powers to impede these movements, short of imposing enormously expensive monitoring standards at the boundary or simply implementing an unpopular closed-border policy.

Neither of these scenarios has occurred at the U.S.–Mexico border. In fact, if one examines the institutional dynamics surrounding maintenance of the border from the U.S. perspective, one sees that the battle to regulate the boundary has escalated in the last decade, yet the resources needed to impede the flow of people, capital, and commodities have been unable to match the volume of cross-border movement. In the case of transfrontier workers, for example, it is well known that thousands of Mexican border residents with shopping card crossing privileges are illegally working in the San Diego metropolitan area and in other U.S. border cities. The Immigration and Naturalization Service admits that this problem exists, but also recognizes that it does not have the resources to monitor the activities of border crossers once they are cleared at the border gate (Mittan, 1983). Equally, with the flow of illegal drugs into the United States, the U.S. Customs Service has lamented the lack of funds needed to monitor the border. Some customs officials have even gone so far as to claim that "one fact is clear: our country has lost control of its borders" (Associated Press, 1986).

The boundary has increasingly become an imaginary line over which people and goods move in response to supply-and-demand relationships that transcend it. In more densely populated areas, these relationships occur in greater magnitudes. In the case of San Diego–Tijuana, Chapter 6 showed that over one hundred thousand people cross the border each day, traveling either north or south. More than three-fourths of the crossings consist of origin-destination moves *within* the San Diego region.

In the transboundary ecosystem model, the "built environment" level represents a medium ground between the natural environment and the social environment. In order to engage in a basic set of social and life support activities (production, consumption, reproduction, and so forth), people modify the natural environment to fit their needs. The result of that modification is manifest in the built environment, the outcome of people-land relations expressed through technological innovations, and the construction and reconstruction of the cultural landscape. In an urban ecosystem, built artifacts such as transport systems, housing, office buildings, factories, sewerage infrastructure, and parks are all elements of the built environment. What is most important about the built environment is that it expresses a set of *political* acts channeled through the state apparatus (local, state, and national government) to alter the natural or built environment (Harvey, 1978). It is one level of the urban ecosystem that can be altered through state intervention in urban planning. The built environment can generate serious problems for an international boundary area, where land-use decisions, normally the exclusive domain of the local or national jurisdiction, can suddenly have international implications when externality effects extend beyond the political boundary in a densely populated region.

Given the three generalized dimensions of the ecosystem model— natural, social, and built environments—a second important feature of this model is that, at each level, positive and negative externalities are introduced into the ecosystem. "Spillover effects," or externalities, refer to a circumstance commonly described in microeconomics and public choice theory (Bish, 1971) in which an event occurring in one political jurisdiction spills across that jurisdiction's boundaries into a neighboring unit of government. In a typical national context, when externalities are negative, two policy solutions might be envisioned: first, local imposition of a tax or penalty charge upon the source of the externality; or second, imposition of standards or quality controls on the externality-generating activity by authorities (Sayer, 1982). Such an arrangement is complicated when externalities are generated in an urban ecosystem at an international boundary. Finding a policy solution that "internalizes" negative externalities becomes more than a local policy issue; it becomes a matter of foreign policy. It has been pointed out, for example, that if nations act only to penalize heavy-polluting firms *within* national boundaries, then it becomes profitable for firms to locate on international frontiers where pollution spills across the borders, and where they will not be penalized for negative externalities located beyond national jurisdiction (ibid.). This problem has received much attention in western Europe, where transfrontier air and water pollution are significant problems along the Rhine River and at numerous national borders.

The Tijuana–San Diego Ecosystem

Data for the Tijuana–San Diego ecosystem were gathered within the framework of the generic model outlined above. An archival search of newspaper reporting in San Diego region print media sources produced the data summarized in Figure 19. Using newspaper reports on border-related problems, Figure 19 documents the incidence of various transfrontier externalities over time. Problems are grouped into the three categories of the model: social, built, and natural environments. One can see generally that the cross-boundary problems with the longest history (at least from the point of view of U.S. newspaper reports) are those associated with the region's hydrological system. Both the sewage and flooding problems plaguing the boundary between Tijuana and San Diego date to the pre-1960 period and involve the watershed of the Tijuana River. Another problem with a history of several decades in the region has been the smuggling of narcotics and other contraband, something that received attention in the local newspapers as early as 1960.

What is also clear from Figure 19 is that many of the externality effects began to intensify as the region urbanized rapidly in the 1960s and 1970s. Problems such as air pollution, management of the Tijuana River, and border crime became significant as more population filtered into the region between 1960 and 1980. One can also see that the *number* of spillover issues in the built environment category rose in the mid-1970s as more urban growth took place. Rapid urbanization on each side of the border created externality effects with real and potential cross-border impacts. Changes in Tijuana—such as the development of the River Zone, the coast, and the Mesa de Otay—had an impact on San Diego. Functional connections between the built environments of the two cities could be discerned, among them, the construction of a light rail transit system (trolley) from downtown San Diego to the border, the opening of a second border crossing, the completion of flood control devices in the Tijuana River

Figure 19. Chronology of News Reporting on Boundary Issues

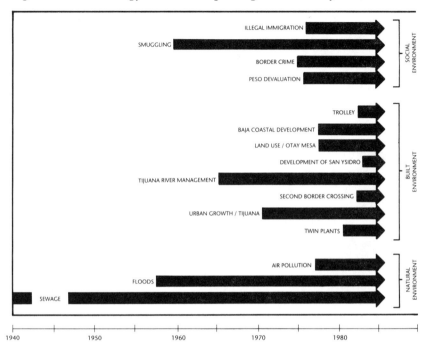

Source: San Diego Union-Tribune and Los Angeles Times, 1950–1984.

valley, the planning of sewage control facilities along the border, and twin-plant industrial development. Let us now examine each level of the transboundary ecosystem in more detail.

Elements of the International Physical Environment

Water. Clearly, the most serious transboundary externality problems have been associated with the watershed of the Tijuana River. Problems facing the watershed (sewage, flooding) are exacerbated by the complex topography of the region, a topography that does not conform to the contours of the humanly created boundary line. The Tijuana River is formed by two principal tributaries, Cottonwood Creek and the Río de las Palmas (Figure 20). From the confluence of its two tributaries, the river flows about 11 miles until discharging into the Pacific Ocean just north of Imperial Beach in San Diego County. Of the overall watershed, about 70 percent lies in Mexico

Figure 20. Basin of the Tijuana River

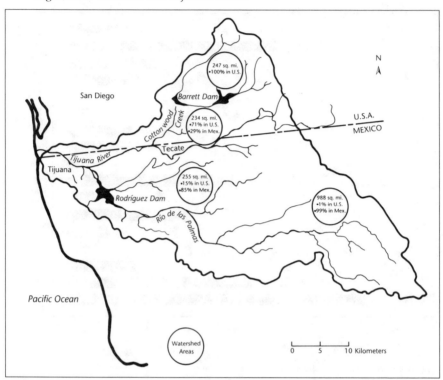

and 30 percent in the United States (Pryde, 1986). When the Tijuana
River crosses the boundary into the United States, the river channel
meanders through a wide flood plain and eventually opens up into
an estuary where the river meets the Pacific Ocean. From the point of
confluence in Mexico where the Tijuana River begins at an elevation
of 215 feet above sea level, there is a gradual slope the next 11 miles
downhill. At the international border the valley cut by the river has a
width of 1.5 miles and opens to 3 miles at the Pacific Ocean (International Boundary and Water Commission, 1976).

Another factor important in understanding the operation of the
watershed is the topography of lands around it. The eastern bank of
the river is flanked by a high mesa, the Mesa de Otay, which runs
along the river's course in Mexico and half of its length in the United
States. On the Mexican side, all of the water drainage from the Mesa
de Otay flows naturally into the Tijuana River and across the boundary into the United States. On the western bank of the river, a cluster
of steep hills rises over the valley floor. These hills are densely populated and most of the drainage from these communities flows naturally toward the lower elevations to the north, mainly the Tijuana
River valley in the United States. Several natural watercourses flow
directly into the valley across the boundary, including Stewart's
Drain, Cañón del Sol, Smuggler's Gulch, and Goat Canyon (Figure 21).

The topography of the Tijuana–San Diego border zone determines
the behavior of the area's hydrology and drainage systems. Because
Tijuana occupies a higher elevation than San Diego, surface drainage,
in the form of urban runoff or sewage discharge, flows toward San
Diego. Furthermore, since 70 percent of the watershed of the Tijuana
River basin lies within Mexico, much of the flood control during periods of heavy rainfall comes from Mexico.

The dynamics of a border ecosystem are vividly illustrated as one
traces the history of the border sewage problem in the San
Diego–Tijuana region. During the 1920s, effluent from septic tank
systems in Tijuana was discharged directly into the Tijuana River,
where it passed into the Pacific Ocean, and was eventually diluted.
But as the population of Tijuana grew in the 1920s, due to the boom
in tourism and gambling, the sewage treatment system quickly became inadequate. During the early and mid-1930s, complaints were
registered by San Ysidro farmers whose truck farming crops and
domestic water wells were being contaminated by sewage spilling
into the Tijuana River. In 1935, Mexico built a larger septic tank

Figure 21. Raw Sewage Discharges along the Border

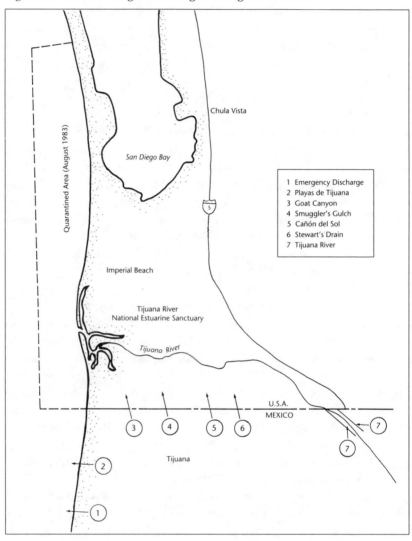

system and made provisions for chlorination. This would be the last completed sewage facility in Tijuana until nearly five decades later (Lowry and Associates, 1983).

Shortly after the septic tank system was completed, Tijuana's growth generated far more waste than could be treated by the system. Thus began a long period of urban expansion in Tijuana in which new neighborhoods (*colonias*) would expand while a large proportion of the houses in the *colonias* would remain unconnected to any sewage facility, creating a steady volume of "renegade" flows of sewage into the Tijuana River watershed, and into San Diego County. In the late 1930s, this problem was recognized in San Diego, and eventually garnered the attention of the State Department of Health and the International Boundary and Water Commission. Through a jointly funded project with Mexico, a series of trunk sewer lines between Tijuana and San Ysidro were completed in 1939. The project, dubbed the "International Outfall," was designed to carry septic tank effluent from the city of Tijuana and from buildings around the core of San Ysidro to the coast, before dumping it into the ocean for disposal. The outfall followed the river for about 6.5 miles from San Ysidro and terminated less than one mile north of the international boundary.

By the late 1940s, the International Outfall project was already in jeopardy. As Tijuana's population expanded to well over fifty thousand, the septic tank system became obsolete. Large amounts of sewage entering the outfall pipes on the U.S. side went untreated. In 1951, the San Ysidro Sanitation District was formed, and monies were allocated to chlorinate the untreated sewage entering the outfall from Tijuana. In 1953, the flow of poorly treated and untreated sewage entering the outfall from Tijuana had increased to 3.5 million gallons per day (ibid.). Both the Governor's Office of the State of California and the International Boundary and Water Commission became involved in the search for a solution to the sewage spill problem. In 1954, the U.S. Department of State filed a protest with Mexico urging the government to "achieve the earliest possible elimination of public health problems caused by the International Outfall" (ibid., p. 5). By the mid-1950s, state and county health departments were conducting bacteriological surveys along the beach between the international border and the city of Imperial Beach. Of the more than 4 million gallons per day (mgd) of untreated sewage flowing into the area, most of it came from Tijuana—with only about 0.2 mgd coming from San Ysidro.

After a brief attempt in 1958 at cooperative treatment and chlorination of the sewage spills entering the water basin, the problem continued. By 1959, the San Diego County Health Department declared all beaches from the border to the northern end of Imperial Beach under indefinite quarantine until the sewage problem could be corrected. In 1961, Mexico partially constructed a sewage facility that would dump wastewater in the ocean at a point 4.4 miles south of the border. Four years later (1965), an agreement was made between Tijuana and San Diego whereby San Diego would accept Tijuana's sewage on an emergency basis. Yet by 1975, Tijuana was producing nearly twenty mgd of untreated sewage, which was sent to the San Diego Metro Sewerage Authority for treatment, not on an emergency basis, but daily. The beaches at Imperial Beach and vicinity were quarantined in 1975, again in 1980, and throughout most of the 1982–84 period.

The sewage spill problem persists at the border between Tijuana and San Diego. Studies show that by 1986 about 4.4 mgd of raw sewage were still entering the United States from Tijuana. Potential water-borne health problems have been avoided thus far, but should not be ignored as one long-range externality effect of these raw sewage spills (Conway, 1986). Renegade spills are likely to continue, as Tijuana's sewage infrastructure is highly fragmented territorially, and vast areas of the city remain without any connection to a sewage discharge line (Salcedo Leos, 1986). Although San Diego has built some defensive sewage facilities along the border, and Mexico has recently opened a new treatment facility to the southwest of Tijuana, the problem is still perhaps the most troublesome in the twin city region. Many U.S. officials have expressed doubt about the new Tijuana treatment facility, claiming that it was built in the wrong location—sewage must be pumped over very steep hills to reach the facility, and that it was built on an unstable landfill that is susceptible to cracking. A second proposed treatment facility for Tijuana has been opposed by U.S. officials because its location near the confluence of the Alamar and Tijuana rivers will mean sewage is dumped back into the Tijuana River, which eventually flows into the United States. The renegade flow problem is likely to continue, and it is probable that breaks in the antiquated pipes near the inner city will continue to occur, causing renewed spills into the canyons that eventually cross into San Diego.

Flooding at the Border. Although sewage spills represent perhaps the most visible negative externality effect along the boundary between Tijuana and San Diego, other environmental problems have surfaced as well. As mentioned above, with 70 percent of the basin of the Tijuana River located in Mexico, the problem of flooding originating south of the border has been a continual concern since the late 1950s. If one again looks at the watershed's geography, the cross-border dimensions of the problem become clearer. Not only does 70 percent of the water come from Mexico, but the largest source area of the basin, that which flows from Tecate Creek into Tecate, runs through an area about which very little hydrological information exists—there are no meteorological gauges or gauging stations to measure the flow of water. Unlike river systems in San Diego County, the flow of water on the Mexican side is mainly uncontrolled. During heavy rains, there is no way of knowing how much water will drain into the basin. Nor are there dams controlling the flow of water into Tecate Creek and Cottonwood Creek below the Morena and Barrett dams on the north side of the boundary (Figure 20). Equally, there are no means of controlling the flow of water into the Tijuana River below the Rodriguez Dam. During heavy storms, enormous amounts of water flow unimpeded through the Mexican watershed into the United States (Pryde, 1986).

Despite the lack of drainage interceptor facilities in Tijuana, the Mexican government did build an expensive concrete channelization facility at the point where the river passes through the most densely populated area of the city. Through an agreement reached by the International Boundary and Water Commission, the United States agreed to construct a facility of equal magnitude on its side to assure that the flows of water would not spill back across the border into Mexico, particularly during peak flow periods. However, completion of the project was delayed several years, and when it finally was completed, the project was not fully complementary with the Mexican flood control channel. On the U.S. side, instead of building a concrete channel, the city opted for what was later described as a "minimum plan" (Kennedy, 1978), a series of earthen dissipator barriers to the floodwaters from Tijuana.

The reasons for selecting the dissipator flood control plan are complex, but can be synthesized for the purposes of this discussion. The decision process underlying the flood control channel basically reflected local politics in the south bay area of San Diego in the mid-1970s. During this period, one interest group, composed of de-velopers, business leaders and south bay municipalities (particularly Imperial Beach), sought to promote the need for a concrete control channel integrated with the commercial and recreational develop-ment associated with a marina and boat basin. They argued that such a development would bring jobs and economic vitality to the south bay area. A second interest group, the "ecologists," sought to pre-serve the lands surrounding the Tijuana River estuary, arguing that the area was one of the last genuine saltwater marshes, with rare fauna and flora. Because the lands were located within the jurisdic-tion of the city of San Diego, its city council became an important force in the decision process. In the end, some observers felt that the city council, influenced by a mayor who had built a platform around "growth management," opted for the "minimum plan" for flood con-trol, thus preserving the physical environment of the south bay. Shortly after the dissipator facility was built, the U.S. government designated the Tijuana River Estuary a national wildlife sanctuary.

The important point here is that the decision regarding the flood control facility was made on the basis of *local* politics within San Diego County, and did not really take cross-border impacts into seri-ous consideration (Duemling, 1981; Kennedy, 1978). In fact, if one looks at the use of land in the basin of the Tijuana River, one sees a pattern of incompatibility between land uses in the United States and Mexico. The flood plain of the river on the U.S. side houses agricul-tural properties, horse farms, and a wildlife refuge. A dissipator facil-ity absorbs water during heavy flooding, or spreads it out over the surrounding undeveloped terrain. Just across the border, the river is channelized in a concrete conduit. Around this is the most densely populated portion of the city of Tijuana. In addition, whereas the United States legislated that lands around the river be preserved for open space and wildlife sanctuary status, Tijuana, in building the concrete channel, expropriated the lands along the river and created an enormous urban development plan for the riverbed area. The first phase of that plan called for the development of office complexes, commercial development, roads, and other public facilities. The River Zone has become a major subarea of development in the city and houses a large proportion of all new commercial, office, and tourist developments, as well as most of the recently built government buildings. In some ways, it has become the new business district of the city, designed more for freeways and automobiles than was the old pedestrian-oriented downtown. Thus, it is ironic that the development of the river basin on one side was oriented toward high-density urban development (Mexico), whereas a short distance away, the river plain was converted to open space and an ecological preserve (United States).

Air Pollution and Toxic Wastes. A third element of the transboundary ecosystem is the common air basin. San Diego and Tijuana are located within a single air circulation system, or *cuenca* (basin). It is an area defined in terms of marine air flow, mountain air currents, local climatic conditions, and the effects of local topography such as rivers and canyons, which channel the air toward certain subregions. The natural air basin encloses an area extending from southern Orange County to Ensenada and eastward to the continuous mountain chain formed by the Santa Ana Mountains to the north, the Laguna Mountains to the east, and the Sierra Juárez to the south (Alvarez, 1986).

The Tijuana–San Diego air basin is integrated by daily exchanges of air. High pressure over the Pacific Ocean causes a constant flow from the northwest toward the interior. Yet air flow also varies by time of day, and with the seasons. Tijuana lies in a northward-facing canyon, which accentuates the flow of air from San Diego. During the day, the ocean breezes push air toward Tijuana; on days when the prevailing winds are north to south and Los Angeles smog is particularly strong, it can reach Tijuana. This is especially prevalent between April and September. At night, the sea breezes ebb, the ground cools, the air in contact with the ground cools down and drains through the river basin toward San Diego (Brown, 1986).

Thus, there is a natural exchange of air between the two cities. This has led to a recognition by both governments of a need to jointly manage the air pollution problem. Communication between representatives of San Diego's Air Pollution Control District and Mexico's Sub-secretaría de Mejoramiento del Ambiente (Subsecretary for Environmental Improvement, disbanded in 1983, with air pollution control responsibility transferred to the Secretaría de Desarrollo Urbano y Ecología, Ministry for Urban Development and Ecology) began in the mid-1970s. Observers on the U.S. side expressed frustration with two things: the centralized nature of the Mexican bureaucracy—most of the government officials are in either Mexicali or Mexico City, not

Tijuana; and the turnover in management personnel that occurs after each six-year presidential term (*sexenio*) (ibid.). Both sides agree that cooperative management is difficult, given the differences in language and culture, as well as what one observer has termed the "asymmetry of power and governance" (Nalven, 1986).

Still another environmental problem that has recently plagued the Tijuana–San Diego region is illegal toxic waste dumping. The problem occurs when either a U.S. or Mexican company tries to dump toxic wastes on the opposite side of the border without informing local environmental regulation authorities. One of the worst recent cases documented in the Tijuana–San Diego area was that of a U.S. ink-manufacturing company shipping thousands of gallons of toxic chemicals to an illegal Mexican recycling operation in Tijuana. The company illegally recycled the chemicals into a constituent of paving asphalt in the La Gloria section of Tijuana, causing serious lead poisoning in the neighborhood (Carson and Larue, 1986). When the operation was shut down, it reappeared later outside of nearby Tecate at the border in east San Diego County. U.S. and Mexican environmental investigators ultimately pressed felony charges against several companies for falsification of customs documents, mail fraud, and other crimes (Larue, 1986). Later, the U.S. Environmental Protection Agency signed an agreement with Mexico to ban all U.S. toxic exports not having Mexican approval. As more industries and other economic activities locate in the rapidly urbanizing regions of southern California and northern Baja California, the question of toxic waste storage and dumping around the international border may become more acute, since some companies will continue to look for cheap ways to avoid the high costs of regulation.

The Built Environment

Most of the externalities associated with the Tijuana–San Diego built environment are of a positive nature and reflect actions in which government and the private sector on either side of the border transform the built landscape partly in response to cross-border demands. It is difficult to argue that these responses are created solely with regard to transboundary relations; still, they offer evidence that the effects of the boundary are occasionally strong enough to mold or transform selected land uses and development projects near it. Two important cross-border transportation projects serve as examples: the light rail transit system, and the second border crossing. Both were designed in the early 1980s to facilitate movement between the two cities.

Another important project that brought the two cities together was the development of Otay Mesa/Mesa de Otay. The growth of the Otay Mesa, a plateau of nearly seventy square miles that straddles the international boundary to the east of the main border gate at San Ysidro, had been seen as a project of mutual interest to the United States and Mexico for more than a decade (Comprehensive Planning Organization, 1978). The mesa remained largely undeveloped on both sides of the boundary until Mexico began to utilize the lands in the early 1970s. Over time, both sides recognized that the morphology of the two cities was such that it would be logical to locate a second transport conduit through the center of the mesa, since both nations had plans to build residential, industrial, and commercial developments on its flatlands, and since each side would benefit from interaction across the plateau.

A number of built environment projects near the boundary garnered mutual interest as well. These included the development of the River Zone, the planning of the Tijuana River estuary, and the redevelopment and expansion of San Ysidro. The development of the River Zone in Tijuana attracted considerable interest in the United States, not the least of which emanated from its easy access for American consumers—its location was quite close to the border crossing and connected to a modern road system. Commercial development in the River Zone was designed to imitate U.S. shopping malls, and it even contains large U.S. commercial outlets like Sears. The River Zone mall was designed by a U.S. architect. Its proximity to the border crossing at San Ysidro has made it possible for Americans, lured by low prices and the strength of the dollar against Mexican currency, to travel south on the two main freeways in San Diego (I-5 and I-805), cross the border at San Ysidro, continue along a recently built arterial road network, and within ten minutes arrive at the Plaza Río Tijuana shopping mall.

On the U.S. side, land-use planning for the Tijuana River flood plain has been greatly intertwined with events south of the border. Even though the dissipator system does not directly conform to the concrete channelization design in Tijuana, politicians and planners who worked on the plan for the estuary were forced to be acutely aware of events in Mexico (Duemling, 1981; Kennedy, 1978). Many of the proponents of a large-scale channelization project and south bay marina argued that such a project would better match the character of the boundary region, given that Tijuana's downtown was only a few hundred yards across the border (Bilbray, 1983).

The development of San Ysidro, the town lying at the international border crossing into Tijuana, is another example of a binational boundary project. A survey of land developments in San Ysidro in the last two decades makes it clear that this community is strongly tied to Tijuana. Most of the developments—warehouses, currency exchange houses, retail stores, hotels, restaurants, Mexican insurance sales offices, post offices, moderate income housing—are tied to economic activities associated with the border location. San Ysidro has multiple roles as a border community: gateway for tourists visiting Mexico and returning to the United States, service and retail goods center for Tijuana residents, center for U.S. border law enforcement agencies and boundary maintenance institutions (U.S. Customs, INS, Border Patrol), and residential enclave for Mexicans and Mexican Americans. A recent study of San Ysidro emphasizes the importance of its cross-border planning connections with Tijuana and recommends creating some form of highway toll or other tax to reimburse the city for the strain that boundary traffic imposes on it, while also recommending that a binational urban design task force be formed with Tijuana to promote tourism, improve roads and other physical plant features, expand employment development, and improve the image of the border crossing community (American Institute of Architects, 1987).

The Social Environment

The nature of the transboundary social environment was examined in some detail in Chapter 6. Figure 19 makes it clear that one of the most significant dimensions of transborder social exchange involves the illegal movement of commodities and people across the boundary. Smuggling of narcotics has been a regional problem in Tijuana–San Diego since 1960. Illegal immigration, of course, is one of the most troublesome and complex problems facing the boundary region. Not only is control at the border a local externality effect, but so is the impact of illegal or undocumented immigrants on the U.S. side. In the last two decades, much concern has been expressed about the potential impacts of Mexican immigrants on the labor force, housing market, and tax-supported social services in the United States. In general, studies have shown that, during the 1970s, Mexican illegal workers shifted out of the agriculture and construction sectors of the southern California labor market and into urban services, light manufacturing, and retail commerce. There is some evidence that a majority of these jobs are undesirable to U.S. citizens and, therefore, that illegal workers do not take jobs from U.S. citizens (Cornelius, Chávez, and Castro, 1982). A study of an estimated twenty-five thousand undocumented Mexican workers in San Diego in 1980 showed that their participation in the regional labor market only increased unemployment by 0.5 percent (Community Research Associates, 1980).

Most available data show that illegal immigrants do not have a serious impact on housing markets in southern California, nor do they make much use of public services such as welfare, food stamps, or unemployment compensation (Cornelius, Chávez, and Castro, 1982). The 1980 study in San Diego revealed that only 0.1 percent of the total county welfare payments went to illegal Mexican immigrants. The same study concluded that undocumented immigrants' impact on services amounted to between 1 and 2 percent of the total costs for all San Diego County hospital patients, and between 1.9 and 3.7 percent of the total costs of all public school systems in San Diego County (Community Research Associates, 1980).

Two other areas of spillover within the social environment of the border region have been border crime and peso devaluation. The problem of border crime has received considerable attention, including a best-selling book (Wambaugh, 1984). Criminals hiding in the canyons near the boundary between San Diego and Tijuana prey on Mexicans trying to sneak across the border, especially in the evening. Robberies, rape, and murder have been committed by criminals who flee back into Mexico, making law enforcement even more difficult. In 1985, ten boundary area murder cases were documented by the San Diego Police Department; nine of them remain unsolved (Fike, 1986). In general, the question of criminal justice in a densely populated border area such as Tijuana–San Diego raises complex and unanswered questions about jurisdiction. How do law enforcement agencies protect citizens from crime when criminals cross an international boundary after having committed the crime?

The peso devaluation problem is another socially derived spillover effect near the boundary. It has equally complex implications in space. The boundary line creates social and economic trauma when it separates the currency of two nations at very different economic levels. In the 1970s, many Mexican border residents, especially the middle class and stable wage earners, had begun to establish credit in retail stores on the U.S. side of the border. No study has documented the amount of credit established, but it is known that Mexicans spent in the neighborhood of $300 million in retail purchases in San Diego each year (see Chapter 6). When the 1976 peso devaluation hit, the effects along the border were staggering. Retail trade in San Ysidro and other south bay area stores dropped by nearly 40 percent (Stoddard and West, 1977). The 1982 peso devaluation was equally devastating to south bay retail trade. It has had other effects as well: more *casas de cambio* (currency exchange houses) have opened since the 1982 devaluation and have remained in business as entrepreneurs speculate in dollars and pesos while the Mexican economy falters. This has been accompanied by clandestine operations that illegally launder monies from the sale of narcotics and other contraband, often using San Ysidro banks. The growth of financial institutions at the border is part of the social environment that evolves in an ecosystem where metropolitan centers of a wealthy country abut those of a developing one.

Comparative Aspects of U.S. and Mexican Local Politics and Planning

Given the evolution of shared social, ecological, and built environments, it is not surprising to discover that an array of institutional responses to this phenomenon has evolved. On the San Diego side of the border, a recognition of symbiotic relations permeated a number of government studies done in the early 1970s. For example, one document commented: "San Diego thinks of itself as a border town, but in reality it is part of the functioning metropolitan region of San Diego/Tijuana. . . . The relation between these two halves of the landscape, belonging to two separate nations and to two vastly different economies, goes far beyond this report. But we hope that officials and citizens will begin to see the division, to understand that it is critical, and that it is urgent that they attend to it" (Lynch and Appleyard, 1974, p. 38).

In the 1970s, the increases in cross-border retail trade, tourism, real estate transactions, labor migration, and proposed industrial development prompted various public officials and bureaucrats in the

United States to seek ways of addressing the connection with Tijuana through public policy. In 1976, a coalition of U.S. and Mexican institutions sponsored a bicentennial conference series called the "Fronteras Project," which brought together public and private officials from both sides of the border to describe the common problems and opportunities of the Tijuana–San Diego region (Fronteras, 1976). The next year, construction began on a sixty million–dollar light rail transit system connecting downtown San Diego with the Mexican border. An important rationale for building the "Tijuana trolley" was that it allowed mass transit communication between two cities that were both growing and interacting more (Metropolitan Transit Development Board, 1977).

In the late 1970s, great attention was placed on the escalating economic interaction between the two border settlements. In a study commissioned by the state of California and the U.S. Economic Development Administration, the various economic sectors of the region were examined and areas of cross-border reciprocity were identified (U.S. Department of Commerce, 1978). In another study, the San Diego Chamber of Commerce sought to better understand how its future economic opportunities were linked with Baja California (San Diego Chamber of Commerce, 1978). There was considerable interest at the local government level in enhancing economic development activities tied to Tijuana. For example, both city and county officials agreed that the vacant land on Otay Mesa represented an opportunity for economic development of an international nature. Local government sought to have the mesa declared an economic development district, and thus be eligible for funding from the U.S. Department of Commerce, Economic Development Administration (Office of the Governor, State of California, 1978). The construction of the second border crossing at Otay Mesa became another policy instrument that recognized the "Mexican connection" (Comprehensive Planning Organization, 1978).

On the Mexican side of the border, recognition of economic and planning ties with California can be documented. In the 1970s attendance by Mexican officials at planning meetings, luncheons, and other functions increased substantially. Meanwhile, in the late 1970s, the federal government in Mexico City was busy allocating millions of pesos for the development of tourist and retail trade infrastructure in Tijuana. Such developments as the $9 million open air market and tourist complex, the Plaza Agua Caliente twin towers, a $25 million, five-story shopping center, the new Cultural Center, the Plaza Río Tijuana shopping center, and the $200 million industrial park on the Mesa de Otay reflected what many observers called "the New Tijuana" (Chavira, 1982). These developments make it clear that the Mexican government recognized the economic opportunities associated with the border and, like its U.S. counterpart, sought to create policies that facilitated U.S. consumption in Tijuana or other forms of economic development.

Despite the emergence of a stronger border consciousness, reflected in public policies in both San Diego and Tijuana during the decade of the 1970s, numerous conflicts continued to separate the two cities. These differences severely limited ongoing cooperation efforts, to the point that it would be accurate to state that the notion of "transfrontier cooperation" was more rhetoric than reality in the local ecosystem. The immigration problem, for example, has been divisive. It has been a constant source of controversy in San Diego County, and, at times, media reaction has created hostility on the Mexican side. The local U.S. media have often engaged in what some observers term "Mexico bashing." One example involves a front page story in a local newspaper that ran a headline of "Corruption in Mexico Assailed" (Stern, 1986). The story dealt with a U.S. Senate Foreign Relations Subcommittee investigation of links between cocaine trafficking and Mexican law enforcement agencies. This story caused the mayor of Tijuana to cancel a scheduled visit to the newly elected mayor of San Diego in the fall of 1986.

There have been other more serious and long-lasting points of contention. Politics at the national level works against local cooperation. When the United States and Mexico clash over Central American policy, petroleum sales, payment of international debt, trade relations, or drug enforcement, relations at the border suffer. When the United States was investigating the death of one of its drug enforcement agents in Guadalajara in 1985, discovery of possible collusion between narcotics smugglers and the Mexican police led to a protest move by the United States—heightened searches by U.S. customs agents at the border—a move that nearly paralyzed the Tijuana–San Diego region. Traffic delays of up to ten hours at the border crossing occurred over a period of several days. In another instance, a loan by the Inter-American Development Bank to Mexico to help cover the costs of construction of the Colorado River Aqueduct to Tijuana was nearly canceled because the Mexican government felt the United

States was trying to pressure it to agree to finish a sewage facility as a stipulation in granting the water facility loan (Gandelman, 1985).

Still other areas of contention have marked relations between the two border cities. Some of the environmental problems plaguing the area have been mentioned. The sewage spill problem from Tijuana to San Diego has outraged many San Diegans and certainly not improved the twin city relationship. When the United States offered to give Mexico monies to repair several broken pipes from which raw sewage was spilling down the canyons and into San Diego, Mexico refused, claiming that it would resolve the problem through its own mechanisms. The toxic waste dumping problem also engendered bad feelings.

One of the biggest sources of contention has been the problem of smuggling. Many U.S. officials feel that the Mexican government does not do enough to prevent smuggling or to prosecute large-scale drug traffickers. Some elected officials feel that local government ought to take on the responsibility for patrolling and monitoring the border. As mentioned, a San Diego County law enforcement official even went so far as to suggest that the U.S. Marines should be called in to patrol the border (Meyer, 1986). Declaration by Reagan administration officials of the border as a "crisis zone" (*Newsweek*, 1986) or even as a "war zone" (Moyers, 1986) has not helped matters locally.

One can conclude that there are many impediments to binational cooperation along the boundary. The mere existence of policy documents that speak of border interdependence is no proof that formal cooperation can actually take place. It usually does not. Many studies, reports, and public meetings generate a rhetoric created to foster the interests of businesses on either side of the border, with the implicit support of the government. Aside from the difficulty of achieving cooperation, one must realize that Mexico, being the unequal partner, is very cautious about such ventures with the United States. For example, when asked to allow U.S. Drug Enforcement Agency helicopters to fly into Mexican airspace to pursue potential traffickers, the Mexican government refused, claiming that this was a violation of Mexico's sovereignty.

We can suggest that, in fact, the decision processes at the border have remained bifurcated along national lines, despite the existence of an ecosystem. At a meeting of public officials from both sides of the border, U.S. officials unanimously rejected a proposal to create a joint San Diego–Tijuana Planning Commission (Herzog, 1986b), saying it was unrealistic and ahead of its time and noting that "it is unlikely that institutionally we are going to be able to share political power across the border" (Hedgecock, 1986). Thus, if border deci- sions are, in fact, made within governments confined to their national jurisdiction, to understand the politics of space along the border, we must really understand the politics of space in each *separate* border entity—San Diego and Tijuana. Let us examine the comparative poli- tics of space in two border cities.

Local Politics and Planning in Mexico

To begin, one cannot divorce the question of local politics in Mexico from the Mexican political system more generally. The Mexican sys- tem places a number of constraints on the ability of local government to operate autonomously. For one, there is an enormous shortage of public revenue to build infrastructure, distribute vital services, and provide other urban development projects. Local governments lack the ability to control their own destinies. This condition is reinforced by the political process.

The Mexican political system has been defined as a "monolithic power pyramid," built around one party (the PRI, Partido Revolu- cionario Institucional) and the power of the president. There is a sub- stantial social science literature that addresses the inordinate power of the president, his vast centralized cabinet and federal bureaucracy, and the manner in which the PRI has been able to legitimize this con- centration of authority (Fagen and Tuohy, 1972; Needler, 1971; Padg- ett, 1976; Scott, 1964; Ward, 1986). The PRI basically has evolved into a political party with three functions: to provide a career structure for politicians and bureaucrats, to oversee the cyclical process of political patronage, and to maintain government legitimacy by controlling voting patterns (Ward, 1986).

Also unique to the Mexican political system are complex forms of power brokerage and power sharing. It has been argued that major decisions in government are often reached secretly through a process of bargaining among elites at the top of the social hierarchy (Grindle, 1977; Purcell, 1975). Power relationships form around groups of po- litically aligned colleagues, creating a process that has been labeled "fluid clientalism" (Purcell and Purcell, 1980). The client-patron rela- tionship, or *camarilla* system, tends to create a career advancement mentality among bureaucrats and government officials (Smith, 1979).

This causes bureaucrats to become highly mobile within the governmental superstructure and may work against the development of expertise in substantive professional areas such as local or city planning.

Another element of Mexican politics that works against effective local political organization and planning is the cyclical nature of the political system. Virtually all Mexican political issues revolve around the six-year presidential terms of office. Every six years, when a new president is chosen, large-scale shifts in personnel and in the organizational structure of the ministries take place. This bureaucratic reorganization tends to be structured around the *camarilla* relationships established during the previous *sexenio*. Because of the specter of personnel realignment, there is a tendency toward conservatism in government. Bureaucrats tend not to want to take risks by pursuing controversial policy questions; local (municipal) politicians are not likely to lobby too hard for city programs, for fear of jeopardizing their chances of moving up the political ladder. At the same time, it has been observed that some politicians, recognizing the inevitability of political turnover, favor implementing highly visible policies such as the building of public monuments, parks, or other civic improvements. *"Plazismo,"* as some have labeled this behavior (Fagen and Tuohy, 1972), unfortunately occurs at the expense of badly needed social infrastructure (water, sewerage, drainage, street lighting and paving, schools, and the like), especially in large metropolitan areas.

Thus, there are a number of structural features in the Mexican political system that impede the local political process. This discussion can only expose a few irregularities in the complex fabric of Mexican politics. It must be emphasized that most elements of Mexican government—the one-party system, the monolithic power of the president, elite bargaining arrangements, client-patron relationships, and the six-year rotations of office—are unified through a dramatic centralization of political power, both geographical and hierarchical. The result is that local government is severely limited as an agency of policymaking and change and has very little impact on such matters as urban development and planning.

It is ironic that local jurisdiction in Mexico is referred to as *municipio libre* (free municipality), because it is anything but free. Mexican law guarantees that municipal governments will be controlled by state and federal authorities; no one is obliged to pay local taxes not approved by the state government, and all local transactions and revenue sources must be reported monthly (Fagen and Tuohy, 1972). Local governments have very little income anyway. From 1932, when their share of public income amounted to 8.9 percent of the total, local revenues decreased to only 2.6 percent of all public monies in 1960 (Wilkie, 1967). By 1975, the breakdown was federal government, 86 percent, state government, 12 percent, and municipalities, 2 percent.

There was much talk of legislating a decentralization program in Mexico during the de la Madrid administration (Chapa, 1982; Mazier, 1986; Mori, 1982). In February 1983 a constitutional amendment strengthening municipal government was approved by the Congress. Article 115 of the Constitution was aimed at strengthening municipal finances and political autonomy. Such an objective is laudable, but the actual decentralization of finances will require a major dislocation of political power from central to local government. Judging from history, it is unlikely that such a change will occur in the short term. To date, the restructuring of the public financing system seems to consist mainly of rhetoric. The reality is that the public monies remain at the federal level and, to a lesser extent, at the state level.

Local government in Mexico is restricted in terms of what it can actually accomplish. Municipalities have the resources to build only a few small-scale public works projects—a municipal jail, cemeteries, a public market, and a few schools. Some also engage in garbage collection and provide a fraction of the water and electricity services for residents. The bulk of public services and virtually all major infrastructure, however, is built with state and federal monies. The state usually funds education, hospitals, the judicial court system, agriculture, and water and drainage. Monies for harbor development, airports, highways, major water works, electrification, some schools, public health programs, *ejido* management, and other development projects come from the federal government (Ugalde, 1970).

As a result of both the hypercentralization of monies and the hierarchical imbalance of political authority, a patronage system has emerged in Mexico. It has its most pernicious influence on local government. For example, funds for local projects are often mishandled. Because local political appointments are seen as a steppingstone to higher political office, politicians may use their time to build a power base, establish *camarilla* relationships, and please specialized constituencies, rather than carry out development projects or service-provision programs tuned to the needs of the local population. I have already alluded to the *plazismo* syndrome—the implementation of visible political programs that enhance the image of the local politician. This is one way in which local governments, being on the wrong end of the public financing hierarchy, tend to misspend monies needed for vital services and development projects. Because the political system rewards success by moving professionals up the status ladder, the best politicians and bureaucrats never stay in local government; they end up in the state capitals, or in Mexico City. This only serves to perpetuate the problem of ineptness in local government and the proliferation of such corrupt practices as personalism, graft, and bureaucratic wastefulness (Fagen and Tuohy, 1972; Ugalde, 1970). It is not surprising to learn, furthermore, that higher officials are insensitive to local concerns. The now-classic statement by a former state governor of Baja California who turned down one municipality's request for state funds illustrates this: "*A mí me chinga el gobierno federal, y yo chingo al municipal*" (The federal government screws me, and I screw the municipal government) (Ugalde, 1968, p. 165).

It has been observed that political centralization does not exist to promote more efficient economic planning. Rather, it is the most efficient way the Mexican power elite can maintain the hierarchy of power and reinforce political control through a system of spoils. One obvious loser in this process is local government. With power centralized in the hands of the president, there has been a tendency for him to create a multitude of federal agencies, substate entities, and other organizations, all in Mexico City. This allows further maintenance of control through manipulation of factions in various similar bureaucratic groups and the playing off of one agency against another (Ward, 1986). The president can reward the circle of *camarillas* around him while not allowing any one patronage group to gain too much power. It also means that even more personnel and financial resources end up in central government at the expense of the cities.

Local governments in Mexico are generally understaffed, lack resources, and drift toward poor management. In this context, we can now turn to a consideration of the nature of urban planning in Mexico. Up until the mid-1970s, urban planning was virtually nonexistent in government. Mexico, like most Latin American countries, has had a tradition of economic (sectoral) planning directed from the federal government. Not until 1976, with the passage of the Law of Human Settlements, did the government formally recognize city planning as a public sector priority. Shortly thereafter, the Ministry of Human Settlements and Public Works (Secretaría de Asentamientos Humanos y Obras Públicas, or SAHOP) was created, and a national urban plan initiated.

Still, there have been many obstacles to effective urban planning. For one, even though a federal ministry was created to administer the planning process, "planning" still essentially followed the rationale of the economic sectors, rather than a spatial or regional logic. Furthermore, SAHOP was never given the funding to implement the national urban plan; that task fell to the powerful economic planning agency, the Ministry of Programming and Budget (Secretaría de Programación y Presupuesto, or SPP). Following the López Portillo administration (1976–1982), de la Madrid reasserted the priority given to economic over physical planning. De la Madrid himself was a former SPP minister. His administration quickly disbanded SAHOP, replacing it with an entirely reorganized Ministry of Urban Development and Ecology (Secretaría de Desarrollo Urbano y Ecología, or SEDUE), an agency that observers agree has accomplished little since 1983 (Ward, 1986). Although urban planning was finally recognized as a legitimate state activity in the mid-1970s, it was never given the resources and political clout to achieve its objectives. In addition, the two federal urban planning agencies mainly established policies at the macro level; there was limited urban planning within cities. For example, far more research and analysis of national and state urban systems has been undertaken since 1976 than studies dealing with intraurban problems such as transportation, sewage, and housing. The exception to this is Mexico City, which has been studied extensively. However, most other municipalities did not even have comprehensive development plans until the mid-1980s.

As some observers have noted, the concept of "planning" as a general principle has traditionally been threatening to the Mexican political system. "Plans" represent the possibility of concrete action of the kind that many politicians hesitate to commit themselves to for fear of being "burned" (*quemado*) and thus alienated from the patronage system. As some have noted, political control may be more important than efficiency. Furthermore, plans represent a greater dissemination of information to the public than is usually made in a national political system where decisions tend to be reached behind closed doors (ibid.). But planning may finally have appeared on the scene because the state has recognized that it can legitimize its actions under the guise of planning. This is something that governments in other nations discovered long ago. As one writer stated in another context, planning may become a "sophisticated weapon to maintain existing control under a mask of rationality, efficiency, and science" (Goodman, 1971, pp. 171–172). In Mexico, planning may also have evolved as a new form of what Ward labels "political mediation"— state policies that serve to maintain social control. Given the enormous migration of rural populations to the cities in the three decades following the Second World War, the problems of cities became paramount among the social pressures applied to the Mexican state. "Plans" gave the impression that government was responding to urban problems. They provided a cushion for politicians to safely repel public criticism that urban infrastructure was failing to meet the needs of the population (Ward, 1986, p. 51). Whether the plans actually improved anything is a question that can only be examined on a city-by-city basis.

City planning in Mexico is obviously a highly centralized activity. Both the planning apparatus and the financial resources to implement plans originate in Mexico City. Research has shown that the decision to allocate funds is made on the basis of national rather than local interests (Ugalde, 1978). Or, as others have argued, planning decisions are made in the interests of profit and support of the capital sector (Moreno Toscano, 1979). What is clear is that cities have little input into the planning process; the process is both physically and politically removed from the urban voting public.

The Role of the State in Tijuana

During the period 1950–1980, interregional and international migration were the principal determinants of growth in Tijuana. As the city's population expanded from 65,000 in 1950 to over 165,000 in 1960, a troubling pattern of unbridled growth unfolded in the urban area. Throughout this era, there were very few formal state interventions to address the problems generated by rapid urbanization. The state was ill-equipped to handle these; it lacked the resources, trained professionals, and expertise to engage in serious land-use planning efforts, even if politicians considered such activities desirable. The record of state management of the urbanization process in Tijuana is poor—even when state intervention did occur, until the mid-1970s, it was weak and ineffective.

During the period 1950–1960, the majority of city residents lacked basic residential services such as water, sewerage, and electricity. Water was quickly recognized as a problem requiring immediate attention. In 1961, the governor of Baja California enacted a state law that called for an "Urban District of Tijuana" boundary to be drawn. Outside of that boundary, the state would not authorize urban development. The decree was intended to control urban sprawl and allow the government to build a piped water system that could reach the edges of the developed urban area. This intervention became a moot point, however, since the government lacked a master plan and zoning procedure with which to control and monitor land development. Spontaneous subdivisions of land continued both on the outskirts of the city and in inaccessible canyons, valleys, and steep hillsides dispersed widely throughout the urban area.

The state also drafted a *plan regulador* in 1962, which proposed some guidelines for controlling city growth. The plan was totally ineffective, however. It underestimated population growth and failed to provide policy mechanisms for implementation of its principal objectives. An aqueduct providing water for the city was built during the same era, but it quickly became obsolete as the total population in 1970 far exceeded the ability to supply piped water to the city's households (Padilla, 1985).

By 1970, Tijuana had over 340,000 residents, more than half of whom lived in dwellings that lacked piped water, plumbing, sewerage and drainage facilities, street lighting, and adequate schools. Much of the city remained unpaved and was served by an abysmal mass transit system. State intervention has not so much served to improve the quality of life of disadvantaged neighborhoods in the city as it has to expand economic infrastructure in a few strategic locations. Important state interventions began in 1965, when the federal government initiated the National Border Program (PRONAF), which sought to channel federal funds into projects aimed at beautification of border cities and development of infrastructure for economic growth. In Tijuana, this translated to three things: tourism, assembly plants, and cross-border trade. To construct these forms of economic infrastructure, the state needed to provide better circulation into the profit-yielding areas of the city: downtown, the River Zone, the Mesa de Otay, and the coast.

During the period 1965–1984, state intervention in Tijuana was not organized around a single master plan (there was no such plan until

1984), but around federal funding policies that sponsored developments in tourist zones, industrial growth areas, or shopping centers. In the late 1960s and throughout the 1970s, interurban highway construction was funded, creating freeway linkages to Ensenada and Mexicali, as well as to important development zones within the city. By far the largest state investment was in the concrete channelization and development of the River Zone. This project involved construction of a flood control channel, highways, and physical improvements of land that was then sold or leased to private real estate and development interests for the construction of commercial, office, and residential development. The River Zone has become the new business district of the city. At the same time, government has also redeveloped and enhanced the old downtown, making it more attractive to American tourists. Other development zones aided by state intervention were the industrial park on the Mesa de Otay (Nueva Tijuana) and the Playas de Tijuana coastal area, a zone of tourism and housing for public sector professionals and for upper income residents.

Table 24 summarizes government expenditures in the municipality of Tijuana between 1978 and 1982. This is an important period of state investment in Tijuana, because it is the period immediately prior to the devaluation of 1982; thus substantial monies were available for public projects. One dramatic spending pattern is illustrated here: between 1978 and 1982, nearly one-third of all monies spent by the state (about one billion 1978 pesos) was devoted to large-scale development projects, labeled "urbanization" in Table 24. Urbanization projects in Tijuana included the channelization and development of the River Zone and the development of the Mesa de Otay, including New Tijuana Industrial Park. In addition, nearly one-half billion pesos were spent on another form of economic infrastructure, highways. Yet, of all monies spent by the public sector in the four-year period shown in Table 24, fewer than one billion pesos were allocated for social infrastructure: water and sewerage, electrification, schools, and health centers. Nearly one-half of the households in Tijuana lacked potable water systems and plumbing facilities (SEDUE, 1985), yet the state only spent about 15 percent of all public monies to build water and sewerage facilities. Although a new sewage treatment facility was completed for Tijuana in January 1987, many observers claim that the population has already expanded beyond that project's ability to treat urban waste. Another glaring statistic in Table 24 is

Table 24. Government Investment in Tijuana, 1978–1982 (thousands of 1978 pesos)

	1978	1979	1980	1981	1982	Total
Program infrastructure						
Urbanization	194,899	103,570	75,397	471,611	161,464	1,006,941
Highways	108,951	85,085	88,061	134,775	58,101	474,973
Water & sewerage	10,930	136,244	107,448	178,641	45,455	478,718
Telephone	—	—	17,210	—	98,119	115,329
Electrification	60,596	63,019	11,099	2,302	22,170	159,186
Airports	150	2,206	9,414	9,634	6,944	28,348
Subtotal	375,526	390,124	308,629	796,963	392,253	2,263,495
Public services						
Schools	74,017	105,452	22,237	61,859	37,308	300,873
Public buildings	7,586	5,498	93,312	6,466	334	113,196
Cultural centers	—	5,283	717	74,772	—	80,772
Recreation centers	11,970	39,701	14,746	25,387	137	91,941
Health centers	12,924	1,202	17,991	6,023	3,665	41,805
Trade	—	268	—	—	3,652	3,920
Jails	2,400	1,148	194	1,107	—	4,849
Subtotal	108,897	158,552	149,197	175,614	45,096	637,356
Housing	11,886	15,593	12,132	178,321	—	217,932
Planning	—	—	—	131,679	—	131,679
Total	496,309	564,269	469,958	1,282,577	437,349	3,250,462

Source: Secretaría de Desarrollo Urbano y Ecología, 1985.   Note: Government investment includes federal, state, and local monies.

that only 6.7 percent of the budget was allocated for housing, even though Tijuana is one of the fastest-growing cities in Mexico.

In general, the state has provided infrastructure for three purposes in Tijuana: (1) to achieve the goals of national and state economic planning, (2) to provide the means for profit enhancement in property development by the private sector (and allied government interests), and (3) to provide social-interest housing and infrastructure to achieve one of the social goals of the national political party, the Partido Revolucionario Institucional (PRI). The third objective has clearly been a much lower priority than the first two, judging from the data on state expenditures. Some of the principal state investments, such as the building of industrial parks and the development of the River Zone, represent part of the national strategy to expand the tourism, trade, and industrial economic potential of border cities. Interestingly, national urban plans for investment existed ten or fifteen years before local city plans were written. This reinforces the top down nature of the system of urban planning and development. The state makes decisions at the federal level about the type of investments it seeks for Tijuana. Clearly, there is consultation at the local level with regional elites over urban development projects, but ultimately, investment decisions are reached in the national capital. Monies are then passed down to state ministry offices, through which development projects are implemented in the city. Not only has government sought to achieve its national economic goals, it has engaged in activities that are profit enhancing to a small class of entrepreneurs and investors at the expense of the large majority of residents. The River Zone development, for example, created capital-generating land uses (offices, shopping centers, and the like) while the needs of the city's irregular settlements (paved roads, sewerage, and so on) were neglected.

The state imposes a lasting impact on the spatial structure and landscape of the city. In Tijuana, the state, through its investments in the Mesa de Otay and the River Zone and through the construction of freeway networks, has succeeded in altering the traditional morphology of Tijuana. No longer does the urban area display a monocentric, concentrated morphology. The city has become more dispersed. Secondary central places are evolving (the River Zone, the Mesa de Otay, Playas de Tijuana, La Mesa) to replace the once-dominant centralized functions of the old downtown. The downtown, formerly a symbolic and functional center of Tijuana, is rapidly evolving into a zone of

tourist facilities and services. Many of the important government offices have left downtown and relocated in the River Zone.

The state's provision of social infrastructure has occurred only as
the lowest of policy priorities. As noted in Table 24, only 217 million
pesos (about 6.7 percent of total) were spent on housing from 1978 to
1982. This figure is strikingly low when one considers that this was
the period in which confidence in the Mexican economy grew to an
all-time high and petroleum production increased. In Tijuana, this
did not translate into housing for the multitude of low-income families migrating into the city. In fact, most of the housing units built
with government subsidies (on the Mesa de Otay and in the River
Zone, for example) were built to accommodate the salaried workers
already assimilated into the urban scene; few, if any, of the poorest
residents living in the *asentamientos irregulares* (irregular settlements)
would be touched by government housing schemes. In that sense,
Tijuana typifies a general problem in Mexico: about 65 percent of the
population, the so-called popular sector, "lacks sufficient income to
qualify for government housing programs, and thus cannot live in
conventionally built housing" (Garza and Schteingart, 1978). These
people end up in the *colonias populares*. This may not be altogether
bad, since scholars have long recognized that poor squatters have the
ability to create self-help programs that facilitate neighborhood improvement, usually beyond what the government can do.

If state intervention in urban planning has been uneven, it has
manifested itself in the changing social geography of the city. In addition to reordering the spatial structure of the city through its
development strategies, the state's actions (or lack of them) have reinforced and extended the spatial polarization of social classes. The
profit-generating zones have been transformed and modernized; at
the same time the *colonias populares* have not improved their lot significantly. Unpaved streets dominate the cityscape in the *colonias
populares*, and vital services are still lacking.

The state has also been pitted against the residential dwellers of
the city in what might be termed the "politics of expropriation." Expropriation, the taking of privately owned land by government in the
public interest, is a technique widely used in Mexican cities. Public
law gives the state the right to expropriate land if the purpose of the
expropriation is acceptable by law. Taking land for the construction
of airports, harbors, highways, social-interest housing, and industrial
parks represents legally acceptable uses of expropriation policy.

The state, under Mexican law, also has jurisdictional rights over land in river flood plains, along the coast, and along international boundaries.

The River Zone offers an example of expropriation politics. Before 1970, several thousand families occupied a cardboard shantytown settlement in the riverbed, a community that eventually became known as Cartolandia. In the late 1960s, the Mexican government put together a development plan for the River Zone; the plan was actually prepared by a U.S. company (Ruhlow, 1975). It called for a concrete channel to control the floodwaters of the Tijuana River, followed by large-scale commercial, residential, and institutional development of the previously unusable lands in the riverbed. In 1972, the government ousted approximately three thousand families from Cartolandia; three years later low-cost multifamily housing was built in this area—in an attempt by the state to give the impression that the River Zone would be used for social interest purposes.

In fact, after 1975, state actions would be more direct and more aggressive in managing the development of the River Zone. Beginning in 1978, the state engaged in a well-organized plan to dislodge some forty thousand residents who lived in the *colonias* stretched along the flood plain of the river from downtown toward the southeast part of the city. In 1978, some twenty-five thousand residents were forced from their homes in the River Zone; the homes were quickly demolished, and families were moved into a tent city on the Mesa de Otay (Becklund, 1978). The displaced families, called *"los damnificados"* (the injured) in the Baja California press, were never given adequate compensation by the government for their housing losses.

However, two *colonias,* San Martín de Porres and San José del Río, resisted the state's efforts to displace them. Their resistance received national exposure in the Mexican press and was serious enough to warrant a visit from President López Portillo in 1978. The taking of land in these two communities appeared to be a circumvention of the laws surrounding expropriation. In the first phase of the River Zone project, the state had paid indemnity fees to those displaced. In the second phase, farther to the southeast, the government wished to avoid paying compensation fees to the twenty-five thousand people it sought to displace, so, during a flood in 1978, the government seized the moment. Under the guise of protecting them from the floods, it forced families out of their homes. Both the army and the police were brought in to demolish the homes and to keep the residents from returning. Resident associations organized a series of protests, which became threatening enough that the president paid a visit to the area. The residents claim that the state never gave them a choice on the question of moving, that the floods were not really that threatening, and that the whole process of relocation was part of government's effort to avoid paying indemnity fees to those displaced (Juaregui, 1982). The residents were not further compensated for their claimed losses. In the end the River Zone expropriations illustrate how the state engages in a form of urban planning that is highly selective and oriented toward generating income in the national interests, and in the interests of assisting private sector forces closely allied with state interests.

Rosarito, a coastal settlement within the municipality of Tijuana, just to the south of the Playas section of the urbanized area of the city, offers a second example of the politics of expropriation. Since 1980, the question of landownership in Rosarito has become quite controversial in northern Baja California. Most of Rosarito was, at one time, part of Ejido Mazatlán, one of thousands of rural cooperative landholdings created by the land reforms of the 1920s and 1930s throughout Mexico. The question of the use of *ejido* land at the edge of Mexican cities has been controversial in the last two decades. In Rosarito, the stakes of landownership were particularly high—much of the land is prime real estate, lying adjacent to the Baja California coastline.

In 1981, the Mexican government suddenly announced that it was expropriating large portions of land in Ejido Mazatlán and that it would then determine proper landownership. Those whose documentation was in order would be given back their properties; those without proper papers would lose the land, and it would revert to the state. This unleashed popular dissent and the formation of community action groups in Rosarito among the squatters and townspeople who had been leased or sold land by the previous owners (Chavira, 1981; Montemayor, 1981). As the investigations got under way, many speculated about the real interests of the government (Romero, 1985). Several motivations were suspected: (1) the state wished to clarify landownership so that it could gain access to valuable properties for state projects, especially tourist developments; (2) the state wished to assist the private sector in gaining access to valuable lands for profitable use; and (3) the government wished to protect lands that were already developed, especially those leased to U.S.

residents, ten thousand of whom lived along the coast south of Tijuana (ibid.). The last fact is particularly resented by some Mexicans, who feel that the government is favoring the presence of foreigners, because they bring dollars into the local economy, and ignoring the needs of its own citizens (Acevedo Ramírez, 1985). Much like the case of the River Zone, it is clear that state intervention in Rosarito did not occur so much to bring rational planning to the area, as to promote the narrowly defined interests of the state and its alliances in the private sector, including North Americans.

Local Politics and Planning in the United States

Local governments began as the weak link in the U.S. political system. The Constitution gave explicit powers to the federal government, and the states were given jurisdiction and residual powers over their regions. The Constitution did not even recognize local government. In the nineteenth century, as cities began to grow in the United States, local governments had very small budgets and virtually no authority to administer the lives of their citizens. State governments provided most of the major services, such as water, sewerage, police and fire protection, and highways.

Structural changes affecting local government were slow to come, given the bias toward federal and state authority in the Constitution. In the late nineteenth century, residents of U.S. cities lacked both the motivation and the skills to participate in local government. This vacuum of leadership would open the way for a period of local governance highlighted by ethnic political machines and the use of patronage, influence, and bribes (Erie, 1987).

A second important force in the evolution of local government was the "home rule" movement, which evolved in the latter part of the nineteenth century. It grew out of a desire of some citizens to protect themselves from "big government" by achieving local control over public matters. Its intellectual rationale came from Jeffersonian democracy and the idea that local governance was the purest form of democracy. In the 1880s, as cities grew through immigration and economic development, communities evolving at the edges of cities sought autonomy from the inner city. Thus was born the movement for "suburban autonomy," the notion of "home rule," and the idea of incorporation for suburban towns, leading to the formation of independent governments outside the jurisdiction of the inner city

(Markussen, 1976). By the 1930s, most state governments had adopted some form of legislation approving the incorporation of suburban political units and making it difficult for central cities to absorb peripheral lands through annexation. The home rule movement directly contributed to the evolution of autonomous suburban governments, which, over time, would yield the highly fragmented political organization of space one finds in U.S. metropolitan areas today (Cox, 1973).

As a result of legislatively induced changes in political organization and in financing mechanisms, municipalities in the United States today possess abundant resources for providing services. Few countries in the world can match their fiscal and decision-making powers. The severe Depression of the 1930s was an important stimulus for the gradual evolution of the machinery of local public management. It put local governments in a weakened financial state, so to provide services and other local needs, they began borrowing heavily. This set the stage for the development of expertise and interest in local financing mechanisms. After the 1930s, local governments would gain access to legal powers that allowed them to become powerful and autonomous units of government. For example, they acquired the "police powers" to plan and zone land within their boundaries, the right to obtain and sell property, the authority to provide services and enforce regulations (such as building codes, housing ordinances, and zoning laws), and, most important, the power to raise revenue by imposing charges or by collecting taxes. Today, local governments operate under the "corporate city" principle derived from English feudal law, whereby the crown granted charters to local towns to make them independent from landed gentry. Local governments use their corporate powers to operate in a manner similar to higher levels of government. They tax and collect fees to allow themselves to carry out a vast array of service activities, ranging from police and fire protection, sewerage, public welfare, education, and housing to management of airports, parks, utilities, and hospitals. By 1975, municipal governments were generating one-half of their income through local property taxes, local sales taxes, and other locally created income transfer techniques (Yeates and Garner, 1980, p. 422).

The origins of planning in the United States can be traced back to the colonial era. During this time, plans were drawn for a number of cities, including Philadelphia, Savannah, and Washington, D.C. There was an emphasis on designing cities that preserved open space and a sense of community. At the same time, planning in the United States faced obstacles, not the least of which was that U.S. society, from its origins, was rural. The nation's founding fathers did not view urban life as essential. Thomas Jefferson is known to have commented that cities were "pestilential to the morals, the health, and liberties of man." This antiurban bias carried into the nineteenth century, during which no formal planning emerged and urban growth became a speculative business, as the real estate industry evolved in U.S. cities. Not until the very end of the nineteenth century would any response to the lack of planning in U.S. cities emerge.

Some planning historians have suggested that a significant urban planning movement in the United States started in the late nineteenth century with the "Crusade for Improvement," a citizens' group movement to reform housing in cities and to plan for parks. The passage of the "tenement laws" in 1901 in New York City, bringing better sanitation controls to tenements in the lower-income districts, represents one of the first institutional acts to recognize the need for urban planning. Another comes from the tradition of "park planners," who argued that government ought to play a role in the provision of open space in order to assure a healthy urban physical environment. Frederick Law Olmstead, whose classic design for Central Park in New York City was adopted by many other cities in the United States, is regarded as one of the catalysts of this movement. In 1893, the Columbia Exhibition at the Chicago Fair brought architects from all over the nation to display designs for the future city of America. Many regard this as the key moment in the revival of urban planning and the dawn of its modern era (Reps, 1965).

In the twentieth century, many of the institutional bases of the planning profession were established. Zoning was legislated into law in different states in the second and third decades of the century. Planning commissions and zoning boards were set up across the nation. In 1954, the passage of the National Housing Act represented the federal government's first significant recognition of the need for city planning policies. Municipalities were required to submit master plans to receive federal monies for housing and urban renewal. Today, every local government has a planning department and zoning board and produces a comprehensive or master plan that sets out the objectives of the city in areas such as land use, housing, parks, transportation, energy, and public services.

Despite the importance of urban planning as a legitimate tool of government, it remains highly politicized in the United States. Planning decisions, although typically buffered within the local government arena, are strongly influenced by the political environment. Two key constraints upon planning can be identified: (1) the institutional reduction of planning to a technical science divorced from politics; and (2) power structures that supersede the formal planning apparatus, especially those derived in the private sector and through the land market.

In city and regional planning in the United States urban space is commonly viewed as an objective, pure, and scientifically grounded surface on which technical planning decisions are made. This has led to the development of a profession, university training programs, and a body of knowledge that assumes that planning decisions can be reached in a non-political manner. Most planning theory, models, and methods proceed under this misleading assumption. Regional science, for example, operates largely under the neoclassical assumptions of rational economic behavior and neutral space. The problem, of course, is that political-economic motivations penetrate to the core of decisions affecting the use of urban space. The planning profession in the United States is actually one part of a complex circuit of political actors having an impact on the use of urban land. These actors may include banks, financial institutions, elected officials, landowners, investors, community groups, firms, households, and others (Harvey and Chatterjee, 1974). One by-product of the creation of a planning profession divorced from the political process is that planning lacks sufficient community power to become a tool of the public interest in opposing land-use changes that represent narrow interests. Instead, it becomes a tool of the state, used to achieve its interests, which may ultimately coincide with those of the property owners, financial powers, and other members of the capitalist class.

The role of government (planning) in cities in the United States may, therefore, have been restricted by the way the profession defines its responsibilities. One thing is clear: unlike many European nations, such as France and England, the U.S. government has never legislated urban land-use policy. The judiciary, for example, has essentially failed to establish a consistent meaning for the "public interest" that could be reliably utilized in conflicts over land developments affecting private property interests (Herzog, 1983). Private property law continues to protect the rights of the landowner over those of the community or "public interest." No significant urban land policies have been established at the national level. The same can be said about housing policies.

In much of what goes on in U.S. cities, "planning" has failed to impede the development of a consistent pattern of land-use change—the dominance in all land-use decisions of the interests of a class of private investors, developers, and owners, all bent on profit. This trend was most incisively revealed during the "urban renewal" era of U.S. planning (1960s), in which study after study documented the fact that "renewal" was framed by a coalition between government and private interests to extract the "highest and best use" from downtown land. The needs of the *people* who lived on the land were hardly accounted for during this period. As one observer noted: "Competent land-use planning and implementation is wealth creating, that is, the system of land use which arises under a system of controls often creates more wealth from a given area of land than would a system of no land-use controls" (Clawson, 1975, p. 482).

It would appear from these kinds of statements that urban planning in the United States serves the interests of a capitalist class of land developers, investors, corporations, banks, and other actors who seek to utilize the urban arena as a setting for production and profit. Planning becomes another tool to rearrange the spatial structure of urban areas to allow for the most efficient and profitable circulation of goods and services. That these elements may be at variance with the needs of communities for adequate housing, healthy environments, transportation, services, and community facilities is one of the ongoing dilemmas of city planning in the United States.

The Role of the State in San Diego

In the early 1980s, the city of San Diego, together with state and federal funding sources, built a light rail transit line between downtown San Diego and the Mexican border. The project was heralded in the local and national press as a successful example of good transportation planning. Ironically, however, from an urban planning point of view, the "Tijuana trolley" would not have been expected as the first mass transit project in San Diego County. Given the growth patterns of the region (see Chapter 5), the most serious traffic congestion clustered along the I-8 corridor running east-west through Mission

Valley, or along I-94 running parallel to I-8. Regional planners were predicting that by the end of the century the traffic density on the I-8 corridor, and perhaps on some freeways running from central San Diego through north county, would be comparable to that of some of the most congested freeways in Los Angeles. Why then, one has to ask, did the city government choose to build the transit line to the Mexican border first? A tempting answer would be that the city wished to expand its diplomatic and functional ties with Tijuana, its southern neighbor, a rationale that was expressed in some planning documents (Metropolitan Transit Development Board, 1977). This explanation falls far short of the truth, however. The primary reason for building the downtown-Mexican border light rail transit line was profit. Downtown San Diego was being developed into a major commercial center for the region, and a connection to the border would enhance its role as a functional tourist zone for the city's thriving visitor industry.

The role of the state in San Diego's planning and development is linked to economic interests. It is well known, for example, that prior to 1950 San Diego was controlled by a small, elite power structure consisting mainly of families with a long history of ties to the region. Between 1950 and 1980, the power structure was realigned. The axis shifted toward groups tied to the property development, construction, and building industries that became the driving force of the San Diego economy (Keen, 1977). In San Diego in the post–World War II period, activities involving land and the physical environment became central to the region's economy. A study of the San Diego economy in the mid-1970s, for example, showed that some of the most dynamic economic sectors were tied to land and the landscape: agriculture (the land); military and trade (the natural harbor); the visitor industry and retirement, and research and development (the environment); and, of course, the growth and property development industry (land, environment). The visitor industry, for example, generated $916 million in revenue in 1976, and building and construction brought in over a billion dollars, as did the military sector (Economic Research Bureau, 1978).

Urban planning in San Diego County has essentially functioned to enhance the profitability of key economic sectors, such as the military, the trade sector, the visitor industry, and the growth and property development sector. One example of how planning accommodates the military (the navy) is the decision to build a new

Naval Hospital in Balboa Park's Florida Canyon. The city charter of San Diego forbids the acquisition of parkland for uses other than cultural or recreational, except by a two-thirds vote of the public. No public vote was ever taken, yet the city decided to allow the navy to build a new hospital on parkland (G. Smith, 1979). Ultimately, the hospital location decision involved a network of local, state, and national politicians aligned with the navy in overriding the opposition of planners, environmentalists, and citizens.

Perhaps the most striking characteristic of the role of the state in San Diego is the degree to which urban planning decisions have served to benefit the growth and property development industry. Three of the key planning decisions since 1960 have served this vital economic sector: the development of Mission Valley, the development of north county, and the redevelopment of downtown. Mission Valley's development, for example, is thought by some planning scholars to have been a grave error in the overall design of the San Diego region. By developing this geographical resource, the city lost valuable open space and created a corridor of smog-generating, high-density automobile traffic flowing into the El Cajon Valley, a major suburban population cluster (Lynch and Appleyard, 1974). Yet Mission Valley has served a diverse array of property owners in the hotel, restaurant, shopping center, and office building businesses. The redevelopment of downtown and the development of north county have also served the growth and property development sectors; although a mass transit linkage connects downtown San Diego with the border, no such connection, as yet, exists with north county, even though this area is the fastest-growing subregion of San Diego County.

One planning technique that has received considerable attention in San Diego is growth management. Responding to the pressures of rampant population expansion in the 1960s and early 1970s, the city of San Diego formally designed a growth management program, the objectives of which were to reduce urban sprawl, manage new growth in areas that would not impose excessive costs on government in the provision of services, and limit automobile-induced pollution, energy consumption, and inefficient land-use patterns (Rick, 1978). Yet, despite the rhetoric of growth management, the city of San Diego continued a pattern of sprawling development in the 1970s, especially to the north. As one observer noted, typical of sprawl development, 60 to 75 percent of all growth in the city of San

Diego was channeled into outlying areas (Remer, 1977). Growth management gave the impression that the state was actually doing something about inefficient urban development; in fact, it could not control it.

Another feature of state intervention in San Diego has been the inability to undo a gradual pattern of social segregation in the region. Much of San Diego's poverty is concentrated in a single wedge running from southeast San Diego through National City and Chula Vista to the border. Although the San Diego Unified School District has implemented policies that integrate the school system, the city has failed to provide land-use, housing, or business development policies that alter the social-geographic pattern of the city. In 1976, the south bay area was home to 11.7 percent of San Diego's unemployed males and had a median household income of only ninety-six hundred dollars, well below the county average of nearly eleven thousand dollars (U.S. Bureau of the Census, 1975).

A Comparison of Location Conflicts

One way of understanding the differential impacts of politics and planning on cities is to analyze urban conflicts reported in the media. These problems have been collectively labeled "locational conflicts"—conflicts over the use of land, the location of facilities, services, and other changes in land use. This approach to planning problems has received considerable attention from geographers (Cox and Johnston, 1982; Herzog, 1983; Ley and Mercer, 1980).

Tables 25 and 26 offer a snapshot of locational conflicts documented for San Diego and Tijuana during comparable time periods. Table 25 summarizes media reporting of locational conflicts in San Diego during the 1970s and the 1980s. In both time periods, a dominant location conflict was suburban growth/management (22 percent of conflicts in the 1970s, 16 percent in the 1980s). During this period, concerns about peripheral growth and leapfrog development in such areas as North City West, Carmel Valley, Escondido, San Marcos, and San Dieguito dominated news reports. The question of annexation and incorporation in such places as Poway, Del Mar, Solana Beach, and San Dieguito also found its way into numerous local reports.

A second crucial issue in the San Diego region was the environment. Environmental issues captured the largest share of reporting in both periods (32 percent in the 1970s; 23 percent in the 1980s). Some

Table 25. Media Reporting of Location Conflicts in San Diego

Conflict	1970s Number	%	1980s Number	%
Environment/flooding/sewage	44	31.7	23	23.0
Suburban growth/ growth management	31	22.3	16	16.0
Transportation	21	15.1	15	15.0
Public facility siting (airports, nuclear plants)	5	3.6	3	3.0
Zoning conflicts	11	7.9	2	2.0
Housing	5	3.6	1	1.0
Downtown/commercial redevelopment	5	3.6	14	14.0
Education/desegregation	5	3.6	11	11.0
Harbor/coastal development	7	5.0	6	6.0
Public services/crime	5	3.6	9	9.0
Total	139	100.0	100	100.0

Source: Urban Studies and Planning Program, 1983–1985.

Table 26. Principal Location Conflicts in Tijuana, Media Reports, 1970–1985

Conflict	Number	%
Environment	5	13
Squatters: invasions, landownership	10	26
Land disputes	15	38
Lack of service	7	18
Transportation	2	5
Total	39	100

Sources: Newspaper articles from *San Diego Union, Evening Tribune, Los Angeles Times, El Mexicano, El Heraldo, ABC Baja California.*

of the issues included air pollution from automobiles and industry, the pollution of Mission and San Diego bays, the sewage problem, offshore oil drilling, noise pollution, and nuclear plant siting. This reporting pattern is not surprising when one realizes that preservation of the environment in a recreational city is a key policy issue. A clean physical environment is vital to many economic activities in

San Diego—tourism, trade, research and development, retirement, real estate, and so on. Other important issues that surfaced in the local news reporting included transportation, downtown/commercial development, and education/desegregation.

As Table 26 suggests, the kinds of planning conflicts one finds in Tijuana are rather different. The leading reported planning problem has been land disputes (38 percent of reports), mainly involving disputes over land expropriated by the government, especially in the River Zone and Rosarito. Squatter settlements and regularization of land represent a second major location conflict theme (26 percent). Equally problematic has been the lack of urban services, which has generated 18 percent of media reports. Finally, 13 percent of the reports stressed environmental conflicts, such as the lead-processing plant problem in La Gloria, sewage spills along the coast, and the problem of contaminated water throughout the city.

When one contrasts the location conflicts discovered in San Diego with those in Tijuana, one discovers that the differences derive from cross-cultural contrasts that go beyond the planning of cities; the differences are societal. San Diego is a wealthy, postindustrial city. It depends heavily on tertiary and quaternary economic activities like tourism, trade, research and development, and real estate. These enterprises in turn depend on San Diego's physical environment. It is not surprising, therefore, that the principal location conflicts in the city fall within areas related to the physical environment (zoning, suburban growth, environmental pollution). With so much at stake, interest groups (building industry, real estate, and residents) often compete over land-use issues. They also disagree at times over policies related to transportation and public facility location.

Tijuana, on the other hand, is a Third World border city experiencing one of the fastest growth rates on the continent. Its population base has been doubling every ten years, fed mainly by migration from Mexico's interior. Its planning problems are tied to the government's unwillingness to devote more resources to the social planning needs indigenous to a less-developed metropolis with more than a 5 percent annual growth rate. Some of Tijuana's locational conflicts reflect problems deeply ingrained in the Mexican political system, a system that has, to date, failed to produce an adequate urban planning mechanism. Thus, the principal location conflicts of Tijuana express the problems of the socially marginal urban dwellers—squatter communities, their lack of services, and land disputes with the government.

What is very clear then, is that urban planning in the two cities operates within dramatically different social, political, financial, and structural contexts, which are determined by location north or south of the national border. Yet, at the same time, one cannot entirely ignore environmental phenomena that cross the border, as well as the increasing reciprocity in land-use relationships near the boundary. We are therefore left to wonder: how do border cities like Tijuana and San Diego deal with planning problems located adjacent to the border, when those problems seem to warrant some form of direct cooperation between the two nations? A case study, outlined below, may shed light on the problem.

The Case of Otay Mesa/Mesa de Otay

A sixty-square-mile plateau straddling the international boundary midway between Tijuana and San Diego provides an ideal setting for a comparative analysis of U.S. and Mexican land-use planning. Otay Mesa (Mesa de Otay in Mexico) is located at the edge of two expanding urban areas (see Figure 22). Half of the land area lies on each side of the border. Twenty years ago, the plateau was a huge, vacant site attracting the interest of planners and government officials in both countries. Its location between two rapidly urbanizing and economically dynamic cities and the flat grade of the land made it an ideal growth center for both cities. The story of Otay Mesa's development on each side of the boundary provides a precise glimpse into the machinery of urban planning in each nation and a barometer of the possibilities of cross-border planning.

In the Mesa de Otay, Mexican officials saw the opportunity to provide housing, jobs, commercial development, and public facilities on perhaps the largest parcel of land suitable for development in the city. Tijuana, unfortunately, is not blessed with a horizontal surface for urban development; it is laced with canyons, riverbeds, steep sloping hills, and flood-prone indentations. The Mexican government also saw a second opportunity on the Mesa de Otay—gradually to move key urban land uses east of the old downtown. This would break the traditional dependence on the city center, relieve the stress on the chaotic and overcrowded traditional central business district,

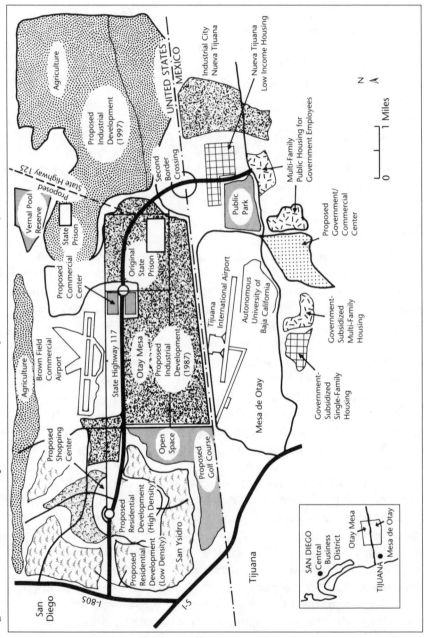

Figure 22. Current and Proposed Land Uses, Otay Mesa/Mesa de Otay, 1987

and allow for lower densities and better planning. Given the general move toward more technocratic policies in Mexico, it is not surprising that planners and politicians wished to achieve a more efficient spatial structure. The development of the Mesa de Otay fit into the overall government strategy to rearrange the spatial structure of Tijuana, moving the city's center of gravity eastward and spatially integrating key land uses, including the River Zone development, the Mesa de Otay Industrial City, and the airport.

Under a different set of circumstances, San Diego determined that Otay Mesa's value to the region would be realized through the development of a peripheral regional growth center. The idea was to provide moderate-income housing and jobs to the south bay subregion (San Ysidro, Chula Vista, National City), one of the lower-income zones of the urban area. In the 1960s, the city of San Diego completed a study of the real estate potential of several south bay land areas, Otay Mesa included. By the early 1970s, the city and county were doing extensive research on the options for Otay Mesa development. A recurrent theme in policy studies was the question of functional linkages between Otay Mesa and Tijuana. Discussions of a new border crossing, an international airport, and other transboundary facilities began. By 1980, city officials were convinced that Otay Mesa's industrial, residential, and commercial developments would bring substantial benefits to the region.

Both the United States and Mexico recognized that Otay Mesa/ Mesa de Otay could become a zone of binational planning, despite the lack of local precedent. Not only was the plateau a geographic formation that physically transcended the boundary, its location offered the possibility of a second major corridor of transport and interaction between San Diego and Tijuana. This would help relieve the congestion at the San Ysidro border crossing while creating a bicultural economic growth center at the edge of two expanding border cities (Comprehensive Planning Organization, 1978).

Given the cross-boundary nature of Otay Mesa's ecology, it is not surprising that, as each nation began to plan and develop its side of the boundary in the late 1970s, a host of cross-border land development externalities emerged. These spillover effects were intensified by the fact that a population of nearly one-quarter million was expected to occupy the area by the year 2000 (ibid.). Residents on either side of the mesa would share noise, air pollution, and water contamination problems. Sewage spills on the Mexican side of the boundary, for example, could drain into the Alamar River and eventually flow across the boundary into the Tijuana River estuary on the U.S. side. Air pollution from industrial parks on either side of the boundary could blow into residential areas on the mesa, and toxic waste spills could potentially contaminate residents on both sides. The impact of the international airport on the Tijuana side of the boundary clearly spilled across the boundary to proposed residential developments in the United States.

Transfrontier linkages in the social and built environments of Otay Mesa/Mesa de Otay could also be envisioned. The mesa's role as a transport corridor between the two cities created a need to construct a compatible transport system. In fact, this did not occur. In the late 1970s, the two nations disagreed on the exact location of the second border crossing. For several years, the U.S. agency negotiating the crossing (General Services Administration, GSA) and various Mexican government entities struggled to agree on a site (General Services Administration, 1979). Once the governments reached agreement on the site, other problems ensued. For example, as the United States completed the access road to the crossing during the 1982–1984 period, the Mexican government informed San Diego officials that, because of the peso devaluation, a shortage of public monies would delay completion of the facilities on Mexico's side. The border crossing did not actually open until 1985.

Other externality effects for the mesa's development also emerged. Given both the large quantity of residents expected to occupy the subregion and its relative isolation from other urbanized zones, there was a clear need for commercial facilities. Ideally, rather than duplicate services and retail facilities, each side might have planned to develop facilities to complement its neighbor's. On the Mexican side, the lack of adequate commercial outlets on the Mesa de Otay had already become evident in the early 1980s. Other forms of common service needs might have included police and fire protection, hospital services, or park facilities (Graizbord, 1986). Equally, such issues as industrial development, illegal Mexican immigration, and legal Mexican labor migration created a need for a transborder approach to land-use planning. The type, density, and location of land uses on either side of the boundary on the Otay Mesa were inextricably linked across the border. Although this observation seems indisputable, the fact is that land-use decisions reached on either side of the boundary at Otay Mesa diverged sharply. Decisions were essentially the domain of the two nation-states sharing the boundary. Analysis of land-use decisions as part of both a historical and a political-geographic process serves to provide a measure of the cross-cultural differences between U.S. and Mexican land-use planning. In the following sections, these differences are empirically analyzed on three levels: (1) the objectives of land-use planning, (2) the scale of government authority, and (3) the instruments of land-use planning.

The Objectives of Land-Use Planning.   Land-use planning is a systematic process of government intervention to regulate and guide the quality of urban development in the public interest (Chapin and Kaiser, 1979). The first important barometer one can apply to the process is a determination of its goals. Interviews with key officials and politicians in the United States and Mexico revealed the priorities assigned for land-use planning on the Otay Mesa/Mesa de Otay by the public sectors in the two nations.

Contrasts between U.S. and Mexican land-use planning objectives are apparent. On the U.S. side, key issues identified by decision makers in a 1981 survey involved controversies tied to the completion of specific facilities that, at certain points in time, delayed the process of land development on Otay Mesa. These controversies included the completion of the second border crossing, the access road to the border crossing, and the state correctional facility. That these issues were ranked highest is not surprising. Land-use planning in the United States typically seeks to facilitate the maximization of profits derived from the land. On Otay Mesa, the completion of a major transport facility into Mexico would be profitable to landowners, investors, and the city's tax base. The underlying motives of those with power over the land-use decision process are to resolve local conflict and get on with the business of developing the land.

Secondary issues of concern to U.S. officials included environmental impact, jobs, and housing prices. These might be termed the "soft," or social, aspects of land-use planning. They received attention from decision makers, but only as secondary items on the land planning agenda.

In Tijuana, officials regarded as important the construction of housing, industry, and public services, as well as highway and mass transit access to the Mesa de Otay. Unlike in San Diego, where the development of Otay Mesa was one of a dozen major zones of peripheral urban expansion, the Mesa de Otay in Tijuana was perhaps the most important "suburban" development zone in the city. Its land would house vital industrial and residential land uses, as well as public facilities. These would serve the state's need to appease the public sector by providing some "social interest" housing (mostly for the upper middle class, however) and some assembly-plant industry jobs. It would also serve capital's interests by opening up lands for commercial, office, and industrial development. It is noteworthy that neither the San Diego nor the Tijuana officials placed cooperation with the neighboring country high on the priority list, although it was mentioned by both sets of decision makers.

Scale of Government Authority. Analysis of the political structures involved in land-use planning on the Otay Mesa shows that, during the period 1970–1984, there are significant U.S.–Mexican contrasts in the location of authority over land-use decisions. In Mexico, the scale of authority is tilted toward the federal and state levels. Most of the important intervening agencies in Mesa de Otay's development were either federal or state. The key planning agency, the Ministry of Human Settlements and Public Works (SAHOP) was based in Mexico City and Mexicali (the state capital of Baja California). The key housing development agencies, the National Institute for Community Development (INDECO) and the National Institute for Housing Promotion (INFONAVIT), were both federal as well. Of the local agencies involved, neither of the two municipal offices (Office of the Mayor, Office of Public Services and Works) had substantial input into major funding or land-use location decisions, except insofar as they were able to negotiate with the governor of Baja California during that period. In the United States, the planning process and funding decisions tended to favor local government entities. The key decision-making structures in San Diego during the period 1970–1984 included the Office of the Mayor, the City Council, the County Board of Supervisors, and the City Planning Department, all locally based. Most of the instances of intervention at higher levels of government occurred because of the proximity to an international boundary—the General Services Administration manages all international border facilities (the second border crossing), and the Economic Development Administration was involved in funding a federal program aimed at creating an economic development center at Otay Mesa. The only truly important higher level of government intervention was in the area of transportation funding, for which San Diego depended on both the state and federal governments for support in building the highway to the second border crossing.

Land-Use Planning Instruments.   Analysis of the land-use decision process reveals significant cross-national variation in the nature of intervention, the legal bases for that intervention, and the methods for planning and regulating the use of land. We might term these differences the "instruments" of land-use planning. One way of studying these kinds of disparities is to focus on the unique policy histories of land planning on each side of the border. Tables 27 and 28 summarize the policy histories of development planning on each side of the boundary across the Otay Mesa.

In San Diego (Table 27), we observe that the planning process was built around legally defined, standardized instruments of planning, such as the Community Plan (or Master Plan) and the Environmental Impact Analysis. New land development in the United States must conform, by law, to zoning restrictions and land-use regulations defined in a comprehensive or master plan for the city. In San Diego, community-level plans are also now institutionalized for most densely populated subregions. We also see a planning process that moved from the level of studies, to analysis through standardized planning instruments (environmental impact reports, community plans), leading up to local legislative approval—the final layer of the planning process. At each major stage of land-use decisions, the role of government was to review the feasibility of specific land-use proposals (second border crossing, freeway, international airport, correctional facility). These reviews suggest that planning in the United States is very much a "policing" mechanism; that is, it serves more to prevent harmful land-use decisions than to promote positive ones.

The Mexican land-use planning process is quite distinct, as the policy history of Mesa de Otay's development hints (Table 28). First, government planning of important land-use districts like the Mesa de Otay typically involves state expropriation of land. Although most of the Mesa de Otay lands were once part of two *ejidos*, Mexican law allows the government to expropriate land if it is to be developed in the "public interest." In 1970, the government expropriated most of the Mesa de Otay, separating it into two public trusts (*fideicomisos*), one for industrial development, the other for residential use. Not only does government often become the owner of land for development, it engages in planning only as it determines that properties are

Table 27. Otay Mesa Development Planning, San Diego

	Type of Policy Action	Description	Government Agency Involved
1965–70	Planning report: *Border Area Plan*	Study of future development of south San Diego, including Otay Mesa	City of San Diego (local)
1971–72	Planning report: *Second Border Crossing Planning Report*	Evaluation of feasibility of second border crossing at Otay Mesa	General Services Administration (federal)
1973	Legislative approval of public works project	San Diego City Council and County Board of Supervisors endorse second border crossing project for Otay Mesa	City Council; County Board of Supervisors (local)
1973	Planning report: *Feasibility of International Airport on Otay Mesa*	Detailed report on the fiscal, environmental, and social consequences of building an international airport on Otay Mesa	Comprehensive Planning Organization (local)
1974	Planning report: *Environmental Impact Analysis*	Environmental study of the impact of the proposed freeway to the second border crossing on Otay Mesa	County of San Diego (local)
1977	Planning report: *Otay Mesa Correctional Facility*	Recommendation for construction of a medium-security correctional facility on Otay Mesa	State of California Dept. of Corrections (state)
1980	Legislative approval of community plan	Formal approval of the Otay Mesa Community Plan (Land-Use Element and Environmental Impact Report)	City Council (local)

Source: Herzog, 1985b, p. 38.

Table 28. Mesa de Otay Development Planning, Tijuana

	Type of Policy Action	Description	Government Agency Involved
Pre-1970	Taking of land by federal government to form *ejidos*	Mesa de Otay lands are organized into agricultural cooperatives (*ejidos*)	Ministry of Agrarian Reform (federal)
1970	Taking of land; creation of public trusts by federal decree	Mesa de Otay *ejidos* expropriated and two public trusts (*fideicomisos*) are formed: one for residential development, the other for industry	Commission for Border Development (federal); National Institute for Community Development (federal); Office of Governor (state)
1970–76	Planning and engineering reports, various projects on the Mesa de Otay	Feasibility studies of road construction, the new airport, residential development, and the university	Ministry of Transport (federal); Ministry of Human Settlements and Public Works (federal, state)
1972– present	Residential development	Construction of multi-family attached residential units for approximately 10,000 persons on the Mesa de Otay	National Institute for Community Development (federal, state); National Institute for Housing Promotion (federal)
1977– present	Industrial development	Construction of an industrial park (New Tijuana) on the eastern edge of the Mesa de Otay	Industrial Parks Program (federal); New Tijuana Industrial City (state); Ministry of Human Settlements and Public Works (federal, state)
1981–82	Formation of a new "substate" planning agency	Creation of the Urban Development Office to administer development on the Mesa de Otay	Office of the Governor, State of Baja California (state)

Source: Herzog, 1985b, p. 39.

suitable for certain types of development. Unlike its U.S. counterpart, the lands on Mesa de Otay were never submitted to any standardized test for development feasibility (for example, a master plan, environmental regulation format, or subdivision plan). The government in Mexico City simply formulated a plan for the development of the mesa and then hired engineers and consultants to study the feasibility of the intended uses. A simple analogy can be made. The Mexican government functions more like a private developer: it owns the land and formulates a plan of action for development; it studies that development from a marketing point of view, not a regulatory one (as in the United States). As the government determined that its intended land uses for Tijuana's Mesa de Otay were economically feasible, it launched into the construction phase with residential development (starting in 1972) and industrial development (beginning in 1977). Nearly one hundred factories occupy the New Tijuana Industrial Park on the Mesa de Otay today.

The Mexican government's role in the planning process is considerably more authoritarian than that of the U.S. government. The Mexican government is given considerable legal power over land-use decisions; few standardized sources of community input exist to balance the decision-making process. The fact that most of the decisions are made outside the city (at state and federal government offices) further removes municipal residents from land-use decisions that affect their city. Although most of the policy decisions in San Diego were of a regulatory nature, those in Tijuana were not; they were oriented toward facilitating development decisions that had already been reached. The land-use decision process mirrors the structure of Mexican politics more generally: many decisions are made secretly and then legitimized through the government machinery. Mexican planning is not so much about regulation of urban development as it is about state intervention in promoting the goals of those in power who decide how urban space will be transformed. It is a process that is largely determined in state capitals and in the seat of the federal government.

Divergent Land-Use Outcomes

The best way to demonstrate that land-use planning is different in two places is to observe the outcomes of the planning and decision-making processes. I have argued that the use of land on both sides of the boundary at Otay Mesa was filtered through very different political machinery in two cities, San Diego and Tijuana. If a common understanding of the inherent cross-border impacts of land use existed, it would not be unreasonable to expect that some complementarity of land-use decisions might have taken place. On the other hand, if the processes of land development unfolded in a virtually independent manner, then the outcome could be two very different land-use patterns. We can apply this simple test to the case of Otay Mesa/Mesa de Otay.

In fact, the land patterns at Otay Mesa are very different. The first obvious difference is in the timing of construction. Mexico is more than ten years ahead of the United States in developing its side of the mesa. By 1985, Mexico had already built an international airport, two universities, an industrial park, and substantial residential development on the mesa. More recently, a large regional shopping center and new industrial sites, as well as residential development, have been placed on the mesa. In the United States, before 1985, the only developments there were a few scattered residences, a small commercial airport (Brown Field), and a handful of light-manufacturing establishments near the airport. Most of the U.S. side of the border was either vacant or under lease to tenant farmers for the cultivation of truck farm crops. Since 1985, the United States has begun to build a large facility near the border called Otay International Center, which eventually will house customs agencies, warehouses, restaurants, and other border-related land uses (Kjos, 1986). There are also plans for a major industrial park west of the second border crossing, and much of the state correctional facility to the north has been completed. Otherwise, however, the mesa remains a vast landscape of agricultural and vacant lands, windswept and decidedly rustic in character.

Not only have there been differences in the timing of development, but land-use decisions on one side have been incompatible with uses across the border. Mexico's decision to build an airport so near the boundary is one example. Of course, it was built when the U.S. side of the border was vacant, thus it was not incompatible at that time. The location of the industrial park directly on the boundary, without a buffer land use, is another possible incompatibility. On the U.S. side, a number of land-use conflicts with Tijuana's development pattern can be identified. At one time, U.S. officials were considering building a Disneyland-style amusement park on the mesa. A second land use under consideration, more recently, is a Grand Prix racetrack. This facility is being seriously considered by the county of San Diego, despite the fact that it is probably not compatible within an area that will have dense residential development, offices, and commercial facilities, and that will require monitoring by U.S. boundary maintenance organizations, such as the Border Patrol and Customs. Such monitoring would be hampered by the construction of a facility like a major racetrack, which would attract large crowds, making boundary vigilance a difficult task.

Perhaps the most serious example of incompatible land-use planning is the location of the State Correctional Facility on Otay Mesa. The original location for this facility was on a site only one hundred yards from the border crossing gate (see Figure 22). Because the state of California had purchased this land in the late 1960s, it assumed it would build a prison there. The prison facility was incorporated into the city's land-use planning agenda until the late 1970s. For nearly a decade, no one really questioned the logic of placing a prison at an international border crossing with Mexico. Finally, in the late 1970s, the City Council of San Diego recognized that this was probably not an appropriate use of the land, and several years later, the idea of a land swap with the state allowed the city to relocate the prison site away from the border. But the startling point is that throughout the period of planning for Otay Mesa's development, no formal mechanism existed on the U.S. side of the border to consider the impact of land uses close to the boundary with Tijuana. Equally, no such mechanism existed in Tijuana to consider land-use impacts on San Diego. Each nation developed its own land and then, in the last instance, considered whether any diplomatic problems might grow out of a particular land use. There was clearly very little coordination of land uses as they were planned and developed on either side of the boundary.

Conclusion: The Political Economy of Urban Space on the U.S.–Mexico Border

8

> *'Good fences make good neighbors.'*
> —Robert Frost, "Mending Wall"

IN THE LAST THREE DECADES, a prolific agenda of social science research questions has emerged as a result of the demographic transformation of the U.S.–Mexico border zone. Among the topics inspired by this important region is the relationship between international borders and human settlements. As this book has repeatedly pointed out, the appearance of sizable urban areas along the political boundary line throws into disarray the traditional economic geographer's view of boundaries. Borders no longer repel; they attract economic activities and inhabitants. The transformation of the U.S.–Mexico borderlands from a rural, frontier outpost to an urbanizing interface between two expanding nations unleashes a range of important spatial and regional questions, a number of which have been addressed in this volume. These questions are not exclusive to the U.S.–Mexico border. Cities and towns have evolved along other borders, notably those in western Europe and between the United States and Canada, although in smaller magnitudes. Their growth is symptomatic of changing political-economic and technological relationships between and across nation-states. The scale of trade, transportation, production, communication, and decision making has led to a necessary abandonment of traditional theories of political geography and territorial politics. Among the by-products of a new political "spatiality" is a world system that does not operate solely on the basis of nation-states. In this light the formal edges of nation-states—political boundaries—blur, and in an era of fading political boundary lines, we must rethink their meaning and reconsider the changing human geographic formations around them.

Macrolevel forces—economic, technological, and political—have ushered in a global territorial metamorphosis, which in turn generates new theoretical questions. The changing human geography of the international border between the United States and Mexico carries with it two broad, intersecting conceptual challenges: first, explanation of the changing role of international borders; and second, analysis of the unique spatial configurations, or "transfrontier metropolises," evolving along the border. The latter topic requires an understanding of the cross-cultural elements of spatial structure. These cross-cultural features become central to understanding the political economy of space in the U.S.–Mexico borderlands. Here, one finds a border zone that is shared by a First and a Third World nation. The confrontation between these two disparate societies, as expressed in space, is abrupt. Urbanization intensifies the geographic juxtaposition of two cultures; a built environment spills across the artificial boundary; urban planning problems float freely across the border between two sovereign nation-states. The "transfrontier metropolis" becomes a geographically determined microcosm of U.S.–Mexico relations.

The Social Ecology of the Transfrontier Metropolis

To date, scant scholarly literature exists on the notion of a bicultural urban spatial configuration, or transfrontier metropolis. Such an entity has evolved along the U.S.–Mexico border. It displays a social ecology that is substantially shaped by two nations. Only a few scholars have recognized this phenomenon (Dillman, 1969; Gildersleeve, 1978; House, 1982). Geographers have perhaps been slow to respond conceptually to border urbanization because of first, a reluctance to move beyond the ideas of classical economic geographers (for example, Christaller and Losch), who emphasized the debilitating effects of boundaries; and second, a discipline-wide reluctance, following several decades of reaction against idiographic approaches to the study of regions, to engage in systematic regional analysis oriented toward the construction of theory. This should elicit concern among those who believe that "regional geography is the highest form of the geographer's art" (Hart, 1972).

A spatially unified, transborder ecological structure is evolving along the international boundary. In nearly every site where urbanization has occurred, it has unfolded not on only one side of the border, but on both. Urbanization has become a boundary-transcending process. It is fueled by common social history, overlapping physical environments, and the forces of capital. This book has examined two different roles a boundary can play: it divides two cultures and two urban structures, yet it houses regions that have become socially and ecologically unified over time and across space.

The spatial dynamics of border settlements reflects the contradictions that are built into the organization of social life in this unique region. We might label the urban political-geographic pattern as one in which there is a "friction/fusion" relationship. Many frictions grow out of the confrontation between the postindustrial North and the industrializing South. Not only are U.S. and Mexican cities structured differently in a morphological sense, they place radically different values on location *within* the city. Among the salient differences in urban structure outlined in this volume are land-use patterns, transport networks, and social geography. The political processes that shape cities also vary considerably on both sides of the border. Mexico's highly centralized, one-party system produces urban structures molded in the interests of the national government and filtered through the investments of a private sector greatly constrained by the wide-reaching net of regulations, trusts, and other intervention forms the government imposes on the urban scene. At the same time, changes in the urban landscape are produced by local and regional elites in concert with the ruling party power structure. In the United States, planning is highly regulatory, and the private sector has more freedom to develop and maximize profits gained from land-use change. There is considerable lobbying and exercise of power and authority at the local level. In Mexico, power struggles are elevated to the level of state and often national politics.

Although cities on both sides function independently, there is much evidence of "fusion" in the spatial organization of twin city areas like Tijuana–San Diego. The juxtaposition of city structures has been encouraged by historical and territorial linkages, cycles of migration and family ties, economically motivated cross-boundary travel, and reciprocal environmental processes. Geographic proximity appears to be a major catalyst of these integrating processes and should not be underestimated as a force in the emergence of transfrontier ecological systems.

The Political Economy of Border Urban Space

Urban space is never devoid of political influence, especially not at the U.S.–Mexico border. The common living space encircled in "twin city" regions is a geographic arena for the clashing of interests between two very different nations. Negotiation of common border problems is increasingly tied to the foreign policy agendas of the two nations.

Despite many forms of transboundary interaction, the political economy of urban space on the U.S.–Mexico border is marked by a high level of inequality. Spatial structures and cityscapes contrast sharply. The differences are not merely visual and geometrical—they derive from a more profound economic asymmetry that is at the root of the political economy of international border space. In regions like Tijuana–San Diego, the visual landscape, divided at the border, serves to underscore the vast economic gap separating the two nations. We have seen some of the dimensions of this inequality: consumer behavior (the drain of Mexican income into the United States), assembly-plant territorial impacts (the lack of long-term regional economic benefits for Mexico), and the political economy of Mexican American neighborhoods in the United States (which are the by-products of waves of Mexican immigration to the United States).

One measure of the economic asymmetry between U.S. and Mexican border cities can be gleaned from Table 29. It offers a simple comparison of public sector capital improvement budgets for Tijuana and San Diego in three different years. The figures, although not entirely comparable because of differences in funding categories and public financing systems, are, even in their crude form, revealing. In 1978, Tijuana's budget of $17.3 million was mainly devoted to urban development projects (principally the construction of the River Zone channelization project and the development of Mesa de Otay) and highways. By 1981, just prior to the peso devaluation, Tijuana had doubled its capital improvement budget to $32.1 million, again spending heavily on urban development (nearly 60 percent of total capital improvement monies) and highways, but also allocating over $7 million toward upgrading its antiquated water and sewage infrastructure. Following the peso devaluation of 1982, capital improvements dwindled to only $4.1 million.

Although it is true that this figure slightly undervalues the resources available to the Mexican government at that moment (Mexico

Table 29. Public Sector Capital Improvement Budgets, Tijuana and San Diego (millions of dollars)

Category	1978	1981	1982
Tijuana			
Urban development	8.6	19.2	2.3
Highways	4.8	5.5	0.8
Water and sewerage	0.8	7.3	0.6
Electrification	2.7	0.1	0.3
Airport	0.4	—	0.1
Total	17.3	32.1	4.1
San Diego			
Community development	11.6	12.2	15.9
Downtown/city redevelopment[a]	17.1	35.7	54.0
Transportation			
City	18.1	19.5	19.1
MTDB[b]	—	12.2	24.3
CALTRANS[c]	117.0	49.3	75.5
Water utilities	26.8	35.6	19.9
Parks and recreation	5.7	22.0	24.1
Other	4.0	8.0	12.7
Total	200.3	194.5	245.5

Sources: Tijuana: Secretaría de Desarrollo Urbano y Ecología, 1985; San Diego (unless otherwise noted): City of San Diego, 1978, 1981, 1982.

Notes: Peso exchange rates used to calculate dollar equivalency: 1978, 22.50:1; 1981, 24.50:1; 1982, 70:1. Figures include federal, state, and local monies spent.

a. Redevelopment Agency of San Diego, 1978, 1981, 1982.
b. Metropolitan Transit Development Board, 1983.
c. California Dept. of Transportation, 1987. Data for city and county of San Diego.

could buy more urban infrastructure immediately following the devaluation than the dollar conversions indicate), the figure still contrasts dramatically with the neighboring U.S. city. San Diego spent more than ten times as much as Tijuana in 1978 ($200.3 million), six times as much in 1981, and over forty times as much in 1982. One government agency alone—the California Department of Transportation (CALTRANS)—allocated more money for highway transportation in 1982 ($75.5 million) than was spent in all categories for Tijuana for all three years (1978, 1981, 1982) combined. San Diego's water utilities budget in any one year was greater than all capital improvement monies together in Tijuana in that year. The figures simply confirm the enormous difference between the economies of the two nations, including the cities that meet at the border.

These asymmetries have political expressions as well. Glaring differences exist with respect to the impact of political systems on urban space. In Mexico, the federal government exerts an imposing control over urban space. In the United States, this power lies with the incorporated local governments. Suburban municipalities have gained considerable clout in U.S. cities, because of the resources they control through locally collected property taxes. In Mexico, urban conflicts grow out of the social problems embedded in the urban fabric—lack of landownership, services, and adequate housing. In the United States, the principal location conflicts—political control (annexation), growth management, pollution—derive from the decentralized political organization of space. Government intervention in cities ("planning") also varies cross-culturally.

A clear pattern of segmentation of social space is characteristic of cities on both sides of the border. But the magnitude of difference in social inequality is enormous. Perhaps this fact alone is ultimately the single most important socioeconomic feature of the U.S.–Mexico borderlands. If we compare the socioeconomic levels of two border cities, like San Diego and Tijuana, we confirm that the international boundary's most profound meaning is that it continues to divide a Third World nation from a First World one. Table 30, for example, offers a simple comparison of social groups, stratified by income, for Tijuana and San Diego. We see that in Tijuana more than 50 percent of the economically active population (people who are employed or looking for work) earned less than $3,456 per year in 1980. This contrasts sharply with San Diego, where the bottom 50 percent of the urban area's households earned $20,000 or less, nearly seven times the amount the bottom half of the Tijuana population earned. In general, there were large clusters of Tijuana's population earning between $1,885 and $6,336 per year, whereas in San Diego the largest proportions of urban households fall in the income range $10,000 to $34,999, or five times the average income recorded in Tijuana. The Tijuana figures were recorded in 1980, before the beginning of a financial collapse in Mexico, so today they may be even worse by comparison with San Diego. Furthermore, the recorded 1980 incomes in Tijuana do not capture the magnitude of poverty as it affects thou-

Table 30. Income Breakdowns, Tijuana and San Diego, 1980 (dollars)

Tijuana[a]			San Diego[b]		
Annual Income	Number	% Total	Annual Income	Number	% Total
$0	15,321	9.4	Less than $5,000	74,605	11.1
1–300	2,532	1.5	5,000–7,499	52,590	7.8
301–564	2,748	1.7	7,500–9,999	56,219	8.4
565–1,032	5,449	3.4	10,000–14,999	109,200	16.3
1,033–1,884	11,401	7.0	15,000–19,999	94,255	14.1
1,885–3,456	47,732	29.5	20,000–24,999	81,015	12.1
3,457–6,336	29,580	18.3	25,000–34,999	104,623	15.6
6,337–11,592	10,814	6.7	35,000–49,999	62,207	9.3
11,593 +	4,912	3.0	50,000 +	35,920	5.3
Not reported	31,575	19.5			
Total	162,064	100.0		670,634	100.0

Sources: Tijuana: Instituto Nacional de Estadística, Geografía e Información, 1983, p. 20; San Diego: U.S. Bureau of the Census, 1983, p. 269, Table P 11.

a. Economically active population.
b. Data for households in the San Diego Standard Metropolitan Statistical Area (SMSA).

sands of marginal residents who are not among the economically active population, and who ultimately earn their income through the informal economy, working as vendors and occasional employees, including illegal ventures.

Another measure of the socioeconomic chasm dividing Tijuana from San Diego can be found in the conditions of housing and neighborhood life. An example is offered in Table 31, which shows that in Tijuana in 1980, only 56.8 percent of all private households had piped water inside their homes. In fact, 27.1 percent of Tijuana's population in 1980 had no running water in their homes. Some observers feel that these figures underestimate the severity of scarce water services. In San Diego, only 1.1 percent of all households in 1980 lacked complete plumbing facilities.

The Management of Border Urban Space: Policy Considerations

Can border space be cooperatively managed? This is not an innocuous query. The scale and structural dimensions of border urban space generate a need for some form of U.S.–Mexico cooperation that

Table 31. Comparison of Water Service, Tijuana and San Diego, 1980

	Number	%
Tijuana		
Total private households	96,833	100.0
With piped water inside house	55,051	56.8
Without piped water in house, but in building	13,163	13.6
Without piped water in house, but in public tap	1,595	1.7
Without water	26,271	27.1
No data	753	0.8
San Diego		
Total housing units	720,346	100.0
With complete plumbing facilities	712,273	98.9
Lacking complete plumbing facilities	8,073	1.1

Sources: Tijuana: Instituto Nacional de Estadística, Geografía e Información, 1983, p. 35; San Diego: U.S. Bureau of the Census, 1983, p. H-1.

may lead into a new area of foreign policy. A number of the conceptual foundations for such a policy area have been addressed in this volume. These can be viewed at both the micro and macro levels of analysis.

At the micro level, this study has demonstrated that a binational set of problems now plagues border city regions like Tijuana–San Diego. These problems stretch across three levels of the border ecosystem: the social, physical, and built environments. At the micro level of analysis, border spatial planning involves the regulation of negative externalities that originate on either side of the boundary, spilling over to the other side. In the built environment, a rather large agenda of transborder issues has emerged, including land-use planning, transport development, sewage control, river channelization, housing, and industrial policy.

Despite the sizable inventory of common border issues, evidence suggests that most border problems are resolved on an ad hoc basis. They are dealt with by different bureaucracies in each nation, often working independently of each other. In some cases, there is little if any cross-border communication. Joint urban planning simply does not occur at the border. In the case studies outlined in this book, we have seen that, despite considerable spatial reciprocity, San Diego and Tijuana approach the governance of space in different ways. Differences stem not only from vastly dissimilar political systems, but from contrasting socioeconomic and cultural contexts, which lead officials to carry dissimilar objectives into the urban development process. For example, Table 32 summarizes the responses of two sets of decision makers to the question: What are the major issues facing the Tijuana–San Diego region? Reacting to their unique sociopolitical context, Mexican leaders expressed the most concern about the economic benefits that might result from changes along the border—the second border crossing, construction of a trolley system, and economic development. They were also concerned about population growth. U.S. leaders responded to the negative impacts associated with the border connection—undocumented aliens, water quality, sewage, air quality, and flood control. They also considered cross-border communication important, despite Tijuana's negative image and the lack of a federal policy toward the border.

On a more macro level, it is clear that the management of border problems has become a salient item on the agenda of U.S.–Mexican relations. Ronfeldt and Sereseres (1983) regard borderlands questions as one of the eight major categories of bilateral negotiation between the United States and Mexico. The others are: international credit,

Table 32. Major Issues Facing the Tijuana–San Diego Region, 1980–1985

Mexican View (Tijuana)	U.S. View (San Diego)
1. Economic development (32%)	1. Undocumented aliens (79%)
2. Construction of San Diego–Tijuana Trolley (30%)	2. Cross-border communication (62%)
3. Second border crossing (30%)	3. Economic development (47%)
4. Population growth (30%)	4. Water quality (45%)
5. Río Tijuana Urban Development Project (24%)	5. Sewage control (43%)
6. Economic interdependence (24%)	6. Air quality (32%)
7. Unemployment (20%)	7. Lack of federal policy (32%)
8. Narcotics traffic (20%)	8. Tijuana's negative image in San Diego (30%)
9. Industrial development (18%)	9. Second border crossing (28%)
10. Tourism (18%)	10. Flood control (23%)

Source: Consejo Tijuana and San Diego Council, 1981.

petroleum/natural gas, trade and protectionism, in-bond industries, tourism, undocumented workers, and drugs/narcotics. Rico (1983) has suggested that border problems represent not only one of the more crucial themes in U.S.–Mexican relations in the post–World War II era, but also one of the most revealing, if one attempts to understand the complex and often misunderstood notion of interdependence. A leading Mexican expert on relations with the United States has noted that the border is the one feature that separates U.S.–Mexican relations from those between the United States and all other Latin American nations (Ojeda, 1976).

What is the nature of the border decision-making process across the two thousand–mile boundary? Two broad approaches to intergovernmental negotiation can be identified: formal and informal. Formal negotiations between the governments of the United States and Mexico are normally channeled through agreements reached in three ways: treaties, presidential meetings, and interparliamentary conferences (Mendoza Berrueto, 1984). For the most part, formal cooperative arrangements between the two nations have not been terribly successful along the border. With the exception of the International Boundary and Water Commission—which has been successful in negotiating border flood control, salinity, water pollution, and water management issues—most formal organizations, like the U.S.–Mexico Trade Commission (formed in 1965) and the U.S.–Mexico Commission for Border Development and Friendship (1966), have fallen by the wayside. A major impediment to border problem solving has been that key decision makers on both sides of the border are located in the national capitals. As one inside official has observed: "There is often the perception along the border that bureaucrats in the two capital cities are out of touch, disinterested, or not understanding of border matters" (Storing, 1984, p. 3). Given that formal decision-making has often been unable to resolve ongoing border problems, local leaders have turned to informal negotiation. Informal dialogue between officials in bureaucratic organizations on either side of the border has led to cooperative arrangements on boundary matters such as criminal justice, firefighting, pollution control, and traffic management (Sloan and West, 1976).

Despite these intermittent forms of cross-border dialogue, the enormous political-economic polarization between the United States and Mexico has impeded the evolution of any sustained form of transboundary cooperation in the management of city growth problems. Instead, radically different bureaucratic structures, government systems, and policy instruments end up being marshaled toward urban spatial planning on either side of the border. More profound barriers to joint resolution of the impacts of urbanization also exist. The two nations cling to their sovereignty and, at this time, seem reluctant to trade off control over national territorial destiny for the recognition of a transboundary "community of interests."

This places the U.S.–Mexico borderlands in a very different category from western European borders. For the past two decades there has been increasing attention paid to the organization of formal transborder planning mechanisms in western Europe. Some observers have even suggested that this approach could be applicable to the U.S.–Mexico border region (Hansen, 1983). The western European model has been successful in creating not only mechanisms for dialogue and research, but legal instruments for transboundary coordination. Formal agreements have been reached on such matters as cross-border pollution control, river navigation, road and air transport engineering, public health planning, and regulation of frontier workers (Council of Europe, 1982).

The western European transfrontier planning model owes its success to the multistate, interparliamentary political structure. The Council of Europe, an advisory social and juridical arm of the more powerful European Economic Community (EEC), administers the transfrontier coordination process. Clearly, in Europe there is greater recognition of the advantages of cross-border cooperation, growing out of the complementarities of trade and economic interaction reinforced through the EEC.

No such interparliamentary structure has emerged between the United States and Mexico, in part because of the obvious political-economic disparities. Thus, the likelihood of creating such cross-boundary cooperative mechanisms is small. Even when a land formation such as the one reviewed in Chapter 7 literally overlaps the boundary between two border cities, urban development will be differentially timed, and of a completely distinct character. At this time, binational land-use planning does not seem possible along the U.S.–Mexico border.

These circumstances, however, may not be entirely counterproductive. Observing the transfrontier ecological dimensions of border cities, Friedmann has distinguished between a "spatial-economic region" (which may transcend a political boundary) and a "territorial political community" (which should not). In a border metropolitan area, notes Friedmann (1984, p. 147), it is necessary to preserve the two political jurisdictions created by the boundary, because "territorial politics should precede economics and the political will of a community should, in every instance, prevail over economic interests."

National sovereignty may, therefore, provide a buffer against abuses of border relationships by business and capital, which, after all, are for the most part controlled by forces in the north. Sovereignty may represent one way for a country to withstand the forces of global capital that threaten to undo centuries of evolution of national political culture and its by-products, including cities. Thus, there is a paradox in the urbanization of the borderlands: although this geographic zone is one of the most important places in the world where ecological, social, and economic processes challenge traditional ideas about boundaries, especially with respect to spatial organization, the political-economic differences between the two neighboring nations create formidable and perhaps reasonable barriers to cross-border planning. Do good fences make good neighbors on the U.S.–Mexico border? This question will continue to represent a great challenge to politicians, writers, and scholars, and to the inhabitants of the growing cities along the only corridor of land in the world where North meets South.

REFERENCES

Abu Lughod, J. 1984. "Culture, Modes of Production and the Changing Nature of the Arab World." In J. Agnew et al., eds., *The City in Cultural Context*, pp. 94–119. Boston: Allen & Unwin.

Acevedo Cárdenas, C., D. Piñera, and J. Ortíz. 1985. "Semblanza de Tijuana, 1915–1930." In D. Piñera, ed., *Historia de Tijuana*, pp. 93–105. Tijuana: Centro de Investigaciones Históricas, UNAM-UABC.

Acevedo Ramírez, R. 1985. "20 mil extranjeros se apoderan de la costa en el estado." *El Heraldo*, November 21.

Adams, J. 1970. "Residential Structure of Midwestern Cities." *Annals of the Association of American Geographers* 60: 37–60.

Agnew, J. 1978. "Market Relations and Locational Conflict in Cross–National Perspective." In K. Cox, ed., *Urbanization and Conflict in Market Societies*, pp. 128–143. Chicago: Maaroufa Press.

Agnew, J., J. Mercer, and D. Sopher, eds. 1984. *The City in Cultural Context.* Boston: Allen & Unwin.

Allinson, G. 1984. "Japanese Urban Society and Its Cultural Context." In J. Agnew et al., eds., *The City in Cultural Context*, pp. 163–185. Boston: Allen & Unwin.

Alonso, W. 1965. *Location and Land Use.* Cambridge: Harvard University Press.

———. 1971. "The Economics of Urban Size." *Papers of the Regional Science Association* 26: 67–83.

Alvarez, J. 1986. "Contaminación atmosférica: Cuenca Tijuana–San Diego, un estudio de caso." In J. Alvarez and V. Castillo, eds., *Ecología y Frontera/ Ecology and the Borderlands*, pp. 137–156. Tijuana: UABC.

Alvarez, R. 1984. "The Border as Social System: The California Case." *New Scholar* 9: 119–133.

Amato, P. 1969. "Environmental Quality and Locational Behavior in a Latin American City." *Urban Affairs Quarterly* 9: 83–101.

———. 1970. "Elitism and Settlement Patterns in the Latin American City." *Journal of the American Institute of Planners* 36: 96–105.

American Institute of Architects. 1987. *Regional Urban Design Assistance Team Briefing Book.* San Diego: City of San Diego.

Amin, S. 1974. *Accumulation on a World Scale: A Critique of the Theory of Underdevelopment.* New York: Monthly Review Press.

Anderson, J., N. Clement, and K. Shellhammer. 1980. "Economic Importance of the U.S. Southwest Border Regions." Working Paper No. 1. California Border Area Resource Center, San Diego.

Anderson, M. 1982. "The Political Problems of Frontier Regions." *West European Politics* 5: 1–17.

Anthony, H. 1979. *The Challenge of Squatter Settlements.* Vancouver: University of British Columbia Press.

Appendini, K., and D. Murayama. 1972. "Desarrollo desigual en México, 1900–1960." In D. Barkin, ed., *Los beneficiarios del desarrollo regional,* pp. 125–150. Mexico City: SEP/Setentas.

Associated Press. 1986. "Customs Unionist Says Border Control Lost." *San Diego Union.*

Baker, M. 1980. "San Ysidro: A Case in Metropolitan Colonialism." M.A. thesis, California State University, Long Beach.

Banamex. 1983. *México social 1983.* Mexico City: Banco de México.

Banco de México. 1987. *Indicadores económicos.* Mexico City: Banco de México.

Barkin, D. 1970. *Regional Economic Development: The River Approach in Mexico.* New York: Cambridge University Press.

Barnet, R. J., and R. E. Muller. 1974. *Global Reach: The Power of Multinational Corporations.* New York: Simon & Schuster.

Barrera, M., C. Muñoz, and C. Ornelas. 1972. "The Barrio as an Internal Colony." In H. Hahn, ed., *People and Politics in Urban Society,* pp. 465–498. Beverly Hills: Sage.

Bath, R. 1986. "Environmental Issues in the United States–Mexico Borderlands." *Journal of Borderlands Studies* 1: 49–72.

Beals, R. 1953. "Social Stratification in Latin America." *American Journal of Sociology* 58: 327–339.

Becklund, L. 1978. "Tijuana Demolishing Homes of 25,000." *Los Angeles Times,* March 18.

Beckmann, M. 1984. "Borders as Locations of Economic Activities." In A. Corona R. and L. Gibson, eds., *Regional Impacts of United States–Mexican Economic Relations,* pp. 333–339. Mexico City: Colegio de México.

Bell, D. 1976. *The Coming of Post Industrial Society.* New York: Basic Books.

Bennett, V. 1987. "Urban Water Services and Social Conflict: The Water Crisis in Monterrey, Mexico, 1973–1985. Ph.D. dissertation, University of Texas, Austin.

Berry, B. J. L. 1959. "Ribbon Developments in the Urban Business Pattern." *Annals of the Association of American Geographers* 49: 145–155.

———. 1961. "City Size Distributions and Economic Development." *Economic Development and Culture Change* 9: 573–587.

———. 1967. *Geography of Market Centers and Retail Distribution.* Englewood Cliffs: Prentice-Hall.

Berry, B., and F. Horton. 1970. *Geographic Perspectives on Urban Systems.*

Englewood Cliffs: Prentice-Hall.

Bevans, C. I., ed. 1972. *Treaties and Other International Agreements of the United States of America 1776–1949.* Vol. 9. Washington, D.C.: U.S. Government Printing Office.

Bilbray, B. 1983. Field interview, San Diego.

Bish, R. L. 1971. *The Public Economy of Metropolitan Areas.* Chicago: Markham Publishing Co.

Boggs, S. W. 1940. *International Boundaries—A Study of Boundary Functions and Problems.* New York: Columbia University Press.

Bolton, H. 1921. *The Spanish Borderlands: A Chronicle of Old Florida and the Southwest.* New Haven: Yale University Press.

Borah, W. 1954. "Race and Class in Mexico." *Pacific Historical Review* 23: 331–342.

Borchert, J. R. 1967. "American Metropolitan Evolution." *Geographical Review* 57: 301–322.

Bourne, L. 1982. "Urban Spatial Structure: An Introductory Essay on Concepts and Criteria." In L. Bourne, ed., *Internal Structure of the City,* pp. 28–45. New York: Oxford University Press.

Bowden, M. J. 1971. "Downtown through Time: Delimitation, Expansion, and Internal Growth." *Economic Geography* 47: 121–135.

Brookfield, H. 1975. *Interdependent Development.* Pittsburgh: University of Pittsburgh Press.

Brown, H. 1986. "Air Pollution Problems in the Tijuana–San Diego Air Basin." In L. Herzog, ed., *Planning the International Border Metropolis,* pp. 39–44. La Jolla: Center for U.S.–Mexican Studies, monograph no. 19.

Bustamante, J. 1975. "El programa fronterizo de maquiladoras: Observaciones para una evaluación." *Foro Internacional* 16: 183–204.

———. 1978. "Commodity Migrants: Structural Analysis of Mexican Immigration to the United States." In S. Ross, ed., *Views across the Border,* pp. 183–203. Albuquerque: University of New Mexico Press.

———. 1985. "Surgimiento de la Colonia Libertad." In D. Piñera, ed., *Historia de Tijuana,* pp. 316–331. Tijuana: Centro de Investigaciones Históricas, UNAM-UABC.

Cabrera Fernández, C. 1978. "El desarrollo económico de Tijuana en relación al suministro de agua y la contaminación atmosférica, marina y acuática." *Natural Resources Journal* 18: 11–27.

Calleo, D., and S. Strange. 1984. "Money and World Politics." In S. Strange, ed., *Paths to International Political Economy,* pp. 91–125. London: Allen & Unwin.

Camarillo, A. 1979. *Chicanos in a Changing Society.* Cambridge: Harvard University Press.

Cameron, G. C. 1973. "Intraurban Location and the New Plant." *Papers of the Regional Science Association* 31: 125–143.

Caplow, T. 1949. "The Social Ecology of Guatemala City." *Social Forces* 28: 113–133.

Carrillo Huerta, M. 1981. "Notas sobre un marco analítico para el estudio de los fenómenos fronterizos México–Estados Unidos." Tijuana: CEFNOMEX.

Carson, D., and S. Larue. 1986. "Firms Accused in Shipping of Toxic Waste to Mexico." *San Diego Union*, February 12.

Castellanos, A. 1981. *Ciudad Juárez: La vida fronteriza.* Mexico City: Editorial Nuestro Tiempo.

Castells, M. 1974. *Monopolville.* Paris: Mouton.

———. 1977. *The Urban Question: A Marxist Approach.* Cambridge: MIT Press.

Castillo, V. 1986. "Desarrollo regional y frontera norte: Conformación regional 1960–1980." In J. Alvarez and V. M. Castillo, eds., *Ecología y frontera,* pp. 71–87. Mexico City: Universidad Autónoma de Baja California, Escuela de Economía.

Chapa, M. A. 1982. "La rebelión en la aldea." *Nexos* 5: 23–27.

Chapin, F. S., and E. Kaiser. 1979. *Urban Land Use Planning.* 3d ed. Urbana: University of Illinois Press.

Chatfield, W. 1893. "Twin Cities of the Border: Brownsville, Texas, and Matamoros, Mexico, and the Colony of the Lower Rio Grande." Manuscript.

Chavira, R. 1981. "Mexico Seeks Solutions in Land Dispute." *San Diego Union,* November 17.

———. 1982. "The New Tijuana: Now It's a Magnet for Mexicans." *San Diego Union,* February 7.

Christaller, W. 1966. *Central Places in Southern Germany.* Englewood Cliffs: Prentice-Hall.

Christopherson, S. 1983. "The Household and Class Formation: Determinants of Residential Location in Ciudad Juárez." *Space and Society* 1: 323–338.

CIC Research, 1978. "Reasons Why People Move to San Diego: A Survey of San Diego County Households." San Diego: CIC Research.

City of San Diego. 1978, 1981, 1982. *Annual Budget.* Vol. 2, *Capital Improvements.* San Diego: City of San Diego Fiscal Management Department.

———. 1979. *Progress Guide and General Plan.* San Diego: City of San Diego.

Claval, P. 1984. "Reflections on the Cultural Geography of the European City." In J. Agnew et al., eds., *The City in Cultural Context,* pp. 31–49. Boston: Allen & Unwin.

Clawson, M. 1975. "Economic and Social Conflicts in Land Use Planning." *Natural Resources Journal* 15: 473–489.

Clawson, M., and P. Hall. 1973. *Planning and Urban Growth.* Baltimore: Johns Hopkins University Press.

Clement, N., and S. Jenner. 1987. "Location Decisions Regarding *Maquiladora*/In-Bond Plants Operating in Baja California, Mexico." Border Issues Series, no. 3. San Diego: Institute for Regional Studies of the Californias.

Coffelt, B. 1973. "No Man's Land: A Transformation." *San Diego Magazine.* December, pp. 84–89, 106–115.

Cohen, S. 1975. *Geography and Politics in a World Divided.* New York: Oxford University Press.

Collier, D. 1976. *Squatters and Oligarchs: Authoritarian Rule and Policy Change in Peru.* Baltimore: Johns Hopkins University Press.

Collins, E. 1970. *International Law in a Changing World.* New York: Random House.

Community Research Associates. 1980. *Undocumented Immigrants: Their Impact on the County of San Diego.* San Diego: County of San Diego.

Comprehensive Planning Organization (CPO). 1975. *Historical Trends: San Diego, 1930–1975* (map). San Diego.

———. 1978. *International Border Crossing: Otay Mesa/Mesa de Otay.* San Diego: CPO.

Consejo Tijuana and San Diego Council. 1981. *A Binational Opinion Survey of San Diego and Tijuana.* San Diego: Nuffer/Smith Associates.

Conway, J. 1986. "Sewage and Public Health: The San Diego–Tijuana Region." In L. Herzog, ed., *Planning the International Border Metropolis,* pp. 27–31. La Jolla: Center for U.S.–Mexican Studies, Monograph no. 19.

Corbridge, S. 1986. *Capitalist World Development: A Critique of Radical Development Geography.* London: Macmillan.

Cornelius, W. 1975. *Politics and the Migrant Poor in Mexico City.* Stanford: Stanford University Press.

Cornelius, W., L. Chávez, and J. Castro, 1982. "Mexican Immigrants and Southern California: A Summary of Current Knowledge." Research Report Series 36. La Jolla: Center for U.S.–Mexican Studies.

Council of Europe. 1977. "Harmonization of Regional Plans in Frontier Regions." *European Regional Planning Study Series.* Strasbourg: Council of Europe.

———. 1979. "The Place of the Peripheral Regions in a European Concept of Regional Planning." *European Regional Planning Study Series.* Strasbourg: Council of Europe.

———. 1982. "The State of Transfrontier Cooperation between Territorial Communities or Authorities." *Conference of European Ministers for Local Government.* Lugano: Council of Europe.

County of San Diego. 1978. *San Ysidro Environmental Plan.* San Diego: County of San Diego.

Cox, K. 1973. *Conflict, Power and Politics in the City.* New York: McGraw-Hill.

———, ed. 1978. *Urbanization and Conflict in Market Societies.* Chicago: Maaroufa Press.

Cox, K., and R. J. Johnson. 1982. *Conflict, Politics and the Urban Scene.* New York: St. Martin's Press.

D'Antonio, W. V., and W. Form. 1965. *Influentials in Two Border Cities.* Notre

Dame: University of Notre Dame Press.

Day, A. 1982. *Border and Territorial Disputes.* London: Longman.

Dear, M. 1974. "A Paradigm for Public Facility Location Theory." *Antipode* 6: 46–50.

———. 1978. "Planning for Mental Health Care: A Reconsideration of Public Facility Location Theory." *International Science Review* 3: 93–111.

Dear M., and A. J. Scott, eds. 1981. *Urbanization and Urban Planning in Capitalist Society.* New York: Methuen.

de la Rosa, Martín. 1985. *Marginalidad en Tijuana.* Tijuana: CEFNOMEX.

Detwyler, T., and M. Marcus. 1972. *Urbanization and Environment.* Belmont, Cal.: Duxbury Press.

Dialogue Information Services Inc., 1986. *National Newspaper Index.*

———. 1986. *Magazine Index.*

Dietz, H. 1978. "Metropolitan Lima: Urban Problem Solving under Military Rule." In W. Cornelius and R. V. Kemper, eds., *Latin American Urban Research.* Vol. 6, pp. 205–226. Beverly Hills: Sage.

Dillman, D. 1969. "Border Town Symbiosis along the Lower Rio Grande as Exemplified by the Twin Cities: Brownsville (Texas) and Matamoros (Tamaulipas)." *Revista Geográfica* 71: 93–113.

———. 1970. "Urban Growth along Mexico's Northern Border and the Mexican National Border Program." *Journal of Developing Areas* 4: 487–507.

———. 1983. "Border Urbanization." In E. Stoddard, R. Nostrand, and J. West, eds., *Borderlands Sourcebook,* pp. 237–244. Norman: University of Oklahoma Press.

Dotson, F., and L. Dotson. 1954. "Ecological Trends in the City of Guadalajara, Mexico." *Social Forces* 32: 367–374.

Duchacek, I. 1986. *The Territorial Dimensions of Politics Within, Among, and Across Nations.* Boulder: Westview Press.

Duemling, R. 1981. "San Diego and Tijuana: Conflict and Cooperation between Two Border Communities." *Executive Seminar in National and International Affairs.* Washington, D.C.: U.S. Department of State.

Duncan, J. S., and N. G. Duncan. 1984. "A Cultural Analysis of Urban Residential Landscapes in North America: The Case of the Anglophile Elite." In J. Agnew et al., eds., *The City in Cultural Context,* pp. 255–276. Boston: Allen & Unwin.

Dupuy, P. M. 1982. "Legal Aspects of Transfrontier Regional Cooperation." *West European Politics* 5: 50–63.

Economic Research Bureau. 1978. *San Diego Economic Profile, 1977.* San Diego: Chamber of Commerce.

Economic Research Bureau, 1985. "Impact of the Peso Devaluation on Retail Sales in San Diego County." *San Diego Economic Bulletin* 33.

Edwards, C. 1985. *The Fragmented World: Competing Perspectives on Trade, Money and Crisis.* London: Methuen.

Enríquez, B. 1973. "International Legal Implications of Industrial Development along the Mexican–U.S. Border." In A. Utton, ed., *Pollution and International Boundaries*, pp. 88–98. Albuquerque: University of New Mexico Press.

Erie, S. 1988. *Rainbow's End: Irish Americans and the Dilemmas of Urban Machine Politics, 1840–1985*. Berkeley & Los Angeles: University of California Press.

Fagen, R., and W. Tuohy. 1972. *Politics and Privilege in a Mexican City*. Stanford: Stanford University Press.

Fainstein, S., and N. Fainstein. 1978. "National Policy and Urban Development." *Social Problems* 26: 139–144.

Fernández, R. 1977. *The United States–Mexican Border: A Politico-Economic Profile*. Notre Dame: University of Notre Dame Press.

Fernández Kelly, P. 1983. *For We Are Sold, I and My People*. Albany: State University of New York Press.

Fike, E. 1986. "The Border at Tijuana: One Square Mile of Hell." *San Diego Union*, May 11.

Ford, L. 1984. "The Historical Evolution of the San Diego Cityscape." In P. Pryde, ed., *San Diego: An Introduction to the Region*, pp. 189–207. Dubuque: Kendall Hunt.

Ford, L., and E. Griffin. 1981. "Chicano Park: Personalizing an Institutional Landscape." *Landscape* 25: 42–48.

Frank, A. G. 1978. *Dependent Accumulation and Underdevelopment*. London: Macmillan.

Friedmann, J. 1972. "The Spatial Organization of Power in the Development of Urban Systems." *Development and Change* 4: 12–50.

———. 1984. "Place, Politics and the Market: The Loss and Recovery of Territorial Values." *New Scholar* 9: 147–152.

Friedmann, J., and R. Morales. 1984. "Transborder Planning: A Case of 'Sophisticated Provocation'?" Paper presented at the Conference on Borderlands Studies, Tijuana, B.C., Mexico.

Fronteras. 1976. *A View of the Border from Mexico*. San Diego: City of San Diego.

Fuentes Romero, D. 1985. "El desarrollo urbano del municipio de Tijuana y el condado de San Diego en un contexto territorial fronterizo." *Ciencias Sociales*, serie 2, cuaderno 3, UABC.

Galarza, E. 1964. *Merchants of Labor: The Mexican Bracero Story*. Santa Barbara: McNally & Loftin.

Gale, S., and E. Moore. 1975. *The Manipulated City*. Chicago: Maaroufa Press.

Gamio, M. 1930. *Mexican Immigration to the United States*. Chicago: University of Chicago Press.

Gandelman, J. 1985. "Wilson Links Mexico Sewage Curbs, Loan OK." *San Diego Union*, January 16.

Gans, H. 1962. *The Urban Villagers*. New York: Free Press.

García, M. 1975. "The Californios of San Diego and the Politics of Accommodation, 1846–1860." *Aztlán* 6: 69–85.

————. 1981. *Desert Immigrants: The Mexicans of El Paso, 1880–1920.* New Haven: Yale University Press.

Garza, G., and M. Schteingart. 1978. *La acción habitacional del estado de México.* Mexico City: Colegio de México.

————. 1978. "Mexico City: The Emerging Metropolis." In W. Cornelius and R. V. Kemper, eds., *Latin American Urban Research.* Vol. 6, pp. 51–85. Beverly Hills: Sage.

General Services Administration, San Diego Office. 1979. Field interview, San Diego.

Gilbert, A. 1981. "Pirates and Invaders: Land Acquisition in Urban Colombia and Venezuela." *World Development* 9: 657–678.

————. 1982. *Urbanization in Contemporary Latin America.* New York: John Wiley & Sons.

————. 1983. "The Tenants of Self-Help Housing: Choice and Constraint in the Housing Market." *Development and Change* 14: 449–477.

Gilbert A., and P. M. Ward. 1985. *Housing, the State and the Poor: Policy and Practice in Three Latin American Cities.* Cambridge: Cambridge University Press.

Gildersleeve, C. 1978. "The International Border City: Urban Spatial Organization in a Context of Two Cultures along the United States–Mexico Boundary." Ph.D. dissertation, University of Nebraska.

Goldberg, M., and J. Mercer. 1986. *The Myth of the North American City.* Vancouver: University of British Columbia Press.

Goodman, R. 1971. *After the Planners.* New York: Simon & Schuster.

Gottman, J. 1973. *The Significance of Territory.* Charlottesville: University Press of Virginia.

Graizbord, B. 1983. "Integración, diferencias regionales e interdependencia en la frontera norte con Estados Unidos." *Demografía y Economía* 17: 1–20.

Graizbord, C. 1986. "Transboundary Land Use Planning: A Mexican Perspective." In L. Herzog, ed., *Planning the International Border Metropolis,* pp. 13–20. La Jolla: Center for U.S.–Mexican Studies, Monograph no. 19.

Grebler, L., J. Moore, and R. Guzmán. 1970. *The Mexican-American People.* New York: Free Press.

Griffin, E., and L. Ford. 1980. "A Model of Latin American City Structure." *Geographical Review* 70: 397–422.

Grindle, M. 1977. *Bureaucrats, Politicians and the Peasantry in Mexico.* Berkeley & Los Angeles: University of California Press.

Gross, L. 1969. *International Law in the Twentieth Century.* New York: Appleton-Century-Crofts.

Grunwald, J., and K. Flamm. 1985. *The Global Factory.* Washington, D.C.: Brookings Institution.

Hall, P. 1966. *Von Thunen's Isolated State*. London: Pergamon Press.

———. 1984. "The Urban Culture and Suburban Culture: A New Look at an Old Paper." In J. Agnew et al., eds., *The City in Cultural Context*, pp. 120–133. Boston: Allen & Unwin.

Hansen, A. 1934. "The Ecology of a Latin American City." In E. B. Reuter, ed. *Race and Culture Contacts*, pp. 124–152. New York: McGraw-Hill.

Hansen, N. 1981. *The Border Economy*. Austin: University of Texas Press.

———. 1983a. "International Cooperation in Border Regions: An Overview and Research Agenda." *International Regional Science Review* 8: 255–270.

———. 1983b. "European Trans-boundary Cooperation and Its Relevance to the United States–Mexico Border." *Journal of the American Institute of Planners* 49: 336–343.

Hardoy, J. E. 1982. "The Building of Latin American Cities." In A. Gilbert, ed., *Urbanization in Contemporary Latin America*, pp. 19–34. New York: John Wiley & Sons.

Harris, C. D., and E. Ullman. 1945. "The Nature of Cities." *Annals of the American Academy of Political Science* 242: 7–17.

Harris, L. 1974. "The Other Side of the Freeway: A Study of Settlement Patterns of Negroes and Mexican-Americans in San Diego, California." Ph.D. dissertation, Carnegie Mellon University.

Harris, N. 1983. *Of Bread and Guns: The World Economy in Crisis*. New York: Penguin Books.

Hart, J. F., ed. 1972. *Regions of the United States*. New York: Harper & Row.

Hartman, C. 1974. *Yerba Buena*. San Francisco: Glide Publications.

Hartshorne, T. 1980. *Interpreting the City: An Urban Geography*. New York: John Wiley & Sons.

Harvey, D. 1978. "Labor, Capital and Class Struggle around the Built Environment in Advanced Capitalist Societies." In K. Cox, ed., *Urbanization and Conflict in Market Societies*, pp. 9–37. Chicago: Maaroufa Press.

———. 1973. *Social Justice and the City*. Baltimore: Johns Hopkins University Press.

Harvey, D., and L. Chatterjee. 1974. "Absolute Rent and the Structuring of Space by Government and Financial Institutions." *Antipode* 6: 22–36.

Hauser, P., and L. Schnore. 1965. *The Study of Urbanization*. New York: John Wiley & Sons.

Hayner, N. 1944. "Oaxaca: City of Old Mexico." *Sociology and Social Research* 29: 87–95.

———. 1945. "Mexico City: Its Growth and Configuration." *American Journal of Sociology* 50: 295–304.

Hedgecock, R. 1986. "Remarks." In L. Herzog, ed., *Planning the International Border Metropolis*, pp. 75–77. La Jolla: Center for U.S.–Mexican Studies, Monograph no. 19.

Heiges, H., F. Stutz, and P. Pryde. 1984. "The Regional Economic and Energy

Base." In P. Pryde, ed., *San Diego: An Introduction to the Region*, pp. 153–170. Dubuque: Kendall Hunt.

Herrera-Sobek, M. 1984. "Mexican Immigration and Petroleum: A Folklorist's Perspective." *New Scholar* 9: 99–110.

Herzog, L. 1977. "Mexican Americans in the Metropolitan Southwest: A Descriptive Ecological Commentary." Discussion Paper Series, no. 34. Department of Geography, Syracuse University.

————. 1978. "Demystifying the Industrial City: The Case of Monterrey, Mexico." Paper presented at the Association of American Geographers Annual Meetings, New Orleans, Louisiana.

————. 1983. "Politics and the Role of the State in Land Use Change." *International Journal of Urban and Regional Research* 7: 93–113.

————. 1985a. "City Profile—Tijuana." *Cities* 2: 297–306.

————. 1985b. "The Cross-Cultural Dimensions of Urban Land Use Policy on the U.S.–Mexico Border: A San Diego–Tijuana Case Study." *Social Science Journal* 22: 29–46.

————. 1986a. "Mexican-Americans and the Evolution of the San Diego, California Built Environment." *Critica, Journal of Critical Essays* 1: 115–134.

————, ed. 1986b. *Planning the International Border Metropolis*. La Jolla: Center for U.S.–Mexican Studies, Monograph no. 19.

Hiernaux, D. 1986. *Urbanización y autoconstrucción de vivienda en Tijuana*. Mexico City: Centro de Ecodesarrollo.

Hinsley, F. H. 1966. *Sovereignty*. New York: Basic Books.

Hoover, E. 1948. *The Location of Economic Activity*. New York: McGraw-Hill.

House, J. W. 1968. "A Local Perspective on Boundaries and the Frontier Zone: Two Examples from the European Economic Community." In C.A. Fisher, ed., *Essays in Political Geography*, pp. 327–344. London: Methuen.

————. 1982. *Frontier on the Rio Grande*. Oxford: Clarendon Press.

Hoyt, H. 1939. *The Structure and Growth of Residential Neighborhoods in American Cities*. Washington, D.C.: Federal Housing Administration.

Instituto de Investigaciones Económicas y Sociales. 1980. *Compendio de estadísticas básicas de la ciudad de Tijuana*. Tijuana: Universidad Autónoma de Baja California.

Instituto de Investigaciones Sociales, UABC. 1984. Survey of Tijuana: Research Project on Migration and Labor Force. Tijuana: Universidad Autónoma de Baja California (UABC).

Instituto Nacional de Estadística, Geografía e Información. 1982. *Anuario estadístico de los Estados Unidos Mexicanos*. Mexico: SPP.

————. 1983. *Censo general de población y vivienda 1980*. Vol. 1, tomo 2, *Estado de Baja California*. Mexico City: Secretaría de Programación y Presupuesto.

International Boundary and Water Commission (IBWC). 1976. *Tijuana River Flood Control Project, San Diego County, California*. San Diego: IBWC.

James, D. 1983. "Trade and Merchandising." In E. R. Stoddard et al., eds., *Borderlands Sourcebook,* pp. 153–158. Norman: University of Oklahoma Press.

Janelle, D. G., and H. Millword. 1976. "Locational Conflict Patterns and Urban Ecological Structure." *Tijdschrift Voor Economische en Sociale Geographie* 67: 102–112.

Jefferson, D. 1986. "San Ysidro Split on Low Income Housing." *San Diego Tribune,* March 20.

Johnston, R. J. 1982. *Geography and the State: An Essay in Political Geography.* New York: St. Martin's Press.

Jones, R. 1984. *Patterns of Undocumented Migration: Mexico and the United States.* Totowa, N.J.: Rowman & Allenheld.

Jones, S. B. 1945. *Boundary Making: A Handbook for Statesmen, Treaty Editors and Boundary Commissioners.* Washington, D.C.: Carnegie Endowment for International Peace.

Joulia Lagares, A. 1986. "Una restructuración del sistema de distribución de líneas del transporte urbano público." Paper presented at Foro de Análisis del Plan Estatal de Desarrollo. Mexicali, Baja California, Mexico.

Juaregui, S. (president, Tijuana River Evicted Resident Committee). 1982. Field interview. Tijuana.

Kain, J. 1975. *Essays on Urban Spatial Structure.* Cambridge, Mass.: Ballinger.

Keen, H. 1977. "The Great Triple Alliance and Other Power Stories." *San Diego Magazine,* May: 67–71.

Kennedy, W. 1978. "Ecology and the Border: The Case of the Tijuana Flood Control Channel." Paper presented at the American Sociological Association Meetings, San Francisco.

Kjos, K. 1986. "Transboundary Land Use Planning: A U.S. Perspective." In L. Herzog, ed., *Planning the International Border Metropolis,* pp. 21–26. La Jolla: Center for U.S.–Mexican Studies, Monograph no. 19.

Kolinsky, M. 1981. "The Nation-State in Western Europe: Erosion from Above and Below." In L. Tivey, ed., *The Nation-State: The Formation of Modern Politics,* pp. 82–193. Oxford: Martin Robertson.

Korcelli, P. 1982. "Theory of Intra-Urban Structure, Review and Synthesis: A Cross-Cultural Perspective." In L. Bourne, ed., *Internal Structure of the City,* pp. 93–110. New York: Oxford University Press.

Kristoff, L. 1969. "The Nature of Frontiers and Boundaries." In R. E. Kasperson and J. V. Minghi, eds. *The Structure of Political Geography,* pp. 128–131. Chicago: Aldine.

Lapradelle, P. 1928. *La Frontiere.* Paris: Editions Internationale.

Larue, S. 1986. "U.S., Mexico Near Accord on Dumping Toxics." *San Diego Union,* September 22.

Lefebvre H. 1976. "Reflections on the Politics of Space." *Antipode* 8: 30–37.

Leinberger, C., and C. Lockwood. 1986. "How Business Is Reshaping America."

The Atlantic 258: 43–52.

Leonard, O. 1948. "La Paz, Bolivia: Its Population and Growth." *American Sociological Review* 13: 448–454.

Leontief, W., et al. 1977. *The Future of the World Economy.* New York: Oxford University Press.

Ley, D., and J. Mercer. 1980. "Locational Conflict and the Politics of Consumption." *Economic Geography* 56: 89–109.

Little, A., Inc. 1974. *Tourism in San Diego: Its Economic, Fiscal and Environmental Impacts.* San Diego: City of San Diego.

Los Angeles Times. 1986. "These Days, Watch on the Rhine Observes New Perils of Pollution." November 30.

Losch, A. 1954. *The Economics of Location.* New Haven: Yale University Press.

Lowry and Associates. 1983. *Joint International Wastewater Treatment Reclamation and Disposal Project: Facilities Plan.* San Diego: City of San Diego.

Luhman, N. 1982. "Territorial Borders as System Boundaries." In R. Strassoldo and G. Delli Zotti, eds., *Cooperation and Conflict in Border Areas,* pp. 235–244. Milan: Franco Angeli Editore.

Lummis, C. 1925. *Land of Poco Tiempo.* New York: Charles Scribner & Sons.

Lynch, K., and D. Appleyard. 1974. *Temporary Paradise? A Look at the Special Landscape of the San Diego Region.* San Diego: City of San Diego/ Marston Foundation.

Makler, H, A. Martinelli, and N. Smelser. 1982. *The New International Economy.* Beverly Hills: Sage.

Mangin, W. 1967. "Latin American Squatter Settlements: A Problem and a Solution." *Latin American Research Review* 2: 65–98.

Markussen, A. 1976. "Class and Urban Social Expenditures: A Local Theory of the State." *Kapitalistate: Working Papers on the Capitalist State* 4–5: 50–65.

Martin, R. 1965. *The Cities and the Federal System.* New York: Athenton Press.

Martínez, O. 1977. "Chicanos and the Border Cities: An Interpretive Essay." *Pacific Historical Review* 46: 85–106.

———. 1978. *Border Boom Town: Ciudad Juárez since 1848.* Austin: University of Texas Press.

———. ed. 1986. *Across Boundaries: Transborder Interaction in Comparative Perspective.* El Paso: Texas Western Press.

Mazier, J. T. 1986. "Remarks." In L. Herzog, ed., *Planning the International Border Metropolis,* pp. 77–79. La Jolla: Center for U.S.–Mexican Studies, Monograph no. 19.

McConville, J. 1965. "El Paso–Ciudad Juárez: A Focus on Inter-American Culture." *New Mexico Historical Review* 40: 233–247.

McWilliams, C. 1968. *North from Mexico: The Spanish Speaking People of the United States.* New York: Greenwood Press.

Meinig, D. W. 1971. *Southwest: Three Peoples in Geographical Change.* New York: Oxford University Press.

Mendoza Berrueto, E. 1984. "Visión de un marco conceptual para el primer encuentro sobre impactos regionales de las relaciones económicas entre México y Estados Unidos." In A. Corona Rentería and L. Gibson, eds., *Regional Impacts of United States–Mexico Economic Relations*, pp. 33–52. Mexico City: Colegio de México.

Merriam, C. 1972. *History of the Theory of Sovereignty*. New York: Garland.

Metropolitan Transit Development Board (MTDB). 1977. *San Diego–Tijuana: One Region*. Guideway Planning Project. San Diego: MTDB.

———. 1983. *San Diego Trolley: An Overview*. San Diego: MTDB.

Mexico Communications. 1986. *Maquiladora Directory*. Mexico City.

Meyer, J. S. 1986. "Sheriff Urges Posting Marines along Border." *San Diego Union*, April 6.

Minghi, J. V. 1963. "Boundary Studies in Political Geography." *Annals of the Association of American Geographers* 53: 407–428.

Mittan, R. 1983. Field interview. San Diego, California.

Montemayor, R. 1979. "Growth and Grumbling in San Ysidro." *Los Angeles Times*, San Diego County Section. November 18.

———. 1981. "Ownership in Rosarito." *Los Angeles Times*, November 30.

Moreno Toscano, A. 1979. "La crisis en la ciudad." In P. González Casanova and E. Florescano, eds., *México hoy*, pp. 152–176. Mexico City: Siglo Veintiuno Editores.

Morgan, N., and T. Blair. 1976. *Yesterday's San Diego*. Miami: E. A. Seemann.

Mori, A. 1982. "Ciudades: Hacia una reforma urbana." *Nexos* 5: 31–35.

Mörner, M. 1967. *Race Mixture in the History of Latin America*. Boston: Little Brown.

Morrissey, M. 1982. "Ethnic Stratification and the Study of Chicanos." *Journal of Ethnic Studies* 10: 71–99.

Morse, R. 1965. "Recent Research on Latin American Urbanization: A Selective Survey with Commentary." *Latin American Research Review* 1: 35–74.

Moyers, B. 1986. "One River, One Country: The U.S.–Mexico Border." CBS News documentary.

Muller, P. O. 1976. *The Outer City: Geographical Consequences of the Urbanization of the Suburbs*, Resource paper 75-2. Washington, D.C.: Association of American Geographers.

———. 1981. *Contemporary Suburban America*. Englewood Cliffs: Prentice-Hall.

Mumford, L. 1961. *The City in History*. New York: Harcourt, Brace & World.

Mungaray, A., and P. Moctezuma. 1984. "La disputa del mercado fronterizo 1960–1983." *Estudios Fronterizos* 1: 89–111.

Murdie, R. A. 1969. *Factorial Ecology of Metropolitan Toronto 1951–61*, Research paper 116, Department of Geography. Chicago: University of Chicago Press.

Murphey, R. 1984. "City as a Mirror of Society: China Tradition and Transformation." In J. Agnew et al., eds., *The City in Cultural Context*, pp. 186–204. Boston: Allen & Unwin.

Murphy, R. E., and J. E. Vance. 1954. "Delimiting the CBD." *Economic Geography* 30: 189–222.

Murty, T. 1978. *Frontiers: A Changing Concept.* New Delhi: Palit & Palit, 1978.

Nalven, J., ed. 1984. "Border Perspectives: On the U.S.–Mexico Relationship." *New Scholar* 9.

———. 1986. "Transboundary Environmental Problem Solving: Social Process, Cultural Perception." *Natural Resources Journal* 26: 793–818.

Nalven, J., and Frederickson, C. 1982. *The Employer's View: Is There a Need for a Guest Worker Program?* San Diego: Community Research Associates.

Nash, J. 1983. "The Impact of the Changing International Division of Labor on Different Sectors of the Labor Force." In J. Nash and M. P. Fernández Kelly, eds., *Women, Men, and the International Division of Labor*, pp. 3–38. Albany: State University of New York Press.

Navari, C. 1981. "The Origins of the Nation-State." In L. Tivey, ed., *The Nation-State*, pp. 13–38. Oxford: Martin Robertson.

Needler, M. 1971. *Politics and Society in Mexico.* Albuquerque: University of New Mexico Press.

Newton, K. 1975. "American Urban Politics: Social Class, Political Structure and Public Goods." *Urban Affairs Quarterly* 2: 241–264.

Newsweek. 1986. "A Crisis Zone on the Border." April 21.

Norris, F. 1983. "Logan Heights: Growth and Change in the Old East End." *Journal of San Diego History* 29: 28–40.

North, D. 1970. *The Border Crossers.* Washington, D.C.: Transcentury Corp.

Nuttall, Z. 1922. "Royal Ordinances Concerning the Laying Out of New Towns." *Hispanic American Historical Review* 5: 249–254.

Office of the Governor, State of California. 1978. "Economic Development District, Request for Authorization by State of California." Sacramento: Governor's Office.

Ojeda, M. 1976. *Alcances y límites de la política exterior de México.* Mexico City: Colegio de México.

———. 1983. "Mexico and United States Relations: Interdependence or Mexico's Dependence?" In C. Vásquez and M. García y Griego, eds., *Mexican–U.S. Relations: Conflict and Convergence*, pp. 109–126. Los Angeles: UCLA Latin American Center.

Overall Economic Development Program. 1979. *Directory 80: A Plan and Strategy for Regional Economic Development.* San Diego: San Diego Region Overall Economic Development Program.

Padgett, V. 1976. *The Mexican Political System.* 2d ed. Boston: Houghton Mifflin.

Padilla, A. 1985. "Desarrollo urbano." In D. Piñera, ed., *Historia de Tijuana,* pp. 183–201. Tijuana: Centro de Investigaciones Históricas, UNAM-UABC.

Palm, R. 1981. *The Geography of American Cities.* New York: Oxford University Press.

Palmer, R., and J. Colton 1965. *A History of the Modern World.* New York: Alfred Knopf.

Park, R. E., et al. 1925. *The City.* Chicago: University of Chicago Press.

Peattie, L. 1974. *The View from the Barrio.* Ann Arbor: University of Michigan Press.

Perdomo, R. P., and P. Nikken. 1982. "The Law and Homeownership in the *Barrios* of Caracas." In A. Gilbert, ed. *Urbanization in Contemporary Latin America,* pp. 205–229. New York: John Wiley & Sons.

Perlman, J. 1976. *The Myth of Marginality: Urban Poverty and Politics in Rio de Janeiro.* Berkeley & Los Angeles: University of California Press.

Perry, D., and A. Watkins. 1977. *The Rise of the Sunbelt Cities.* Vol. 14, *Urban Affairs Annual Review.* Beverly Hills: Sage.

Petras, E. 1980. "The Role of National Boundaries in a Cross-National Labour Market." *International Journal of Urban and Regional Research* 4: 157–195.

Pickvance, C. G. 1976. *Urban Sociology: Critical Essays.* New York: St. Martin's Press.

Piñera, D., ed. 1983. *Panorama histórico de Baja California.* Tijuana: Centro de Investigaciones Históricas, UNAM-UABC.

————. 1985. *Historia de Tijuana.* Tijuana: Centro de Investigaciones Históricas, UNAM-UABC.

————. 1986. Field interview, Tijuana, Mexico.

Piñera, D., and J. Ortíz. 1983. "Inicios de Tijuana como asentamiento urbano." In D. Piñera, ed., *Panorama histórico de Baja California,* pp. 284–292. Tijuana: Centro de Investigaciones Históricas, UNAM-UABC.

Pirages, D. 1984. "An Ecological Approach." In S. Strange, ed., *Paths to International Political Economy,* pp. 53–69. London: Allen & Unwin.

Pirenne, H. 1952. *Medieval Cities: Their Origins and the Revival of Trade.* Princeton: Princeton University Press.

Pitt, L., 1966. *The Decline of the Californios.* Berkeley & Los Angeles: University of California Press.

Portes, A., and J. Walton. 1976. *Urban Latin America: The Political Condition from Above and Below.* Austin: University of Texas Press.

Prescott, J. R. 1965. *The Geography of Frontiers and Boundaries.* Chicago: Aldine.

Price, J. 1973. *Tijuana: Urbanization in a Border Culture.* Notre Dame: University of Notre Dame Press.

Pryde, P. 1986. "A Geography of Water Supply and Management in the San Diego–Tijuana Border Zone." In L. Herzog, ed., *Planning the International Border Metropolis,* pp. 45–54. La Jolla: Center for U.S.–Mexican Studies, Monograph no. 19.

Purcell, S. 1975. *The Mexican Profit-Sharing Decision: Politics in an Authoritarian Regime*. Berkeley & Los Angeles: University of California Press.

Purcell, S., and J. Purcell. 1980. "State and Society in Mexico: Must a Stable Polity Be Institutionalized?" *World Politics* 32: 194–227.

Quintin, J. M. 1973. *European Cooperation in Frontier Regions*. Strasbourg: Council of Europe.

Ramírez Acosta, J., and V. Castillo. 1985. "La frontera México–Estados Unidos: Estudio de las economías de Baja California y California." *Cuadernos de Economía* 1.

Ranfla, A. G., and G. B. Alvarez de la Torre. 1986. "Expansión física, formas urbanas y migración en el desarrollo urbano de Tijuana, 1900–1984." *Ciencias Sociales*, serie 3, cuaderno 2, UABC.

Rapoport, A. 1984. "Culture and the Urban Order." In J. Agnew et al., eds., *The City in Cultural Context*, pp. 50–75. Boston: Allen & Unwin.

Ratzel, F. 1897. *Politiche Geographie*. Leipzig: Oldenbourg.

Redevelopment Agency of San Diego. 1978, 1981, 1982. *Adopted Fiscal Budget*. San Diego.

Regional Economic Research. 1981. "Estimates of the Degree of Economic Integration of Mexico and the United States Border Cities: Two Cases— Tijuana, Baja California/San Diego, California and Mexicali, B.C./ Imperial Valley, California." San Diego: Regional Economic Research.

Remer, L. 1977. "Los Angelizing San Diego." *San Diego Newsline*, April 2.

Reps, J. W. 1965. *The Making of Urban America: A History of City Planning in the United States*. Princeton: Princeton University Press.

Revel Mouroz, J. 1984. "La frontera México–Estados Unidos: Mexicanización e internacionalización." *Estudios Fronterizos* l: ll–29.

Reynolds, C. 1983. "Labor Market Projections for the United States and Mexico, and Their Relevance to Current Migration Controversies." In C. Vásquez and M. García y Griego, eds., *Mexican–U.S. Relations: Conflict and Convergence*, pp. 325–369. Los Angeles: UCLA Latin American Center.

———. 1984. "A Shift Share Analysis of Regional and Sectoral Productivity Growth in Contemporary Mexico and the United States: Implications for Economic Interdependence." In A. Corona R. and L. Gibson, eds., *Regional Impacts of United States–Mexican Economic Relations*, pp. 71–89. Mexico City: Colegio de México.

Rick, W. 1978. "Growth Management in San Diego." *Urban Land*, April, pp. 3–5.

Rico, C. 1983. "The Future of Mexican–U.S. Relations and the Limits of the Rhetoric of Interdependence." In C. Vásquez and M. García y Griego, eds., *Mexican–U.S. Relations: Conflict and Cooperation*, pp. 127–174. Los Angeles: UCLA Latin American Center.

Ricq, C. 1982. "Frontier Workers in Europe." *West European Politics* 5: 98–108.

Robinson, D. J. 1975. "The Analysis of Eighteenth Century Spanish American Cities: Some Problems and Alternative Solutions." Discussion Paper Series, no. 4. Department of Geography, Syracuse University.

Rokkan, S. 1980. "Territories, Centre and Periphery: Towards a Geoethnic-Geoeconomic-Geopolitical Model of Differentiation in Western Europe." In J. Gottman, ed., *Centre and Periphery,* pp. 163–204. Beverly Hills: Sage.

Romero, F. 1985. "Land Dispute Unsettling to Resort Town." *San Diego Evening Tribune,* May 2.

Romo, R. 1982. *East Los Angeles: History of a Barrio.* Austin: University of Texas Press.

Ronfeldt, D., and C. Sereseres. 1983. "The Management of U.S.–Mexico Interdependence: Drift toward Failure?" In C. Vásquez and M. García y Griego, eds., *Mexican–U.S. Relations: Conflict and Convergence,* pp. 43–107. Los Angeles: UCLA Latin American Center.

Rose, H. 1971. *The Black Ghetto: A Spatial Perspective.* New York: McGraw Hill.

———. 1976. *Black Suburbanization: Access to Improved Quality of Life or Maintenance of the Status Quo?* Cambridge, Mass.: Ballinger.

Ross, S., ed. 1978. *Views across the Border.* Albuquerque: University of New Mexico Press.

Ruhlow, J. 1975. "Tijuana's Dream Becomes a Reality." *Los Angeles Times,* August 10.

Sack, R. D. 1983. "Human Territoriality: A Theory." *Annals of the American Geographers* 73: 55–74.

Salcedo Leos, B. 1986. "Sewage and Potable Water Systems in Tijuana." In L. Herzog, ed., *Planning the International Border Metropolis,* pp. 33–38. La Jolla: Center for U.S.–Mexican Studies, Monograph no. 19.

Sale, K. 1975. *Power Shift: The Rise of the Southern Rim and Its Challenge to the Eastern Establishment.* New York: Random House.

Sampson, A. 1981. *The Money Lenders.* London: Hodder & Stoughton.

San Diego Association of Governments (SANDAG). 1981. *Comprehensive Plan for the San Diego Region.* Vol. 10, series V, *Regional Growth Research.* San Diego: SANDAG.

San Diego Chamber of Commerce. 1978. "The Baja California–San Diego County Linkage." *San Diego Economic Profile.* San Diego: Economic Research Bureau of Chamber of Commerce.

San Diego Union. 1986. "Sheriff Urges Posting Marines along Border." April 6.

———. 1986. "Poisoning of Rhine Makes Case, Again, for International Effort." November 30.

Sanders, R. 1978. "The City: Eclipse of a Geographic Concept." *AAG Middle States Proceedings* 12: 81–84.

Sargent, C. S. 1974. *The Spatial Evolution of Greater Buenos Aires, Argentina, 1870–1930.* Tempe: Center for Latin American Studies, Arizona State University.

Sassen-Koob, S. 1983. "Labor Migration and the New Industrial Division of Labor." In J. Nash and M. P. Fernández Kelly, eds., *Women, Men, and the International Division of Labor,* pp. 175–204. Albany: State University of New York Press.

Sawers, L., and W. Tabb, eds., 1984. *Sunbelt/Snowbelt: Urban Development and Regional Restructuring.* New York: Oxford University Press.

Sayer, S. 1982. "The Economic Analysis of Frontier Regions." *West European Politics* 5: 64–80.

Schnore, L. 1965. "On the Spatial Structure of Cities in the Two Americas." In P. Hauser and L. Schnore, eds., *The Study of Urbanization,* pp. 347–398. New York: John Wiley & Sons.

Schramm, G. 1984. "Regional Effects of U.S.–Mexican Current Account Transactions." In A. Corona R. and L. Gibson, eds., *Regional Impacts of United States–Mexico Economic Relations,* pp. 109–143. Mexico City: Colegio de México.

Scott, R. 1964. *Mexican Government in Transition.* Urbana: University of Illinois Press.

Secretaría de Desarrollo Urbano y Ecología (SEDUE). 1984. *Plan director de desarrollo urbano de Tijuana.* Mexico City: SEDUE.

———. 1985. *Urban Development Plan of the City of Tijuana.* Mexicali: SAHOPE-SEDUE.

Secretaría de Industria y Comercio, 1976. *Indicadores socioeconómicos de las zonas fronterizas.* Mexico City: Secretaría de Industria y Comercio.

Security Pacific National Bank. 1981. *U.S.–Mexican Border Region Economic Report.*

Semple, E. C. 1911. *Problems of Geographic Environment.* New York: Holt.

Shevky, E., and W. Bell. 1955. *Social Area Analysis: Theory, Illustrative Applications, and Computational Procedures.* Stanford: Stanford University Press.

Short, J. R. 1978. "Residential Mobility." *Progress in Human Geography* 2: 419–447.

Sinkin, R., and R. Marks. 1988. "The Second Wave: Developmental Implications of New Forms of *Maquiladora* Investment in Mexico." Research Seminar, Center for U.S.–Mexican Studies, University of California, San Diego.

Sjoberg, A. 1960. *The Pre-Industrial City.* New York: Free Press.

Sklair, L. 1987. "Does Mexico's Maquiladora Program Represent a Genuine Development Strategy?" *Research Seminar on United States–Mexico Relations.* La Jolla: Center for U.S.–Mexico Studies, University of California, San Diego.

Sloan, J., and J. West. 1976. "Community Integration and Policies Among Elites in Two Border Cities: Los Dos Laredos." *Journal of Inter-American Studies and World Affairs* 18: 451–474.

———. 1977. "The Role of Informal Policy Making in U.S.–Mexico Border

Cities." *The Social Science Quarterly* 58: 270–282.

Smith, G. 1979. "The Battle of Florida Canyon." *The Reader*, May 10.

Smith, P. 1979. *Labyrinths of Power: Political Recruitment in Twentieth Century Mexico*. Princeton: Princeton University Press.

Smith, T. 1981. *The Pattern of Imperialism*. Cambridge: Cambridge University Press.

Soble, R. 1985. "Border Town's Bustle Linked to Drug Traffic." *Los Angeles Times*, December 16.

Soja, E. 1971. *The Political Organization of Space*. Resource Paper no. 8. Washington, D.C.: Association of American Geographers.

Spykman, N. J. 1942. "Frontiers, Security and International Organization." *Geographical Review* 32: 436–447.

Stanislawski, D. 1946. "The Origin and Spread of the Grid Pattern Town." *Geographical Review* 36: 105–120.

———. 1947. "Early Spanish Town Planning in the New World." *Geographical Review* 37: 94–105.

Stern, M. 1986. "Corruption in Mexico Hailed: Blamed for Drug Menace, Lawlessness along Border." *San Diego Union*, May 14.

Stoddard, E., and J. West. 1977. *The Impact of Mexico's Peso Devaluation on Selected U.S. Border Cities*. Washington, D.C.: U.S. Economic Development Administration.

Storing, P. 1984. "U.S.–Mexican Border Cooperation and Development: Is a New Border Commission Needed?" Washington, D.C.: Department of State.

Storper, M., and R. Walker. 1984. "The Spatial Division of Labor: Labor and the Location of Industries." In L. Sawers and W. Tabb, eds., *Sunbelt/Snowbelt: Urban Development and Regional Restructuring*, pp. 19–47. New York: Oxford University Press.

Strange, S, ed. 1984. *Paths to International Political Economy*. London: Allen & Unwin.

Strassoldo, R. 1982. "Boundaries in Sociological Theory: A Reassessment." In R. Strassoldo and G. Delli Zotti, eds., *Cooperation and Conflict in Border Areas*, pp. 245–271. Milan: Franco Angeli Editore.

Strassoldo, R., and G. Delli Zotti, eds. 1982. *Cooperation and Conflict in Border Areas*. Milan: Franco Angeli Editore.

Stutz, F. P. 1976. *Social Aspects of Interaction*. Resource paper 76-2. Washington D.C.: Association of American Geographers.

Suárez Villa, L. 1984. "Industrial Export Enclaves and Manufacturing Change." *Papers of the Regional Science Association* 54: 89–111.

Swann, M. M. 1982. *Tierra Adentro: Settlement and Society in Colonial Durango*. Boulder: Westview Press.

Tagil, S. 1982. "The Question of Border Regions in Western Europe: An Historical Background." *West European Politics* 5: 18–33.

Tamayo, J., and J. L. Fernández. 1983. *Zonas fronterizas (México–Estados Unidos)*. Mexico City: CIDE.

Taylor, M., and N. Thrift. 1982. *The Geography of Multinationals*. New York: St. Martin's Press.

Taylor, P. J. 1985. *Political Geography: World-Economy, Nation-State and Locality*. London: Longman.

Teitz, M. 1968. "Toward a Theory of Urban Facility Location." *Papers of the Regional Science Association* 21: 35–52.

Tilley, C. 1975. "Reflections on the History of European State-Making." In C. Tilley, ed., *The Formation of Nation-States in Western Europe*, pp. 3–83. Princeton: Princeton University Press.

Tivey, L., ed. 1981. *The Nation-State*. Oxford: Martin Robertson.

Turner, F. J. 1969. "The Significance of the Frontier in American History." In R. Kasperson and J. Minghi, eds., *The Structure of Political Geography*, pp. 132–139. Chicago: Aldine.

Turner, J. F. C. 1967. "Barriers and Channels for Housing Development in Modernizing Countries." *Journal of the American Institute of Planners* 32: 167–181.

Ugalde, A. 1968. "Conflict and Cooperation in a Mexican City: A Study in Political Integration." Ph.D. dissertation, Stanford University.

———. 1970. *Power and Conflict in a Mexican Community: A Study of Political Integration*. Albuquerque: University of New Mexico Press.

———. 1978. "Regional Political Processes and Mexican Politics on the Border." In S. Ross, ed., *Views across the Border*, pp. 97–116. Albuquerque: University of New Mexico Press.

Unikel, L. 1978. *El desarrollo urbano de México*. Mexico City: Colegio de México.

U.S. Bureau of the Census. 1950–1980. *Census of Population and Housing, San Diego*. Washington, D.C.: U.S. Government Printing Office.

———. 1970. *Census of Population: 1970 General Social and Economic Characteristics, California*. Washington, D.C.: U.S. Government Printing Office.

———. 1975. *Special Census of Population and Housing: County of San Diego*. Washington, D.C.: U.S. Government Printing Office.

———. 1983. *1980 Census of Population and Housing: Census Tracts, San Diego, California*. Washington, D.C.: U.S. Government Printing Office.

———. 1984. *Metropolitan Statistical Areas, 1980*. Supplementary Report. Washington, D.C.: U.S. Government Printing Office.

———. 1986. *State and Metropolitan Data Book, 1986*. Washington, D.C.: U.S. Government Printing Office.

U.S. Department of Commerce. 1978. *Economic Problems of the California Border Region, San Diego County*. Washington, D.C.: Economic Development Administration.

U.S. Department of State. 1987. *Treaties in Force: A List of Treaties and Other*

International Agreements of the United States. January 1, 1987, pp. 122–127. Washington, D.C.: U.S. Government Printing Office.

U.S. House of Representatives and Senate. 1983. *Report of the Twenty-Third Mexico–United States Interparliamentary Conference, Puebla, Mexico.* Washington, D.C.: U.S. Government Printing Office.

Urban Studies and Planning Program, 1983–85. "Location Conflict Survey" (unpublished). La Jolla: University of California, San Diego.

Urquidi, V. 1975. "The Underdeveloped City." In J. Hardoy, ed., *Urbanization in Latin America,* pp. 339–366. New York: Anchor Books.

Urquidi, V., and S. Méndez Villareal. 1978. "Economic Importance of Mexico's Northern Border Region." In S. Ross, ed., *Views across the Border,* pp. 141–162. Albuquerque: University of New Mexico Press.

Valdez, L., and S. Steiner. 1972. *Aztlán: An Anthology of Mexican American Literature.* New York: Vintage Books.

Vetter, D., and A. Brasileira. 1978. "Toward a Development Strategy for Grande Rio de Janeiro." In W. Cornelius and R. V. Kemper, eds., *Latin American Urban Research.* Vol. 6, pp. 259–278. Beverly Hills: Sage.

Von Hagen, V. W. 1957. *Realm of the Incas.* New York: Mentor.

Walker, R. 1978. "The Transformation of Urban Structure in the Nineteenth Century and the Beginnings of Suburbanization." In K. Cox, ed., *Urbanization and Conflict in Market Societies,* pp. 165–212. Chicago: Maaroufa Press.

———. 1981. "A Theory of Suburbanization: Capitalism and the Construction of Urban Space in the United States." In M. Dear and A. Scott, eds., *Urbanization and Urban Planning in Capitalist Society,* pp. 384–429. New York: Methuen.

Wallerstein, I. 1974. *The Modern World System.* New York: Academic Press.

———. 1984. *The Politics of the World Economy.* New York: Cambridge University Press.

Walton, J., 1978. "Guadalajara: Creating the Divided City." In W. Cornelius and R. V. Kemper, eds., *Latin American Urban Research.* Vol. 6, pp. 25–50. Beverly Hills: Sage.

———. 1984. "Culture and Economy in the Shaping of Urban Life: General Issues and Latin American Examples." In J. Agnew et al., eds., *The City in Cultural Context,* pp. 76–93. Boston: Allen & Unwin.

Wambaugh, J. 1984. *Lines and Shadows.* New York: Morrow.

Ward, P., ed. 1982. *Self-Help Housing: A Critique.* London: Mansell.

———. 1986. *Welfare Politics in Mexico: Papering over the Cracks.* London: Allen & Unwin.

Warner, B. J. 1962. *Street Car Suburbs: The Process of Growth in Boston.* Cambridge: Harvard University Press.

Warner, S. B., Jr. 1972. *The Urban Wilderness: A History of the American City.* New York: Harper & Row.

Weinstein, B., H. Gross, and J. Rees, eds. 1985. *Regional Growth and Decline in the United States.* New York: Praeger.

West, J. P., and D. James. 1983. "Border Tourism." In E. R. Stoddard et al., eds., *Borderlands Sourcebook,* pp. 159–165. Norman: University of Oklahoma Press.

Wilkie, J. 1967. *The Mexican Revolution: Federal Expenditures and Social Change Since 1910.* Berkeley & Los Angeles: University of California Press.

Williams-Kuebelback & Associates, 1986. *San Ysidro Community Economic Revitalization Study.* San Diego.

Yeates, M. 1965. "Some Factors Affecting the Spatial Distribution of Chicago Land Values, 1910–1960." *Economic Geography* 41: 55–70.

Yeates, M., and B. Garner. 1980. *The North American City.* New York: Harper & Row.

Yujnovsky, O. 1975. "Urban Spatial Structure in Latin America." In J. Hardoy, ed., *Urbanization in Latin America,* pp. 191–219. New York: Anchor Books.

INDEX

ABOUT THE AUTHOR

Lawrence A. Herzog is associate professor of Mexican American studies at San Diego State University, California. He holds a Ph.D. in geography from the Maxwell School of Citizenship and Public Affairs, Syracuse University, and has served as a Fulbright scholar in Peru and consultant to the U.S. Agency for International Development in Peru and Bolivia. He is editor of *Planning the International Border Metropolis* (1986).

Where North Meets South was composed on a Macintosh computer using the program Pagemaker. The text was set in ten point Palatino, with three points of leading; Stone Sans was chosen for display. Camera-ready copy was produced on a Linotronic digital phototypesetter by RJL Graphics, of Austin, Texas. The book was printed offset and bound by Thomson-Shore, Inc., of Dexter, Michigan.

CENTER FOR MEXICAN AMERICAN STUDIES • UNIVERSITY OF TEXAS AT AUSTIN